METHODISTS AND THE
CRUCIBLE OF RACE
1930–1975

Methodists

AND THE

Crucible of Race 1930–1975

Peter C. Murray

University of Missouri Press
Columbia and London

Copyright © 2004 by
The Curators of the University of Missouri
University of Missouri Press, Columbia, Missouri 65201
Printed and bound in the United States of America
All rights reserved
5 4 3 2 1   08 07 06 05 04

Library of Congress Cataloging-in-Publication Data

Murray, Peter C., 1953–
Methodists and the crucible of race, 1930–1975 / Peter C. Murray.
p.   cm.
Includes index.
ISBN 0-8262-1514-9 (alk. paper)
1. African Americans—Civil rights—History—20th century.
2. Civil rights movements—United States—History—20th century.
3. African American Methodists—History—20th century.   4. Methodist
Church—United States—History—20th century.   5. Methodist Church
(U.S.). Central Jurisdiction—History.   6. Racism—Religious aspects—
Methodists—History—20th century.   7. United States—Race relations.
8. Southern States—Race relations.   I. Title.
E185.61.M985   2004
287'.6'089—dc22
2003025333

⊚™   This paper meets the requirements of the
American National Standard for Permanence of Paper
for Printed Library Materials, Z39.48, 1984.

Text design: Stephanie Foley
Jacket design: Susan Ferber
Typesetter: Phoenix Type, Inc.
Printer and binder: The Maple-Vail Book Manufacturing Group
Typeface: Adobe Caslon

For
Mary Cathryn

Contents

Preface

I RECEIVED AN introduction to the Methodist Church structure when my father, a Methodist minister, moved to a two-church charge in rural South Carolina. In the small town there were several Baptist churches, a Presbyterian church, and several Methodist churches, one of which was my father's. Across the street, there was a southern Methodist church that had defiantly formed after most southern white Methodists reunited with their northern counterparts in 1939. Two blocks away from my father's church was another Methodist church. It belonged to the same denomination, but it was in a different annual conference and had a different bishop; also, one congregation was all African American and the other was entirely white. Despite being part of the same denomination, the two churches had no direct contact with one another. It was as if they were worshipping different gods. Even as an elementary school student, I knew enough about Christian teachings to know that there existed a serious discrepancy between professed beliefs and practices. I watched the Civil Rights movement unfold around me knowing that change was occurring in the nation, in my state and community, but I wondered what change, if any, might occur in these two churches, particularly on Sunday morning. It is a question that on an expanded scale animates much of this book.

In writing this book, I have largely focused on Methodists who are part of the United Methodist Church today. This is not to say that African American Methodists who are part of other denominations, particularly the African Methodist Episcopal (AME) Church, African Methodist Episcopal Zion (AMEZ) Church, or the Christian Methodist Episcopal (CME) Church, are not fully Methodists. Nothing could be further from my intent. I have simply used

"African American Methodists" in a more limited sense to simplify the text. In Chapters 1 and 2, I will describe the various divisions and mergers of Methodists that are pertinent to this study. Most African American Methodists became and remain part of these three denominations, but there was also always an African American presence in some part of the "white" Methodist Church. The story of this last group of African American Methodists is integral to this study, but the members of the AME, AMEZ, and CME churches are also legitimately African American Methodists.

Just as important a caveat as affirming the complexity of African American Methodism is explaining the terminology regarding race used in this book. Racial terms, like concepts of race, are fluid and present any thoughtful author with some quandaries. I have chosen what some might consider a mixed bag. I have chosen "African American Methodists" as opposed to "black Methodists," but I have retained the use of "white" as a reference to Caucasians or European Americans. This is not the most logically consistent terminology, but language does not change with such precision. The use of "European American" may become more prevalent in the future, but it still seems vague, while there is widespread acceptance of the term "African American." However, it is worth noting that during this study the major shift in racial terminology was from "Negro Methodists" to "Black Methodists."

Although this book has only one author, in reality, there are many contributors who have made it possible for the manuscript to take shape. I apologize to those not explicitly named, but my intellectual debts span many years and my memory fails me. The problems that remain in this manuscript are not because of the lack of trying or insight on the part of those helping me. The errors that still reside here are addressed in Psalm 139:6.

Rev. Bob Epps as a campus minister at Indiana University–Bloomington set me on this course by suggesting the Central Jurisdiction as a possible dissertation topic. He and his wife, Richie, were very gracious to me during my years in Bloomington. William H. Harris directed the dissertation, "Christ and Caste in Conflict," but he also came out of retirement literally and figuratively to provide numerous suggestions to improve this expanded study. I am very grateful for Bill's dedication.

Archivists and librarians are a historian's best friends, and I have enjoyed the assistance of many at a variety of institutions. I am especially indebted to the staff of the United Methodist Church's General Commission on Archives and History, headquartered on the campus of Drew University. Dr. Charles Yrigoyen, Jr., General Secretary of the Commission, provided me complete cooperation with my research. Archivists L. Dale Patterson, Mark Shenise, and Tracey del Duca each assisted me numerous times, as did William Beal earlier. Archivists at Emory University, both at the Pitts Theology Library and the Robert W. Woodruff Library, guided me through the papers of many Methodist bishops. Wilson Flemister was gracious to me while I was doing research in the James P. Brawley Papers at Atlanta University Center. Small archives not used to academic researchers have also been very accommodating, especially Methodist retreat facilities at Lake Junaluska, North Carolina, and Epworth by the Sea, St. Simons Island, Georgia.

A number of scholars and other professionals have offered their advice to improve the writing and encourage me during difficult stages. Lewis P. Jones offered comments on an early draft chapter. Methodist scholars Russell Richey, Will Gravely, and Kenneth E. Rowe read portions of the manuscript. Arvarh Strickland read the entire manuscript at one stage and corrected several errors. Several anonymous readers recommended changes and avenues to pursue that have added to research and writing. Fayetteville State University colleagues Stanley Johnson and Tom Hennessey read portions of the manuscript and listened to progress reports. Melanie Casey copyedited the manuscript as it approached submission. Jerry Miller and Dr. Kenneth Kastleman both helped me see how to balance various demands so that the manuscript continued to move forward over the years.

Methodist College has provided more than a place to teach and write. Although a small school in prestige and limited in resources, I have enjoyed the company of good colleagues in various disciplines, especially Richard Walsh and Robin Greene, who have shared with me their own woes and joys of the publication dance. Trevor Morris has been a supportive division director and friend. Paul Joseph guided me through the production of an initial set of computer-generated maps. Susan Pulsipher has been a fantastic library director; Kim Hockings, Kathy Chaspell, and Katie Zybeck have been astute as reference librarians; and document delivery officer Helen Graham has obtained obscure books and articles for me for close to a decade. Erik Bitterbaum and especially Tony DeLapa have been very supportive deans, providing a sabbatical and summer research funds. My history department colleagues have been very generous with their time as well as their collegial spirit. Neal McCrillis gave many suggestions to improve the writing of an early draft. More recently, Carl Dyke and Rebecca Wendelken devoted considerable summer time that they could have used for their own professional development to aid me. I also thank Norm Wilson for his years of camaraderie. Last, but not least, as an ordained Methodist minister as well as college president, M. Elton Hendricks has been more than a little interested in this project.

The staff of the University of Missouri Press has been professional, patient, and unfailingly positive. They have been such a delight to work with that I have another reason to write "the next book." I am especially grateful to Julie Schroeder, my editor, for guiding me over the hurdles of publishing.

My debt to my family is colossal. My mother and late father did so much to support my education and development. Vince and Donna have supported the project over the years, and Julie and Thomas opened their home to me numerous times as I did research in Atlanta. My boys, Nathaniel and Adam, have slowed the writing of the manuscript in a variety of ways. These diversions have improved the quality of my thinking and made me a much happier person. I look forward to more diversions with both of them. This book would truly have been abandoned had it not been for the constant love and support of my beautiful wife, Mary Cathryn. We have both had triumphs and crises over the years, but I have been richly blessed by the ways that Mary has persevered in loving me, the boys, herself, and God. I dedicate this book to her with great joy.

Methodist Churches

This is a list of the branches of Methodism most often mentioned in this book. This work deals primarily with the last two listed: the Methodist Church and the United Methodist Church.

Methodist Episcopal Church

Formed at the 1784 Baltimore Christmas Conference. It was led by Francis Asbury and Thomas Coke, the first two Methodist bishops. In 1939, this church joined with the Methodist Episcopal Church, South (see below), to form the Methodist Church.

African Methodist Episcopal (AME) Church

Led by Richard Allen, formed in Philadelphia in 1819. This church quickly became the largest African American form of Methodism. After the Civil War, it spread rapidly in the South.

African Methodist Episcopal Zion (AMEZ) Church

Similar to the AME Church, but formed in New York City, in 1821. It was considerably smaller than the AME Church in the antebellum period.

Methodist Protestant Church

Started in 1830 with a more egalitarian, democratic structure than the Methodist Episcopal Church; it remained a very small denomination throughout its existence. It was a minor partner in the formation of the Methodist Church in 1939.

METHODIST EPISCOPAL CHURCH, SOUTH

Formed in 1845 after its division from the Methodist Episcopal Church over slavery at the 1844 General Conference. It continued to have African American members until after the Civil War, when it encouraged African Americans who remained in its membership to join the CME Church (see below).

CHRISTIAN METHODIST EPISCOPAL CHURCH

Formed as the Colored Methodist Episcopal Church in 1870, largely of African Americans from the Methodist Episcopal Church, South, who chose not to join with the AME, AMEZ, or the northern Methodist Episcopal Church. In 1954, it changed its name to the Christian Methodist Episcopal Church.

METHODIST CHURCH

Formed in 1939 by the reunion of the Methodist Episcopal Church, the Methodist Episcopal Church, South, and the Methodist Protestant Church. This church created jurisdictional conferences to elect bishops and other representatives to church boards and agencies. Five jurisdictional conferences were regional; the sixth, the Central Jurisdiction, included all African American annual conferences, of which there were nineteen in 1939.

UNITED METHODIST CHURCH

Created in 1968 with the merger of the Methodist Church and the Evangelical United Brethren (EUB), a similar church whose roots were among early German-speaking Americans, some of whom were contemporaries of the first American Methodists. The United Methodist Church maintained jurisdictional conferences but did not include the Central Jurisdiction, which met for the last time in 1967.

Overview of Methodist Church Structure

LOCAL CHURCH

The local congregation consists of the laity (church members who have been baptized and confirmed) and the ordained minister. The bishop appoints an ordained local minister in consultation with the district superintendent and the local congregation. The denomination owns all local property, but local trustees administer the property. The congregation elects lay representatives to the annual conference. Depending upon the size of the congregation, a church may have several lay representatives, with each lay representative having full voting privileges. Ordained ministers, called elders in Methodism, are members of the annual conference and also have full voting privileges.

ANNUAL CONFERENCES

This is the basic unit of the church, and it makes decisions regarding social issues and policies in accordance with *The Discipline,* the set of rules and policies of the national church (see General Conference below). Although some cover territories as large as a state, in 2000 there were sixty-four annual conferences in the United States. A bishop presides over an annual conference, but he is not a member of any annual conference and does not vote on issues before the annual conference. Each annual conference creates districts that organize local congregations into arrangements of fellowship and cooperation. Each district has a superintendent, and together these superintendents serve as advisers to the bishop of the annual conference. Every four years, each annual conference elects both ministerial and lay representatives to both its jurisdictional conference and to the General Conference.

Jurisdictional Conferences

This is a collection of annual conferences that quadrennially meets to elect bishops and other representatives to church boards and agencies. The Central Jurisdiction, which existed from 1940 to 1967, was based on race, but the five other jurisdictional conferences were and continue to be regional. The jurisdictional conference assigns bishops to lead one or more of the various annual conferences within its borders, although in theory bishops can serve in any annual conference in the church. Each jurisdictional conference has a college of bishops that meets regularly to consult about issues facing that region of the church. Jurisdictional conferences can have special sessions, but they traditionally gather once every four years after the conclusion of the General Conference.

General Conference

This is the national body of Methodists that determines *The Discipline,* which is the set of church rules and policies. General Conferences are scheduled quadrennially, but special sessions may be held more frequently. Bishops rotate presiding over the General Conference, but bishops do not vote. The Council of Bishops, which consists of all bishops regardless of jurisdictional conference, opens the General Conference with an "episcopal address" outlining their concerns, but the legislative proposals before the General Conferences come in the form of petitions, which Methodists call "memorials," from the various levels of the church. Committees of the General Conference do much of the early work of considering the various proposed memorials. These committees report their concurrence or nonconcurrence with each memorial and then, in what are sometimes long sessions, the entire General Conference considers, debates, and votes on a myriad of issues. From the actions of the General Conference come the church's *Discipline.*

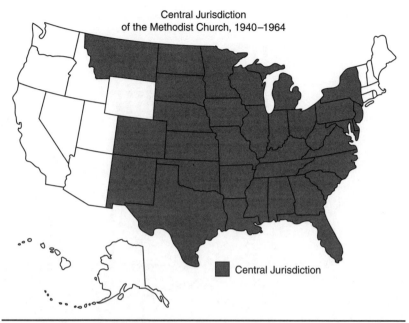

Central Jurisdiction
of the Methodist Church, 1940–1964

■ Central Jurisdiction

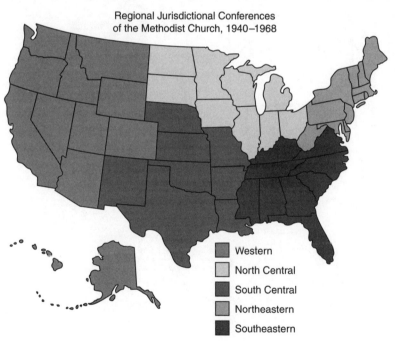

Regional Jurisdictional Conferences
of the Methodist Church, 1940–1968

■ Western
■ North Central
■ South Central
■ Northeastern
■ Southeastern

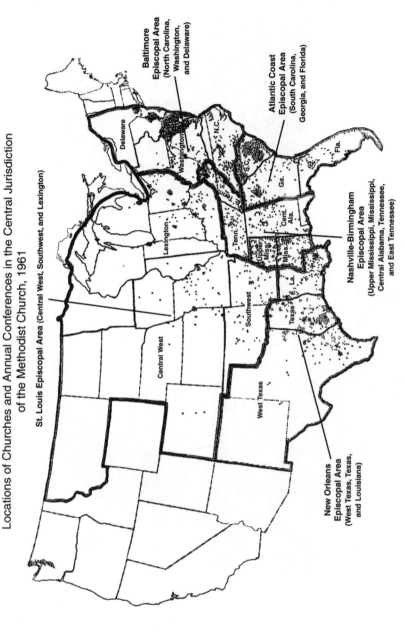

Locations of Churches and Annual Conferences in the Central Jurisdiction of the Methodist Church, 1961

St. Louis Episcopal Area (Central West, Southwest, and Lexington)

Baltimore Episcopal Area (North Carolina, Washington, and Delaware)

Atlantic Coast Episcopal Area (South Carolina, Georgia, and Florida)

Nashville–Birmingham Episcopal Area (Upper Mississippi, Mississippi, Central Alabama, Tennessee, and East Tennessee)

New Orleans Episcopal Area (West Texas, Texas, and Louisiana)

Delaware

Washington

N.C.

E. Tenn.

S.C.

Ga.

Fla.

Lexington

Tenn.

Cent. Ala.

Upper Miss.

Miss.

La.

Southwest

Texas

Central West

West Texas

Based on a map in Ernest T. Dixon Jr., "Negro Americans in the Methodist Church" [leaflet], Division of Human Relations and Economic Affairs, General Board of Church and Society, GCAH.

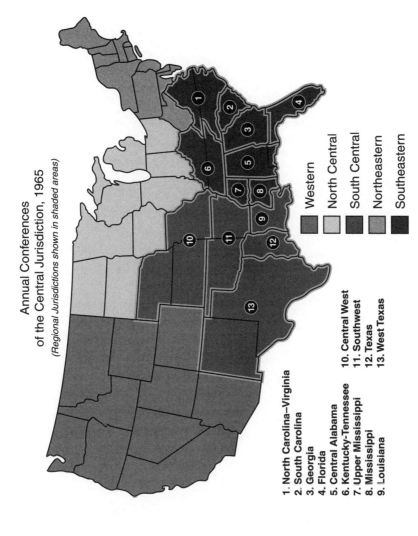

Annual Conferences
of the Central Jurisdiction, 1965
(Regional Jurisdictions shown in shaded areas)

Western
North Central
South Central
Northeastern
Southeastern

1. North Carolina–Virginia
2. South Carolina
3. Georgia
4. Florida
5. Central Alabama
6. Kentucky-Tennessee
7. Upper Mississippi
8. Mississippi
9. Louisiana
10. Central West
11. Southwest
12. Texas
13. West Texas

Based on a map published in the Central Christian Advocate, *April 15, 1963, 5.*

METHODISTS AND THE
CRUCIBLE OF RACE
1930–1975

Introduction

ONE OF THE MOST persistent questions about the origins of the Holocaust, the systematic attack upon Jews and other "undesirables" in Germany, has been why the German people allowed it to take place, especially because it was so antithetical to Christian teachings. Since most Germans of the period were either Lutherans or Catholics, how could Germans allow their government to commit such evil? Most Germans would have denied that they knew the details of what occurred in concentration camps, but they could not claim ignorance of the persecution of Jews. Hitler's campaign against Jews started quickly after he became chancellor in early 1933. Open persecution of Jews escalated in severity numerous times before mass extermination began in wartime concentration camps. Obviously, there were risks involved in opposing Hitler's government from very early in Nazi rule. Nevertheless, Germans either tacitly or enthusiastically supported a government that savagely discriminated against a group of its citizens and then ruthlessly killed millions. Anti-Semitism was not new, but the ferocity and magnitude of the persecution was startlingly different from anything Germans had seen before.

During the same period in the United States, a racist ideology existed and persecuted African Americans, especially across the American South. Throughout the first half of the twentieth century, segregation and legal restrictions on African Americans abounded across the South. Today many of these restrictions seem astounding in their viciousness and absurdity. For example, in Atlanta, Georgia, the public zoo created separate paths for African American and white visitors. In Montgomery, Alabama, the municipal government created bus segregation with an intricate seating system in which white riders

1

sat in the front, African Americans sat in the back, and a middle zone existed that always worked in the favor of white patrons. How could southern white Americans reconcile this vast scheme of state-sponsored discrimination and hate with their professed religion? In a region where Protestant churches, especially Baptist, Methodist, and Presbyterian, were pervasive and influential, why and how did such prejudice and bigotry flourish? In the so-called Bible Belt, how could the Sermon on the Mount make so little impact?

White Americans outside the South knew of the worst features of these attacks on African Americans even if they had not visited the Atlanta Zoo or ridden the Montgomery municipal bus. Lynchings, the most savage form of terrorism against African Americans, still occurred in the South and were publicized across the nation. Although lynchings had declined in the twentieth century from the ghastly period of the 1890s, when on average a lynching took place every other day somewhere in the South, the U.S. Congress never passed a federal antilynching law. Presidents stayed conspicuously quiet in the entire arena of civil rights. The Supreme Court was very slow in revisiting its 1896 *Plessy v. Ferguson* decision that upheld the constitutionality of segregation in public accommodations. In addition, violence against African Americans was not limited to the South. Race riots broke out with alarming regularity in the North. The grisly results showed that northern white mobs could also terrorize their African American neighbors.

In many ways, the distance between Hitler's Germany and the United States was not great. Without the Great Depression, Adolph Hitler might have remained a fringe politician preaching a doctrine of racism not too different from that espoused in the early years of the century by U.S. senators from several southern states. The United States had stronger democratic traditions than did the Wiemar Republic, but anti-Semitism in Germany prior to the Great Depression was not stronger or more pervasive than racist ideology in America at that same time. American institutions, especially churches, need to examine what they did to accommodate or bless racism in American society. Churches in particular could profit from examining when and how they acknowledged the depth of racism in American society and how this consciousness changed their own institutional practices. This review would begin with what churches practiced regarding race relations among their own members. The adage that

Sunday morning at eleven o'clock was the most segregated time in America was never as true as during this period of American history.

For no American church is such a study more revealing than the United Methodist Church, which was known simply as the Methodist Church before 1968. Although the Methodist movement in America began as interracial, Methodists became racially separate early in the nineteenth century. For most Methodists, the distance between African American and white church members increased after the Civil War. In 1939, the southern and northern Methodist churches, along with a far smaller Methodist Protestant Church, formed the Methodist Church, which created the most rigid and segregated church structure of any national Protestant denomination. The details of this structure were new but were the products of years of prejudice and discrimination within Methodism. The new church was a compromise made possible because most Methodists accepted the notion that African American and white Methodists were "separate, but equal" in one church. For a short period, Methodists could congratulate themselves that they had healed the division that in 1844 had divided Methodists into sectional churches. This sectional reunion was an achievement that eluded Presbyterians (reunited in 1983) and Baptists (still divided), who also had split into sectional churches before the Civil War. However, Methodist rejoicing died quickly during the Civil Rights movement, when the church had to confront its own racism.

In 1939, the newly created Methodist Church brought together the largest number of African American members of any predominantly white Protestant church (308,000 in a church of more than 7,000,000). Yet the new church organization created the Central Jurisdiction for "all Negro annual conferences." Equal to five regional jurisdictional conferences, the Central Jurisdiction could elect its own bishops and had representation on national church boards and agencies. The jurisdiction met as a body once every four years, published a twice monthly newspaper, and had various other jurisdictional organizations such as the Woman's Society of Christian Service. However, it was a mechanism for keeping African American Methodists separate from white Methodists, which was particularly important in the Southeast. The majority of African American Methodists lived in this portion of the country, but this area also contained the largest regional (white) jurisdictional conference.

Ironically, once locked together in this Jim Crow church structure, the fate of African American and white Methodists became integrally related as American society changed. Methodists created the Central Jurisdiction as a wall between African American and white members, but this wall slowly crumbled as its foundation eroded.

The creation of the Central Jurisdiction had placed white brotherhood above racial equality. However, this new jurisdictional system quickly became an embarrassment because Jim Crow, although still strong, came under assault from several different directions. During World War II, Americans fought against Nazism, which was rooted in a racist doctrine, but American racism was too obvious to ignore completely. Soon thereafter, the Cold War brought a new reason for Americans to champion themselves as the land of freedom, but Soviet propagandists pointed out the hypocrisy of the American caste system. In the postwar ideological struggle between East and West, people of color across the globe took on new importance. In U.S. foreign policy, American racism was a source of great embarrassment. Domestically, there were a number of points of stress in the Jim Crow system, and parts of its structure began to crumble. In 1944, the Supreme Court ruled that the white-only Democratic primary—a widespread means of disenfranchising African American voters—was unconstitutional; in 1947, Jackie Robinson integrated professional baseball; and, in 1948, President Harry Truman ordered the desegregation of the U.S. armed forces. Churches that divided members according to race began to find that their racism made missionary activity more difficult. Methodists prided themselves upon their evangelism and proclamation of the gospel in distant parts of the world, but church missionaries pleaded for desegregation. With each passing year during the 1950s and 1960s, Methodist Church leaders found it more difficult to reconcile their church structure with these international and domestic changes.

The struggle between African American and white Methodists was about both change and continuity in race relations and leadership in a voluntary organization. Although many Methodists did not know or understand the issues of church organization, there were lay and ordained members deeply engaged in these issues. For several quadrenniums, race relations within the church were one of the largest topics of controversy in the Methodist Church (and after 1968, the United Methodist Church). Church leaders, ordained and lay, women and men, African American and white, worked either to create a new racially inclusive church or to maintain the existing structure. Events such as Supreme Court decisions, sit-ins, and race riots influenced the actions of Methodists, as did their understanding of the Gospel. The issue of race acted as a crucible in the Methodist Church; the changes that occurred were dramatic and propelled the church in directions not initially envisioned by the participants.

As African American and white Methodists dealt with civil rights, the experience transformed them and forced them to jettison many myths that they had about themselves, people of other races, and American society. In particular, the Methodist Church wrestled with its own myth of "voluntarism" as a Christian means of desegregation. Voluntarism, desegregation by a series of two-thirds votes by both white and African American Methodists, emerged during the 1950s when desegregation was in its infancy and massive resistance among southern whites was still a potent force. Amendment IX to the church's constitution allowed for African American Methodist congregations and/or annual conferences to transfer into white annual conferences and jurisdictional conferences if each unit gave its approval by a two-thirds vote. There was great enthusiasm among white Methodist leaders, especially in the South, because desegregation could not occur without their consent.

Voluntarism guaranteed to southern white Methodists that the national church would not force rapid desegregation of the church structure. However, voluntarism was riddled with contradictions from the start. African American Methodists had never "volunteered" for segregation. The Methodist Church imposed a segregated jurisdictional conference upon African American members because they were only a small minority group in a largely white church. The Central Jurisdiction was not created out of any moral commitment, but was a compromise with racial prejudice and bigotry. As time went on and segregation ended across the South, church leaders searched for means to increase the speed of voluntarism.

The Civil Rights movement challenged Methodists and other American churches to examine the American dilemma of race relations. Methodists had no monopoly on prejudice and bigotry, and the denomination had outspoken white liberals as well as African American members who worked assiduously for a racially inclusive church. Among Methodists and other denominations, victories produced new challenges. American churches had to confront the pervasiveness of racism more deeply. They could not simply clean up their structures and ignore the devastation throughout American society created by generations of prejudice. What began as an internal struggle for equality in the Methodist Church became a wider struggle over the purpose of the church in a society that increasingly saw all Christian churches as just one among many voluntary organizations. The Methodist experience mirrored many parts of the experiences of the Catholic, Presbyterian, and Episcopal churches. Although each church had its particular nuances, they all wrestled with their racial policies and practices. Each church attempted to build racial reconciliation within its fellowship as a means of healing the greater racism in American society, but none were completely successful in bridging the gap between African American and white members.

This study builds upon a rich, diverse historical literature on the Civil Rights movement and churches. Exhaustive studies of various locales have uncovered new dimensions of social change in the South and the nation. Several books have explored the role of Catholics, Presbyterians, and Episcopalians in the Civil Rights era, and there is one monograph on Methodist women's activities. These studies show that each church had its own difficulties as it wrestled with racism. African American and white church leaders often moved at different speeds. Women's church organizations often, but not always, pushed civil rights more quickly than did men. In conjunction with the struggle for racial equality, women confronted patriarchy within the church. Youth groups also wanted desegregation at a faster pace than did the church hierarchies. Many youth, African American and white, simply dropped out of churches that changed too slowly. They decided that a gospel that protected the status quo was bad news rather than good news.

Recent scholarship has shown also that the so-called Solid South was not as solidly behind racism and segregation as once presumed. When Methodists created the Central Jurisdiction, southern liberals were attempting to form a coalition of African American and white southerners focused upon economic issues. Even after the Cold War and the *Brown v. Board of Education* decision had contributed to the ascendancy of a new, rabid defense of segregation and conservatism, there continued to be southern white liberals. Often these dissenters consisted of women and young ministers who, at considerable risk to themselves, supported desegregation and civil rights. However, segregationists intimidated and blocked the creation of a strong biracial coalition for civil rights within the South.

Another theme of new scholarship is that the Civil Rights movement energized African American churches, but the goals of African Americans changed. Particularly, the Black Power movement divided African Americans who wanted a new, separate "Black" identity from African Americans who wanted a nonracial American society. The rise of African American nationalism caught many older African American leaders off guard as the Civil Rights movement moved beyond attacking Jim Crow.

Recent scholarship in religious history has also shown that the religious revival of the 1950s did not eliminate liberal and conservative divisions and that conservative, evangelical churches grew faster than national, established Protestant churches. Mainline denominations, like Methodists, grew during the baby boom, but they experienced sharp drops in membership and financial contributions during the tumultuous 1960s. Wrestling with the explosive issues of civil rights, the Vietnam War, poverty, and urban unrest divided mainline churches. Denominations including Methodists found themselves divided between members who insisted upon evangelism and sexual morality and members who demanded greater emphasis upon justice and solutions to social ills, including racism. In their own congregations, churches experienced the decay of center cities and white flight to suburbs. Many Americans, African American and white, rich and poor, expected greater individual autonomy, and they looked less to mainline churches for guidance about moral issues such as divorce and politics.

Events, both internal and external, significantly changed American churches between 1940 and 1975. Catholics experienced a major transformation through the Vatican II Council, and American Protestants experienced their own upheavals. Not every change was related to the Civil Rights movement, but close examination of the Methodist experience illustrates much about how the Protestant establishment moved from a position of strength to one of decline. Methodists became more united and inclusive racially, but also more pluralistic and fragmented as a body. They emerged from the Civil Rights movement far different from what they had been when they started. They changed in ways that few Methodists had envisioned.

1

"In Christ There Is No East or West"

In Christ there is no east or west,
In him no south or north;
But one great fellowship of love
Throughout the whole wide earth.

—hymn by John Oxenham

THE METHODIST MOVEMENT in America began in the 1760s as an offshoot of John Wesley's reform movement in England. John and Charles, his hymn-writing brother, led a religious revival within the Anglican Church to make it more emotional, evangelical, and effective. Early Methodist missionaries particularly arrived in the Middle Atlantic colonies, an area that was remarkably diverse in ethnicity and cultures. These early missionaries found that their small revivals, often attended by only a small number of persons, continually touched the hearts of their hearers. Calvinism was still strong in many colonies, and Methodist preaching must have seemed quite different. Methodists preached that salvation was open to all and was not predestined by God and reserved for a select few. In a land wrestling with questions of political sovereignty, Methodism offered a religious equivalent to political independence in which worshippers chose salvation and God extended spiritual freedom to all. On a more practical level, Methodist itinerant ministers tirelessly traveled and preached wherever they could find an audience, whether friendly or not.[1]

From its earliest days in America, the Wesleyan movement struggled to reconcile its faith with social norms. Methodism began as an interracial fellowship, but early Methodists were not free of racism. Colonial America was a land of barriers including wealth, gender, status, and race. The racial prejudices of colonial American society deeply influenced early American Methodists even as they proclaimed the Gospel open to all. Yet early Methodists, both African American and white, worshipped together, preached together, prayed together, and contended with one another over the breadth and length of God's liberating message.

By 1774, the missionary Thomas Rankin reported to John Wesley that African American Methodists constituted about five hundred members of the nascent movement. That figure was at least 25 percent of the entire American church movement, and Rankin may have undercounted the total African American membership by omitting those who were not free. After the American Revolution, the number of free African Americans in the Midatlantic states increased significantly as some states began to end slavery and more slaves were manumitted by their owners. Methodists were particularly successful in reaching these free African Americans and incorporating them into their classes and churches, although often on a segregated basis. Throughout the late eighteenth and well into the early nineteenth centuries, African American membership hovered around 20 percent of the Methodist Church. Despite segregation in many congregations, African Americans were also exhorters, local preachers,

1. The history of early Methodism in American has had several recent studies of exceptional quality. Dee E. Andrews, *The Methodists and Revolutionary America, 1760–1800;* and John H. Wigger, *Taking Heaven by Storm: Methodism and the Rise of Popular Christianity in America,* are the most recent scholarly accounts. Christine Leigh Heyrman, *Southern Cross: The Beginnings of the Bible Belt,* is not strictly about Methodism but covers much of early Methodist history. William B. McClain, *Black People in the Methodist Church: Whither Thou Goest?* is a brief introduction to the history of African Americans in the United Methodist Church. *Heritage and Hope: The African-American Presence in United Methodism,* edited by Grant S. Shockley, is another starting point. Bishop James S. Thomas's *Methodism's Racial Dilemma: The Story of the Central Jurisdiction* is an inside account of Methodism's segregated jurisdiction, and J. Philip Wogaman, *Methodism's Challenge in Race Relations: A Study of Strategy,* published in 1960, is a contemporaneous account.

and class leaders. To a degree unfathomable a century later, African Americans were integral members of a predominantly white Protestant church in America, both as worshippers and leaders.

Methodism attracted African Americans and white Americans for many of the same reasons. Methodist revivals attracted people from all conditions, although the early church was stronger among the lower classes of society than among the colonial elite. The message delivered by Methodist preachers was that salvation was obtainable to all who confessed their sins and accepted God's grace. Methodists expected a powerful emotional experience, similar to John Wesley's Altergate transformation in 1738, which he described as "I felt my heart strangely warmed." Many early Methodists did have such a rebirth, and this regeneration was so powerful they remembered it decades later as if it had just happened.[2]

This change of heart opened the door to new life for Methodists, a life where economic class, gender, and race no longer defined them. Instead, many Methodists received a new identity based on God's grace that freed them from all other claims. This new status produced a condition of liminality, a threshold of new experience that Methodists shared with one another. This liminality freed persons of "normal" expectations, conditions, and rituals and established an order beyond such concerns. New brotherhood broke the bonds of the old life and introduced Methodists to their new brothers and sisters in Christ. This new Christian fellowship was a tremendous change because colonial America was such a hierarchical society. The Methodist message was an egalitarian one, although Methodists were not completely able to live out this egalitarian ideology. It was a message that was so radical that Methodists encountered a great deal of opposition, especially in the South. Their neighbors found the Methodist liminal experience disconcerting and a challenge to the traditional order. Of course, not every Methodist convert was so radically transformed or experienced such opposition to their new religious identity.[3]

Whether men or women, African American or white, Method-

2. Andrews, *Methodists and Revolutionary America*, 21, 84–92.
3. Donald G. Mathews, "Evangelical America: The Methodist Ideology"; Russell E. Richey, *Early American Methodism*, 2–5; Heyrman, *Southern Cross*, 33–52.

ists supported one another in a close relationship, usually in class meetings. Frequently worshipping together and attending prayer meetings created a separate space outside of the sinful world. Often these hymn singings and prayerful times cut across status and racial lines as family members, servants, or slaves praised their God together. In addition, African American and white preachers often traveled together. For a time, Francis Asbury, an influential early bishop, journeyed with Harry Hosier, an African American Methodist evangelist who Asbury thought was the better preacher of the two. Small group experiences characterized early Methodists as its members supported one another in building a greater sense of holiness. Methodist piety also emphasized a plain and simple life that opposed frivolous and worldly extravagances. This freedom from worldly cares and habits was another way for Methodists to be equal regardless of race, gender, or wealth.

African Americans flocked to the Methodist Church because in its earliest days Methodists opposed slavery. John Wesley became an outspoken critic of slavery in 1772 after reading a pamphlet by antislavery activist Anthony Benezet. Wesley wrote his own antislavery tract in 1774 in which he asserted that "Liberty is the right of every human creature, as soon as he breathes the vital air. And no human law can deprive him of that right." Later, in a letter to William Wilberforce, before Wesley's death in 1791, he labeled American slavery "the vilest that ever saw the sun." Two examples of how the issue of slavery seized early Methodist ministers are noteworthy. In one instance, Freeman Garrettson felt seized by the Holy Spirit just before beginning a family worship service and immediately gave his own slaves their freedom before continuing with the service. In another example, Joseph Everett, whose ministry took him through the Delmarva Peninsula, refused to eat with slave owners until they freed their slaves. In 1780, Methodist ministers meeting in Baltimore declared slavery "contrary to the laws of God, man, and nature, and hurtful to society, contrary to the dictates of conscience and pure religion." Thus, the first Methodist *Discipline*, written by ministers in 1785, condemned slavery unsparingly and gave members two years to free their slaves. Francis Asbury confided in his journal in 1778 that "the more pious parts of the people called Quakers, are exerting themselves for the liberation of slaves. This is a laudable design; and what the Methodists must come to, or, I fear the Lord will depart from them." Many early Methodists were part of a larger antislavery movement going on during and immediately after the American Revolution. The early antislavery position was an important reason that African Americans responded positively to the Methodist Church.[4]

Methodism also appealed to African Americans because of its orality, for it was a religious movement rooted in preaching, praise, and hymn singing. African Americans faced many restrictions on literacy and found in oral communication a power frequently denied them in Revolutionary era society. Methodist evangelicalism was not the only form of oral religion, but it was primarily the oral message that engaged its audience. Biblical knowledge or theological understanding was clearly secondary to the conversion experience for Methodists. While conversion was an internal, emotional experience, Methodists expressed their new faith orally through shouts of joy or words of praise.[5]

Although Methodism grew rapidly during the 1760s and 1770s, the American Revolution was a perilous time for the burgeoning church because John Wesley was so closely associated with the Tory or Loyalist cause. Many Methodist ministers who had come to America returned to the British Isles, and Asbury temporarily stopped traveling. American patriots objected to the refusal of some Methodists to take up arms and fight. There were Methodists who did participate in the fight against the British government, but Methodism experienced a crisis, as many of its leaders were seen as Tories or pacifists. However, peace ended persecution of Methodists, and the church soon recovered. Methodism entered a period of phenomenal growth as itinerant ministers fanned out across the American countryside. In 1784, in Baltimore, Maryland, Methodist ministers held their first General Conference and consecrated Francis Asbury and Thomas Coke bishops of the Methodist Episcopal Church.

4. H. Shelton Smith, *In His Image, But... : Racism in Southern Religion, 1780–1910*, 36, 37, 38, 39–47; Donald G. Mathews, *Slavery and Methodism: A Chapter in American Morality, 1780–1845*, 8, 3–29; William H. Williams, "Attraction of Methodism: The Delmarva Peninsula as a Case Study, 1769–1820," 43–44.

5. Mathews, "Evangelical America," 19–23, 28–30; Andrews, *Methodists and Revolutionary America*, 76–84.

Much of the growth in membership came from the peripatetic missionary activity of Methodist circuit-riding ministers who brought the gospel to many people who lived far from churches. In addition, local preachers who were settled augmented the work of circuit riders. Together, traveling elders and local preachers proclaimed to the local population the Gospel message, inviting all to confess their sins and accept God's grace. In the period after the American Revolution, theirs was a message of hope and renewal that found sympathetic ears.

The Great Revival, begun in 1800 at Cane Ridge, Kentucky, symbolized a new era of religious conversion that Methodists capitalized upon. Methodists led in the invention of new, larger revival methods that reached considerably larger audiences than had earlier revivals. Not only did these revivals involve more people, but also they incorporated armies of preachers to maximize their impact. They employed "anxious benches" for those in the midst of conversion experiences, and deputized guards to patrol the camps to keep order. Methodists were by no means the only Christians to use these conversion techniques or to grow so rapidly as a denomination. However, Methodism emerged as the largest church in the country by the 1830s and became the preeminent example of American Protestantism.

As the Methodist Episcopal Church grew, it also experienced fissures over race and polity. Race was the larger issue and caused the greater division within Methodism. One dimension of the church's racial separation was its retreat from antislavery, which the historian Donald G. Mathews splendidly describes. Methodists suspended their rules against slavery within six months after writing the church's first *Discipline* in 1785. Ministers found that slaveholding members did not experience sufficient religious enthusiasm to free their slaves. In 1800, the General Conference rejected a prohibition against slaveholders joining the church. By 1804, the *Discipline* came in two varieties, with the southern version saying nothing against slavery. The 1816 General Conference lamented the lost opportunity declaring, "little can be done to abolish the practice so contrary to the principles of moral justice." Despite misgivings about the institution of slavery, the Methodist Church decided it was better to grow in the slaveholding South than to rigidly uphold its antislavery position. This alone did not cause a break between African American and white Methodists, but it indicated how white interests dominated the church.[6]

The major schism between African American and white Methodists during the early nineteenth century occurred over ministerial rights, although segregation and paternalism were integrally involved. The segregation of class members had occurred in various parts of the Methodist Church with conflicts between African American and white members over equality. At St. George Methodist Church in Philadelphia in 1792, angry ushers who wanted African Americans to pray last dragged African American leaders Richard Allen and Absalom Jones to their feet while at the altar. Allen and Jones then led in the creation of the Free African Society as a mutual aid society when white leaders objected to their idea of creating a separate African American church. Jones eventually joined the Episcopal Church, but Allen remained committed to Methodism. As he explained, "I informed them [the Free African Society] that I could not be anything else but a Methodist, as I was born and awakened under them." Allen remained a Methodist and arranged for a separate Bethel Methodist Church loosely connected to St. George Methodist Church. This arrangement was outside the Methodist *Discipline*, but it had the active support of Bishop Asbury, who preached the inaugural sermon in 1794. Other African American congregations followed in Philadelphia, New York, and other towns in the Middle Atlantic states.[7]

The critical issue for these African American congregations was the status of their ministers. The Methodist Church ordained Richard Allen and other African American leaders as deacons, but deacons did not have the same rights as elders regarding administration of baptisms, marriages, and communion services. While Bethel and other African American congregations flourished and grew, conflict over ministerial control broke out. When a new presiding elder of St. George Church, James Smith, attempted to appoint a new preacher to Bethel, Allen and his congregation challenged the presiding elder

6. Donald G. Mathews, *Religion in the Old South*, 75; Mathews, *Slavery and Methodism*, 22–28.

7. Andrews, *Methodists and Revolutionary America*, 147, 132–50; Carol V. R. George, *Segregated Sabbaths: Richard Allen and the Emergence of Independent Black Churches, 1760–1840*, 49–71.

in court. Allen had a supplement to the original agreement, "The African Supplement," to further delineate the rights of the Bethel congregation. After nearly a decade of struggle, the issue was settled in 1816 when the Pennsylvania Supreme Court ruled that St. George Church and the white Methodists lost all authority over Bethel. This was a blow to white paternal control and monopoly of church power; Bethel had grown to be one of the largest Methodist congregations in America. Had the Methodist Church made African American ministers elders and accepted them as members of annual conferences, then it might have been possible for Methodists to remain racially unified. However, this would have been a fellowship far outside the norms of American society. Whether one examines racial practices in the free North or the slave South, free African Americans in the early nineteenth century did not enjoy equality. White American society assumed its supremacy over African Americans, slave or free, and the liminal enthusiasm of Methodists became less common and racial prejudice more prevalent. The racial bigotry of American society, North and South, had compromised Methodist brotherhood.[8]

Formation of African American Methodist denominations quickly followed the rise of autonomous African American Methodist congregations. In April 1816, African American Methodists from Philadelphia, Baltimore, Wilmington (Delaware), Attleborough (Pennsylvania), and New Salem (New Jersey) organized the African Methodist Episcopal (AME) Church with a *Discipline* that was virtually identical to the Methodist Episcopal Church. After African American minister Daniel Coker declined, Richard Allen became the first AME bishop. In 1821, in New York City, several African American congregations formed their own denomination after having failed to convince the New York Annual Conference to approve formation of an "African Conference." This church eventually took the name African Methodist Episcopal Zion (AMEZ) to distinguish itself from the Philadelphia-based church. Nevertheless, other African American congregations remained within the Methodist Episcopal Church and continually petitioned the General Conference

8. Will B. Gravely, "African Methodisms and the Rise of Black Denominationalism," 108–17.

until the time of the Civil War for ordination of African American elders.[9]

Defection by a large body of African American Methodists was not the only loss that the Methodist Episcopal Church experienced. The power and authority of bishops also led to challenges by those who wanted a more egalitarian church polity. James O'Kelly launched an early rebellion against the power of bishops at the 1792 General Conference. He demanded a system where ministers could vote to overturn appointments made by bishops. Using rhetoric from the American Revolution, he argued that the ministers would be free only if they held this protection from episcopal tyranny, but the conference sustained the power of bishops. O'Kelly and about thirty ministers subsequently formed their own Republican Methodist Church (later renamed the Christian Church). O'Kelly was an outspoken southern foe of slavery; his departure was significant to the church. A later revolt against the power of bishops produced the Methodist Protestant Church in 1830. It elected presidents rather than bishops, and laity and ministers had equal power in annual conferences.

The rise of modern abolitionism in the 1830s precipitated more splintering of the Methodist Episcopal Church. Although most northern Methodists opposed abolitionism as a dangerous and destructive doctrine, it did have some advocates, led by New England Methodist ministers Orange Scott and La Roy Sunderland. After unsuccessful efforts at restoring antislavery positions in the Methodist Church, a portion of the abolitionists formed the Wesleyan Methodist Church in 1843. However, a sectional split in Methodism occurred at the 1844 General Conference. Here the national sectionalism around slavery came to the fore in the church as a series of slavery issues drove southern and northern halves apart. The General Conference upheld the Baltimore Annual Conference in its decision to deny ordination to a candidate who owned a slave. It also rejected a militant southern effort to strip from both versions of the *Discipline* any condemnation of slavery except for the slave trade. Finally, the sectional conflict reached its apogee over the status of

9. A small African American Methodist denomination emerged earlier in Baltimore, but it never flourished like the slightly later churches; see ibid., 108–26; and Reginald F. Hildebrand, "Methodist Episcopal Policy on the Ordination of Black Ministers, 1784–1864."

Bishop James O. Andrew of Georgia, who, after his election to the episcopacy, had become a slave owner when his wife inherited a slave. After several days of intense debate, a majority of the General Conference voted for a resolution that requested Bishop Andrew to "desist" serving as a bishop while still a slaveholder. Southern Methodists found this unacceptable, and they announced their intent to form a new church, one cleansed of antislavery sentiment. The following year in Louisville, Kentucky, southern Methodists held the first General Conference of the Methodist Episcopal Church, South.[10]

Although the split within the largest Methodist denomination was over slavery, both northern and southern Methodist churches continued to have African American members, albeit with very different types of white paternalism. In the northern church, African American members largely worshipped in their own congregations with supervision by white presiding elders and bishops. Local African American pastors continued to press for full ordination and equal status within the church, but northern white Methodists ignored their petitions. In the South, an effort at bringing more slaves into the church expanded significantly after the sectional division. Many southern slaveholders allowed the Methodist Episcopal Church, South, to organize congregations among their slaves so that their slaves might internalize values of loyalty and honesty. Masters saw Christianity as a means of extending their authority and making their slaves more satisfied. Most slave owners also very much wanted to believe in their own benevolence, and what could be more benevolent than bringing salvation to their slaves?[11]

The outbreak of the Civil War with the firing upon Ft. Sumter in April 1861 came after several of the major forms of Christianity in America had already split over slavery or theological positions that related to slavery. In 1837, Presbyterians split into Old School and New School theological camps, but these positions were related to their respective positions on church structure and reform activity. Methodists, the largest Protestant church in the country, divided as described above, and Baptists broke apart in 1845 over the refusal of its Home Board of Missions (its foreign missions board) to appoint a

---

10. Mathews, *Slavery and Methodism*, 229–33, 246–82.
11. Ibid., 62–87; Hildebrand, "Methodist Episcopal Policy," 132–42.

slaveholder as a missionary. Episcopalians and Catholics avoided an outright split over slavery, although there were sharp regional differences in each church.[12]

The Civil War produced a second American revolution that opened the door for some improvement in the condition and status of African Americans, although racial prejudice remained endemic in American society. Ironically, both sides entered the war denying that slavery was an issue: the Union wanted to keep the border states of Maryland, Kentucky, and Missouri in the federal government, so it did not attack slavery in these states. The Confederates wanted foreign aid from Britain and France, both of which had governments that opposed slavery, so it emphasized states' rights. As the war intensified, Union forces began to include African Americans and Lincoln issued the Emancipation Proclamation after the battle of Antietam in September 1862. In the desperate closing days of the war, Confederate leaders even contemplated granting freedom to slaves if they fought for the Confederacy. Throughout the country, the war challenged assumptions about white supremacy, particularly as African Americans served in the Union army.

Even before the Civil War ended, both white and African American leaders in the North scrambled to organize southern African American churches. Although most southern African Americans chose to join congregational Baptist churches, Methodism was their clear second choice. Many southern African Americans were familiar with Methodism because of its evangelism; and a large number of missionaries came to the South to organize churches. These missionaries were both African American and white and represented the Methodist Episcopal Church, AME Church, and the AMEZ Church.

The northern Methodist Episcopal Church aggressively organized African American churches in the South. After starting work in an ecumenical mission to the South, the northern Methodists quickly formed their own Freedmen's Aid Society, and in 1864, after years of resistance to ordaining African American ministers, the church began doing so in significant numbers. The church's Freed-

12. Sydney E. Ahlstrom, *A Religious History of the American People*, 657–69. For more depth, see C. C. Goen, *Broken Churches, Broken Nation: Denominational Schisms and the Coming of the American Civil War*.

men's Aid Society sponsored schools, colleges, and a seminary as part of its efforts to extend educational opportunities. Even more innovative for the time, the northern church created annual conferences in the South where African American and white ministers served together. Bishop Gilbert Haven, a New England abolitionist who served in Atlanta, Georgia, even praised interracial marriages. There was within northern Methodism an attempt to create in the South a church where there was close cooperation between African American and white Methodists, although this cooperation started at the ministerial level, rather than the congregational level. Still, this was a significant degree of integration and anticaste attitude for the late 1860s and early 1870s. In many ways, the northern church appeared headed toward recovering a portion of the biracial origins of Methodism.[13]

In contrast, the Methodist Episcopal Church, South, rapidly began losing its African American members during the Civil War, and by 1866 its African American membership stood at 78,742, compared to 207,776 in 1860. Desperate to have some continued influence over southern African Americans lest they depend entirely on northern influences, southern Methodist bishops began creating separate annual conferences for the African American members who remained. By late 1870, when the first General Conference of the new Colored Methodist Episcopal Church met, there were five annual conferences organized across the South. This was an independent church, although the leaders of these conferences were African American southerners who had close ties to southern whites. Several early leaders were favorably inclined toward white southerners because these leaders were products of interracial families themselves; none of the early church leaders came from the North. Attacked as being too close to former slaveholders, the Colored Methodist Episcopal (CME; after 1954 known as the Christian Methodist Episcopal) Church appealed to African American southerners who resisted political activity in churches and who believed that cooperative

13. Reginald F. Hildebrand, *The Times Were Strange and Stirring: Methodist Preachers and the Crisis of Emancipation*, 75–100; see also William B. Gravely, *Gilbert Haven, Methodist Abolitionist: A Study in Race, Religion, and Reform, 1850–1880*; Ralph E. Morrow, *Northern Methodism and Reconstruction;* and Hunter Dickinson Farish, *The Circuit Rider Dismounts: A Social History of Southern Methodism, 1865–1900.*

relations with southern whites were necessary for any progress to occur.

Although the Methodist Episcopal Church, South, provided some funds for the support of two Colored Methodist Episcopal colleges, the southern white church had virtually no African American membership and relatively little to do with African American southerners until women's groups within the church started some paternalistic contact with them in the late nineteenth century. Bishop Atticus G. Haygood spoke for improved relations with African Americans within the Methodist Episcopal Church, South, during the late nineteenth century. He advocated public education for African Americans on a segregated basis so they would be better prepared for voting. He also denounced lynchings. The South was still working out issues of public education, suffrage, and civil rights, and Haygood advocated a position that African American and white southerners were integrally related even though not socially equal. In contrast, Bishop John Christian Keener told the 1890 General Conference of the Methodist Episcopal Church, South, that "we now have a solidly white church, for which we thank God."[14]

The chief competitors with the northern church were the AME and AMEZ churches. Both began sending missionaries into the South while the war still raged to assist their newly freed brothers and sisters. Their missionaries brought a message of racial pride and achievement that white northerners seldom conveyed. Although these churches had scarce resources to share with their southern brethren, they built churches and schools at great individual sacrifice. They particularly encouraged freedmen to exercise all facets of their new freedom. They preached not only that southern African Americans should work hard to get out from under white economic control, but they should also be involved politically to defend their civil rights. This was a gospel of freedom that emphasized the dignity of all African Americans.[15]

14. Kenneth K. Bailey, "The Post–Civil War Racial Separations in Southern Protestantism: Another Look," 453; Hildebrand, *Times Were Strange*, 3–27; David L. Chappell, *Inside Agitators: White Southerners in the Civil Rights Movement*, 4–7; Ralph E. Luker, *The Social Gospel in Black and White: American Racial Reform, 1885–1912*, 20–23, 100–101.

15. Hildebrand, *Times Were Strange*, 31–72; William E. Montgomery, *Under Their Own Vine and Fig Tree: The African-American Church in the South, 1865–*

Despite the similarities in these Methodist churches, there were differences that influenced how African Americans determined which church was for them. The northern Methodist Episcopal Church appealed to African Americans because of its anticaste stand. Initially, the missionaries of this church gloried in their biracial annual conferences and even attracted a few ministers from the AME church. The Colored Methodist Episcopal Church took a more conservative stance than the others did; although it was a separate denomination, it recognized that southern whites were not going to go away and that the New South would be more like the Old South than not. Its leaders did not engage in political activity, and they cooperated with southern whites. The AME and AMEZ churches both appealed to freedmen who wanted complete autonomy from white influence. They emphasized their northern independent roots and proclaimed a gospel of freedom that asserted African Americans were equal to white Americans, that economic advance came through work and education, and that political advance required suffrage.[16]

Each form of African American Methodism had geographic areas of strength. The Methodist Episcopal Church was able to establish a considerable following in South Carolina, in part because its missionaries arrived in the state as Union forces seized control from Confederates in 1865 and because South Carolina had such a large African American population. Maryland, Delaware, and New Jersey were also areas where the Methodist Episcopal Church was very successful. Meanwhile, the AME Church became strong in South Carolina, Georgia, and Florida. By 1906, its memberships in these three states constituted 42 percent of the 500,000-member denomination. North Carolina and Alabama were the AMEZ Church's most successful mission fields, and in 1906 these two states contained 55 percent of the 185,000-member church. Because of its later start, the CME Church did not establish a particular dominance in any state, but it became strong in Georgia and along the Mississippi River. Georgia held nearly 20 percent of the entire

---

1900, 38–96; Clarence E. Walker, *A Rock in a Weary Land: The African Methodist Episcopal Church during the Civil War and Reconstruction,* 46–81.

16. Hildebrand, *Times Were Strange,* 15–27, 50–72, 89–100, 111–18; Montgomery, *Under Their Own,* 97–141; Walker, *Rock,* 82–107.

denomination in 1906, and half of the remaining membership lived in Tennessee, Mississippi, Arkansas, and Louisiana. In the post–Civil War period, the Baptist and Methodist churches dominated the Afro-American religious experience. It was said, "If you meet a Negro and he isn't a Methodist or a Baptist, then you know somebody's been messing with him."[17]

The Methodist Episcopal Church retreated from its anticaste position in the mid-1870s, mirroring the northern Republican party's shift away from southern politics. After the initial rush to organize annual conferences in the South subsided, concern for integrated annual conferences waned among many white leaders. Some white Methodists argued that modifying the anticaste element of the church in the South would attract more white members. The 1872 General Conference refused to allow annual conferences to divide along racial lines, but the 1876 General Conference authorized by a large majority such a division if both races consented. Although several African American leaders spoke out against the move, many of their white allies, such as Bishop Haven, were dead. Most annual conferences divided along racial lines during the next quadrennium, although a few waited until later. The northern Methodist Freedmen's Aid Society also metamorphosed into a general southern education fund that no longer devoted its entire funds to African American education.[18]

Throughout the post–Civil War period, white bishops presided over the Methodist Episcopal Church's southern annual conferences, whether the membership was African American or white. Not surprisingly, agitation for the election of an African American bishop began in 1872 when James Lynch, an African American minister and politician in Mississippi, urged the Methodist Episcopal Church's General Conference to elect an African American bishop. The conference instead only affirmed that African American and white ministers were eligible. Nineteenth-century efforts to elect an African American bishop reached their zenith in 1896, when Dr. John Wesley Bowen, the first African American to receive a Ph.D. from Boston University, led all voting on the first ballot for the

17. William H. Wiggins Jr., *O Freedom! Afro-American Emancipation Celebrations,* 83; 1906 Census Bureau, Religious Bodies, 2:450, 458, 480. See also William B. Gravely, "The Social, Political, and Religious Significance of the Formation of the Colored Methodist Episcopal Church."

18. Hildebrand, *Times Were Strange,* 101–18.

episcopacy. However, Bowen was not elected, and episcopal supervision by white bishops remained a grievance among African American Methodists in the northern church.

African Americans in the northern Methodist Episcopal Church were not the only African Americans who experienced discrimination within their own church. African American Catholics, Episcopalians, and Presbyterians confronted many of the same problems. Each church had its own internal issues that affected its African American members, but the major issue, as for Methodists, was how to reconcile white racial prejudice with an African American desire for full participation. Prejudice prevailed, although the form of discrimination differed from church to church.

African American Catholics were only a small percentage of the total American Catholic Church. Throughout the nineteenth century, the chief concern of the American Catholic hierarchy was providing for Catholic immigrants and fighting the widespread anti-Catholic sentiment among Protestant Americans. Since immigrants settled largely in the northern portion of the country and most African Americans lived in the South, the Catholic Church was not particularly strong among African Americans. There were significant numbers of African American Catholics in Louisiana and Maryland, areas where there had been Catholic slaveholders before emancipation. However, because of the severe shortage of priests, Catholic slaves in the Old South received very little religious instruction before the Civil War.[19]

At the Second Plenary Council in 1866, a major council of the American Catholic hierarchy, American Catholic bishops decided to increase evangelism among African Americans. Yet the bishops rejected a proposal to establish a coordinated approach and instead left action to individual bishops, a form of regional autonomy that invited inaction. Southern Catholic bishops were not eager to evangelize among African American freedmen, as they feared this would engender even more hostility from the local Protestant community in the South. The council also approved the establishment of separate churches for African American Catholics where local conditions made this advisable. Separate parishes in the same locale ran counter to the tradition of a parish determined solely by geography,

19. Randall M. Miller, "Slaves and Southern Catholicism."

but the American Catholic Church had already discovered that ethnic tension among immigrants in some cases made separate churches advisable. The most active missionary society among African Americans was the St. Joseph Foreign Missionary Society (Josephites), who in 1871 sent four priests from England exclusively to work among African Americans.[20]

The Protestant Episcopal Church did not have a strong record on civil rights during the late nineteenth century. Writing in 1903, W. E. B. Du Bois judged that the Episcopal Church had "probably done less for black people than any other aggregation of Christians." African American Episcopalians were not numerous before the Civil War, and freedom produced a mass defection to African American Baptist or Methodist churches. In South Carolina, Episcopal priest Alexander Glennie, who labored for years among rice plantation slaves, saw "the labors of his lifetime dissipated and lost in a single day," according to a white associate who noted that once freedom arrived, African American Christians "flatly refused his ministrations." Like other churches, the Episcopal Church created the Protestant Episcopal Freedman's Commission in 1865 to begin educational and missionary activity among former slaves in the South. The commission, renamed the Commission on Home Mission to Colored People in 1868, limited most of its activity to Virginia and the Carolinas, and it was chronically short of funds, with fewer than 20 percent of all parishes contributing to it. By 1877, the commission could only report thirty-seven African American congregations, fifteen ministers, and fourteen candidates preparing for ordination. The only point of pride in the commission's 1877 report was that African American Episcopalians were "chiefly, if not exclusively[,] of the better class of colored population." In 1878, the General Convention decided to end the Commission of Home Mission to Colored People and simply to have outreach to African Americans become another responsibility of the Board of Missions.[21]

20. Stephen J. Ochs, *Desegregating the Altar: The Josephites and the Struggle for Black Priests, 1871–1960*, 9–48.
21. W. E. B. Du Bois, *The Negro Church*, 139; Charles Joyner, *Down by the Riverside: A South Carolina Slave Community*, 229, 230; J. Carleton Hayden, "After the War," 426; Gardiner H. Shattuck Jr., *Episcopalians and Race: Civil War to Civil Rights*, 7–11.

Presbyterians combined some of the features of the Episcopal and Methodist churches in race relations after the Civil War. They, like the Episcopalians, did not have large numbers of African American members, and, like the Methodists, had split into sectional bodies. The southern branch of Presbyterianism, the Presbyterian Church in the United States (PCUS), saw most of its African American members drift away after the Civil War. Its General Assembly held in Augusta, Georgia, in 1865 affirmed that freedom made African Americans no less in need of salvation, but it went on to advise African Americans to expect to take a subordinate role when worshipping with white southerners. African American congregations would have their own leaders, but they initially had no ordained ministers, so final authority rested with white Presbyterian leaders. The Colored Evangelistic Fund was weakly supported, as was the Institute for the Training of Colored Ministers. Many of its African American members were more favorably disposed toward white people than were most southern African Americans. An African American congregation in Louisiana pleaded for assistance from the church, writing, "We have no member capable of expounding to us the Scripture of Truth—we are all poor and have not the means of procuring a white preacher, which we are so anxious for." Under the circumstances, most African American Presbyterians moved to all-African American denominations or associated with the northern Presbyterians, the Presbyterian Church in the United States of America (PCUSA).[22]

Northern Presbyterians joined in the effort to evangelize among southern African Americans after the Civil War and did form several presbyteries. However, financial contributions to the effort were not generous, and church missionaries brought with them a paternalistic attitude. They did ordain a few educated African Americans such as Jonathan Gibbs, who formed a successful Presbyterian church in Charleston, South Carolina, in 1865. Nevertheless, like southern Presbyterians, the northern church had difficulty competing with the more emotional, less theologically inclined Baptist and Methodist churches. The PCUSA took an early, strong stand for interracial

22. Ernest Trice Thompson, "Black Presbyterians, Education, and Evangelism after the Civil War," 178; Montgomery, *Under Their Own*, 74–76.

unity when in 1888 it rejected a plea for creation of racial presbyteries and synods. Yet this stand was not final. The southern Cumberland Presbyterian Church, a small synod in eastern Tennessee, desired to join the northern church in 1904, but only on the condition that the church permit the formation of segregated presbyteries and synods. Despite African American protests, the northern church changed its constitution to allow separate presbyteries and synods in order to unite with the Cumberland Presbyterian Church.[23]

African American Methodists, Catholics, Episcopalians, and Presbyterians sought unsuccessfully to worship God as full members of their churches. They protested being relegated to the gallery, denied ordination, or treated as children under the tutelage of their white counterparts. However, racial prejudice remained stronger than Christian brotherhood. Very few white Christians challenged the racial status quo or denounced racial discrimination as a denial of Christian brotherhood. For Methodists, the brief and imperfect racial brotherhood in its American beginning was a quickly forgotten moment. In different ways, northern and southern white Methodists said no to equality with African American Methodists, and they formed churches that practiced brotherhood for white members only. The northern church did have African American members, but its brief flirtation with equality had ended quickly. Paternalism and separation became the norm. In the southern church, white supremacy reigned, although there were some advocates of benign paternalism. However, talks of reunion between northern and southern Methodists would again raise the issue of race. Advocates of Methodist reunion would face two major questions: How could the two churches resolve their differences? And how would African American Methodists in the northern church influence their white counterparts?

23. Henry Justin Ferry, "Racism and Reunion: A Black Protest by Francis James Grimke"; Montgomery, *Under Their Own*, 76–78; David M. Reimers, *White Protestantism and the Negro*, 136–39.

2

Jim Crow Church

THE TWENTIETH CENTURY opened with race relations in a steep descent, but with sectional relations between white Americans steadily improving. This sectional rapprochement included Methodists, which in turn put new stress on the position of African American members of the "northern" Methodist Episcopal Church. In a period of political disfranchisement and increased segregation, this was a time of peril for African American Methodists who were not part of the all–African American Methodist denominations. Two attempts to unite the Methodist Episcopal Church with the Methodist Episcopal Church, South, ran aground over race, but on the third try Methodists became the first of the three major Protestant denominations to reunite since separating before the Civil War. This merger of Methodism created the Methodist Church, a denomination with a new structure that placed African American Methodists in a "separate but equal" arrangement within the new denomination. This Methodist compromise over race was in some ways unique, but other American churches made their own accommodations with racism and Jim Crow during the first four decades of the twentieth century.

In the last decade of the nineteenth and first decade of the twentieth centuries, the prospects for African American and southern white Methodists returning to the same church were bleak. This time was the nadir of the free African American experience as white southerners, with national concurrence, imposed economic, political, and social hardships upon African Americans. There was also no unified strategy of resistance or response, and little assistance offered to African Americans by white Americans of any region or political party. Booker T. Washington, founder of Tuskegee Institute and leader of the industrial education movement, advocated a policy of accommodation in his 1895 Atlanta Compromise speech. The speech accepted segregation, advocated African American economic development through thrift and hard work, and advanced cooperation with white leadership to gain African Americans the respect and rights of all Americans. Maligned by critics as a pusillanimous response to exploitation and violence, Washington's position initially had many defenders, including W. E. B. Du Bois and African American Methodist leader John Wesley Bowen. By the time of the speech, Washington had established industrial education as a leading way for southern African Americans to gain economic independence and respectability. In sharp contrast to Washington and the policy of accommodation, African Methodist Episcopal (AME) Bishop Henry McNeal Turner advocated a movement back to Africa. Turner argued that America, not just the South, would never accept African Americans as equals and that the only reasonable course was to organize a mass exodus. Although Turner had some popular support, most African American leaders attacked his proposal as impractical and ill-advised. America was their home, and African Americans could be as successful as white Americans if given an opportunity.[1]

Legal rights won in the constitutional amendments after the Civil War had already been limited, but in the 1890s, the U.S. Supreme Court diminished civil rights in two critical ways. In 1896, the Court accepted the concept of "separate but equal" in the *Plessy v. Ferguson* decision. Southern states had already separated African Americans and white citizens in various settings, but this decision gave state legislatures and local governments permission to expand this form of discrimination in a plethora of ways. Two years later, the Court followed with *Williams v. Mississippi*, which eviscerated the Fifteenth Amendment's defense of African American voting rights. The movement to disfranchise African American voters received a green light from the Supreme Court, and a variety of subterfuges such as literacy tests, "good character" requirements, and poll taxes soon became common across the South. Voting fraud and violence destroyed the southern Populist Movement and its attempt to build a coalition of poor African American and white farmers. In its brief history, the

1. Luker, *Social Gospel*, 136; Montgomery, *Under Their Own*, 195, 198, 203–10.

Populist party brought fear to the southern Democratic party; however, when Democrats regained power, they thoroughly disfranchised southern African Americans and many poor whites as well.

The worst crime against southern African Americans during the 1890s was the horrendous practice of lynching, which averaged over 190 per year for the decade. Two important shifts occurred in trends related to lynchings. First, lynchings became strictly regional events and, second, victims became almost exclusively African Americans. Lynchings were a communal form of terrorism to intimidate African Americans and show women, white as well as African American, that white males were in control of society and above the law. While some white southerners adamantly defended the practice of lynching, many others expressed ambiguous positions. For example, Georgia Methodist bishop Atticus Haygood condemned lynchings, but also decried the attacks on white women often cited as the cause of lynchings. Methodist Episcopal Church, South, newspaper editor and later bishop E. E. Hoss charged that attacks by African American men on white women were rampant. However, the northern Methodist Episcopal Church unequivocally condemned lynching at its 1892 General Conference.[2]

Lynchings continued well into the first half of the twentieth century. At the end of World War I, there was a new outburst of lynchings, with seventy instances across the South in one year. Overall, the period between 1919 and 1939 witnessed over five hundred lynchings, with a second wave of lynchings in the early 1930s when the Great Depression hit. This new spate of terror galvanized protests. The 1920 Episcopal General Convention took its first official stand against lynching. Southern Presbyterian, Methodist, and Baptist denominational bodies also began to condemn lynching as lawless, but they held back from demanding a federal antilynching law. More important than denominational statements were sermons in areas where lynchings were likely to occur. Unfortunately, there is little evidence that pulpits regularly denounced lynching or that these sermons were particularly influential.[3]

2. W. Fitzhugh Brundage, *Lynching in the New South: Georgia and Virginia, 1880–1930*, 8; Luker, *Social Gospel*, 90, 95–96, 98–101; see also Donald G. Mathews, "The Southern Rite of Human Sacrifice."

3. Robert Moats Miller, *American Protestantism and Social Issues, 1919–1939*, 131–36.

The most important response occurred among southern white women, who began to reject the argument that lynchings protected them. They began to use data collected on lynchings to show that most lynchings did not occur because of rape and to pressure local law enforcement to stop lynchings. Southern white Methodist women were integral to the formation of the Association of Southern Women for the Prevention of Lynchings (ASWPL) led by Jessie Daniel Ames. Methodist women had been growing in involvement with African American southerners, and many leaders—such as Bertha Newell, Louise Young, and Estelle Haskin, building upon the earlier work of Lily Hammond, Belle Bennett, and Mary DeBardeleben— made race relations fundamental to their church mission work. A meeting with African American women leaders in 1920 in Memphis, Tennessee, had encouraged southern white Methodist women in working with African American women for improved race relations and social conditions in the South. However, Ames, influenced by the southern women's suffrage movement, led the ASWPL to remain a white-only organization and to focus only upon state action and persuasion. Although ecumenical, the ASWPL drew its membership largely from the ranks of Methodist and Presbyterian women. The southern Methodist Woman's Missionary Council endorsed the ASWPL early and provided some of its most energetic members. The organization denied that lynchings ever protected white women because they were lawless acts, and it worked to get local officials to protect potential lynch victims from mobs. Later, in 1934, southern Methodist women leaders even endorsed the Costigan-Wagner bill to give federal authorities the power to prosecute lynchers, a step that the ASWPL never took.[4]

In the North, conditions for African Americans in the early twentieth century were better than in the South, but they were still far from equal. In housing, African Americans lived in the worst sections and paid inflated prices. Health conditions were poor and infant mortality was particularly high. In employment, labor unions and management both created barriers to work and occupational advance, so African Americans worked for low wages in menial jobs when

4. Jacquelyn Dowd Hall, *Revolt against Chivalry: Jessie Daniel Ames and the Women's Campaign against Lynching,* 70–77, 176; John Patrick McDowell, *The Social Gospel in the South: The Woman's Home Mission Movement in the Methodist Episcopal Church, 1886–1939,* 94–98.

they could find work at all. In politics, urban political machines mobilized African American voters but produced little in return for their support. The Social Gospel Movement, a diverse group of liberal Christians concerned with social conditions, attempted to improve conditions for African Americans through institutional churches and the growing settlement house movement, but some organizations that provided aid, such as the YMCA and YWCA, decided to institute segregation rather than to build interracial facilities. There was a growing awareness within the Social Gospel Movement that American society needed racial reform. However, the Social Gospel Movement was widely divided regarding strategies, tactics, and ultimate goals. Some leaders contributed to the formation of the National Association for the Advancement of Colored People (NAACP), but others took a more conservative, gradualist approach.[5]

Among white Americans at the dawn of the twentieth century, there was a growing healing of the sectional rift created by the Civil War and Reconstruction. Elderly Civil War leaders died or retired, and younger men, who had not been as seared by the wartime experience, rose to positions of leadership. Several events that hastened this process were the Spanish-American War; the election of Woodrow Wilson, the first southern-born president since before the Civil War; and, especially, World War I. During the 1917 wartime outburst of patriotism, the *Confederate Veteran*, a journal dedicated to keeping alive the memory of the Lost Cause, found some good even in the "Battle Hymn of the Republic," which during the war had been an anthem of the Union forces. For most northern Americans, the issue of civil rights in the South was now a local issue with only lynchings receiving national attention from time to time. This feeling of connection between previous enemies reached Methodists in both the North and the South. Serious deliberations toward the union of the Methodist Episcopal and Methodist Episcopal Church, South, began in 1916 after initial conversations in 1898.[6]

Southern white Methodists entered these talks attempting to disengage African American members entirely from any united church or, failing this, to put them on a path that would eventually lead to

5. Luker, *Social Gospel*, 160–78.

6. Charles Reagan Wilson, *Baptized in Blood: The Religion of the Lost Cause, 1865–1920*, 161, 176; Frederick E. Maser, "The Story of Unification, 1874–1939," 412–23.

their separation from white Methodists. To expel African American members from the northern church would not be easy, but some southern Methodists expected this as a price for reunion. This position reflected the adamant white supremacy position of a substantial number of southern white leaders. A more moderate southern white Methodist approach was to create for African American Methodists an independent governing body, an associate general conference. Here African American Methodists could toil with a large degree of autonomy while enjoying the encouragement and support of a reunited white Methodist Church. This moderate approach was similar to the way southern church leaders had contributed to the creation of the Colored Methodist Episcopal Church soon after the Civil War. Neither southern position fully accepted African American members as part of the reunited church or provided much contact between African American and white Methodists.

Some white leaders in the Methodist Episcopal Church, including Bishop Thomas Neely and Charles Parkhurst, the editor of *Zion's Herald*, wanted reunion so fervently that they suggested African American members of the Methodist Episcopal Church should voluntarily withdraw. Others, like Bishop Earl Cranston, demurred from suggesting that African American members leave, but he did earnestly desire that nothing imperil reunion. Bishop John W. Hamilton wrote African American Methodist leader Robert E. Jones that he was of the opinion that Cranston would never ask African American Methodists to leave, but "I think he might go into his closet, shut the door and thank the Lord if you volunteered to go out, so as to give the [Methodist] Church South the right of way to come in."[7]

I. G. Penn and Jones represented African American Methodists within the Methodist Episcopal Church in these negotiations. Penn was born in 1867 in New Glasgow, Virginia. He had been a newspaperman for the *Richmond Planet*, the *Knoxville Negro World* and the *New York Age* and since 1908 had led the Methodist Episcopal Church's Freedmen's Aid Society. He had also served on the committee responsible for the African American exhibits at the 1895

7. Henry N. Oakes, *The Struggle for Racial Equality in the Methodist Episcopal Church*, 144–47; Bishop John W. Hamilton to Robert E. Jones, February 14, 1916, Bishop Robert Elijah Jones Papers, Amistad Research Center, Tulane University, New Orleans, Louisiana.

Atlanta Exposition. His book *The Afro-American Press and Its Editors* was one of the first accounts of African American journalism in America. Jones was slightly younger, being born in 1872 in Greensboro, North Carolina. As a youth, Jones received a college education and seminary training. Ordained in the Methodist Episcopal Church in 1894, he soon took a position on the *Southwestern Christian Advocate*, the Methodist Episcopal's church journal devoted to its African American members. A decade later, he became its editor. Jones later founded Gulfside Assembly, on the coast of the Gulf of Mexico near Waveland, Mississippi, one of the first retreat centers for African Americans. Both men had extensive connections among African American Methodists. Together they wanted to defend the interests of African American Methodists without appearing disruptive or unrealistic.

Jones and Penn steadfastly rejected both southern white positions, regardless of whether separation from white Methodists was immediate or at some point in the future. Jones told his fellow commission members, "The time has passed . . . when a man can contract a delivery of Negroes." Instead, Jones and Penn accepted the idea of a separate jurisdictional conference for African American Methodists. African American Methodists would be voting members in the General Conference and would elect their own bishops, although their bishops could preside over only African American annual conferences. Some African American Methodists had proposed the idea of a separate African American jurisdictional conference, and in October 1914 a conference attended by over two hundred ministers and laymen endorsed the idea of a separate jurisdictional conference. Such a separate jurisdictional conference would accept the principle of segregation, but provide some interracial contact at the highest levels of the church. It was a proposal largely in keeping with the ideology of Booker T. Washington.[8]

Despite efforts of Methodist Episcopal Church, South, commission members to force African American Methodists into a separate church or an associate general conference, white Methodist Episcopal commission members stood by Jones and Penn. The final plan, drafted in January 1920, included an African American jurisdictional

---

8. Joint Commission on Unification, *Proceedings,* 2:613; Joint Commission, *Proceedings,* 1:146–49, 153–55; Oakes, *Struggle,* 153–54.

conference with full voting representation at the General Conference. Southern whites received a provision for the creation of an associate general conference, but only African American Methodists could initiate it. Yet the Methodist Episcopal Church, South, also won a provision that African American representation at the General Conferences be capped at 5 percent of the total General Conference. This allowed for some growth in actual African American membership, but it was clearly discriminatory. African American Methodist bishops would preside only over their own annual conferences, but white Methodists would not take part in their election. The proposal clearly segregated African American members, but the arrangement kept them in a new church with southern white Methodists.[9]

The plan emerged in an especially explosive time in race relations because of changes brought about by American participation in World War I. During the war, three to four hundred thousand African Americans left the South to find employment in northern industry. This produced new racial strife in northern cities, where housing was critically short. White residents feared the sudden rise in African American population. The exodus also alarmed southern whites, since it threatened the status quo in race relations. African Americans were anxious to use the war to gain better conditions. Many assumed that the war to make the world safe for democracy would also improve life for them. However, major race riots occurred in 1917 in East St. Louis, Illinois, and in Houston, Texas. Tension increased when the war ended and job opportunities decreased. In 1919, race riots occurred in over twenty-five cities, in which seventy-eight African Americans died during the violence. The largest riot, in Chicago, occurred over four days, took the lives of twenty-three African American and fifteen white residents, and injured over five hundred people. For many Americans it was shocking to see the magnitude of America's racial divide.

It was in this time of racial strife that the proposed plan to unite the churches came before the Methodist Episcopal Church. Because there was still much concern about the creation of jurisdictional conferences, the 1920 General Conference did not adopt the plan but instead appointed a new commission to continue negotiations. The Methodist Episcopal Church also suggested that when a new

9. Maser, "Story of Unification," 434–36.

plan was ready, the Methodist Episcopal and Methodist Episcopal, South, general conferences would meet in a joint session to resolve any differences. While not approving the first plan of unification, northern Methodists did signal that they wanted to keep negotiations going.

For Jones, the 1920 Methodist Episcopal General Conference was especially meaningful because he and Matthew Clair Sr., a minister in the Washington (D.C.) Annual Conference, were both elected bishops. They became the first African Americans elected to the regular general superintendency of the Methodist Episcopal Church (four missionary bishops had been elected earlier). This personal triumph occurred because the northern church decided to elect Jones and Clair via a special ballot restricted to voting for African American candidates and with the understanding that they would administer only African American annual conferences. Nevertheless, they would preside over the General Conference in rotation with other bishops and serve fully on the Board of Bishops. In this arrangement, the Methodist Episcopal Church answered a long-standing grievance of its African American members. It was also significant for unification efforts because now that the northern church had African American bishops, southern white supremacists had a new reason to hold out against union. Most southern white Methodists would not accept an African American in a position of authority over white members, even for a brief period.[10]

Jones and Penn were not members of the new commission to negotiate union between the northern and southern forms of Methodism. The new plan was actually a confederation where each church formed one jurisdictional conference within a united church. The race issue would be an internal matter of the northern jurisdiction, and southern whites would associate with only a few African American Methodists at the General Conference. This plan received the approval of both the Methodist Episcopal and Methodist Episcopal Church, South, general conferences, but it failed to gain the necessary three-fourths majority vote among Methodist Episcopal Church, South, annual conferences. Yet this failure was only a temporary setback. The trend toward strengthening sectional ties continued,

10. Oakes, *Struggle*, 297–301. See also Karen Y. Collier, "An Encyclopedia of Varied Aspects of Race and Episcopacy in American Methodism, 1844–1939."

and forces for union in both the northern and southern churches remained optimistic.[11]

At the same time, however, the issue of racial accommodation became more difficult because Jim Crow and the pattern of race relations that developed in the post-Reconstruction period had begun to wane. Demographically, more African Americans were living outside the South and more southern African Americans lived in urban areas. In both cases, conditions were better than in the rural South where poverty and terrorism kept African American residents largely dominated by white society. Intellectually, racism was no longer "scientific" as it had been in the late nineteenth and early twentieth centuries. Social scientists such as Franz Boas, Ruth Benedict, and Margaret Mead rejected assumptions about racial superiority. During the 1920s, the Harlem Renaissance brought recognition to African American literature and music. The NAACP and the National Urban League, organized in the early twentieth century, provided means of protest against political, civil, and economic discrimination. Although these developments had only a limited impact on American culture by the 1930s, the growth of Jim Crow institutions had stalled by the mid-1930s, partly because Jim Crow laws in the South covered so many aspects of life.[12]

On August 28, 1934, sixty-five prominent Methodist leaders gathered in Chicago, Illinois, to begin discussion of the unification of three Methodist denominations. Among these leaders were Bishop Jones and Rev. Willis J. King, and their presence was conspicuous within this large group. They were the only African American Methodist representatives, and the status of African American Methodists in Methodism had delayed merger for two decades. Since African American Methodists were members in the largely northern Methodist Episcopal Church and the small Methodist Protestant Church, but not part of the Methodist Episcopal Church, South, Jones and King had a difficult task. They wanted to represent faithfully African American Methodists without alienating their northern white allies who were anxious that unification succeed. Jones and King represented over three hundred thousand African American members of

11. Maser, "Story of Unification," 437–38.
12. Harvard Sitkoff, *A New Deal for Blacks: The Emergence of Civil Rights as a National Issue*, 190–97.

the northern church. African American members made up less than 4 percent of the church, so Jones and King could not threaten to derail any unification plans. However, the Methodist Episcopal Church would be embarrassed if the final plan provoked mass defection of its African American members.

Bishop Jones knew the dynamics of unification from experience. He was also so light in pigmentation that to those who did not know him before the meeting, he may have passed for white. However, he was proud of his identification as an African American and at times proclaimed that he chose to be African American. Jones wanted to see Methodist union, but he wanted it to be on honorable terms. Although associated early in his career with Booker T. Washington and a member of the National Negro Business League established by Washington, Jones knew that what had been acceptable to African American Methodists in the early twentieth century was not satisfactory any longer.[13]

Willis Jefferson King was younger than Jones, but he also had distinguished himself early in life. Born in Texas in 1886, he not only received a college and seminary education but also earned a Ph.D. from Boston University in 1921. This made him one of an elite group of African Americans, and he published his first book, *The Negro in American Life,* in 1926. He taught at Gammon Theological Seminary in Atlanta, Georgia, for twelve years before becoming president of the school in 1932.[14]

Methodists considered their union at a time of shifting winds in race relations. Although Methodists could not know it at the time, Jim Crow had reached its apogee of influence in American life. There was a growing dissatisfaction with bigotry even in the South, although during the 1930s southern white liberals largely focused upon the issue of poverty rather than race. Race-mongering demagogues still dominated the southern political scene, and paternalism still prevailed among those white Americans, north and south, who felt uneasy about bigotry. The Methodists gathering in Chicago had the difficult task of reconciling nearly a century of sectional tensions, beginning a move toward racial equality, and maintaining some Jim Crow arrangement. The new commission delegated most of its work

13. Oakes, *Struggle,* 22.
14. *Who's Who in the Methodist Church* (1966), 726.

to a subcommittee of eighteen that quickly revised the basic features of the 1920 plan, including jurisdictional conferences. (Neither Jones nor King were on this subcommittee.) Gone were the most objectionable features, such as the cap on the African American representation at the General Conference and the creation of an associate general conference. Yet segregation was still an integral part of the new plan. The reunited church would have six jurisdictional conferences—five based on geography and one, the Central Jurisdiction, based on race.

African American Methodists, in the Central Jurisdiction, would elect their own bishops and have jurisdictional representatives on all church boards and agencies, but they would remain otherwise segregated from their white brethren. An African American and a white Methodist from the same town or city would encounter each other at a church meeting only if they were both elected to the same national board or agency or if they were both delegates to the quadrennial General Conference. African American and white Methodists who lived in close proximity would still have their own respective congregations and ministers, be part of separate annual and jurisdictional conferences, and have different bishops. The only exceptions to this Jim Crow jurisdictional system were a few African American Methodist congregations in New England and along the West Coast, which were not included in any of the African American annual conferences. This was an extremely small number of churches, but in these cases, African American and white Methodists would be part of the same annual conference and have no institutional barriers to worship or fellowship with one another.

While African American Methodists had endorsed the idea of a racial jurisdictional conference in 1914, it was no longer acceptable in 1934. Jones was especially vocal in opposition. Lloyd Decell, a southern white commission member, reported that at one meeting Bishop Jones said, "A Georgia legislature would not pass as discriminatory an act as this paper." On another occasion he described Jones's speech as "strenuous and we [the commission] went no further." For his part, King suggested that the Colored Methodist Episcopal Church, with which the Methodist Episcopal Church, South, had maintained fraternal ties, be invited into the united church. However, this proposal received a sharp rebuff from Bishop John M. Moore, a leader of reunion in the southern church, who said,

"There would be just too many colored folks at that first General Conference." Moore's comment emphasized that reunion was primarily for white Methodists; the goal was not to have a truly national Methodist Church.[15]

It was clear that the desire for union was very strong among white leaders in all three churches. Several sources report that Jones and King supported the final plan so that African American Methodists would not be blamed if the plan were rejected. Jones reportedly told the commission, "I do not want to be an obstructionist." The *Pittsburgh Courier,* an influential African American newspaper, reported that when the final voting occurred, white Methodist leaders breathed a collective sigh of relief when Jones stood and announced that he was voting for the plan. King also voted for the plan and subsequently campaigned for its approval by African American Methodists.[16]

The proposed Plan of Union immediately brought a cavalcade of condemnations of Jones and King in the secular African American press. Articles accused them of selling out and charged King with betraying African American Methodists in order to be elected a bishop at the next Methodist Episcopal General Conference. African American Methodist leaders who supported the plan were clearly on the defensive. They argued that the plan was the best possible; that it brought African American and southern white Methodists together; and that it permitted African American Methodists even more autonomy than in the Methodist Episcopal Church. A. P. Shaw, editor of the *Southwestern Christian Advocate,* reminded his readers: "An Omnipotent God has not yet made the white race perfect in race attitudes and relations. We cannot do more than God has done."[17]

African American opponents of the plan kept up a barrage of attacks on the compromise the plan made with Christian brotherhood. T. B. Echols, an influential minister in Louisiana, wrote in

15. Lloyd Decell to Bishop Warren A. Candler, April 29, 1935, and Decell to Bishop Candler, March 28, 1935, both in Bishop Warren Akin Candler Papers, Special Collections and Archives, Robert W. Woodruff Library, Emory University, Atlanta, Georgia; Oakes, *Struggle,* 420.

16. Oakes, *Struggle,* 419, 422.

17. *Southwestern Christian Advocate* (hereinafter cited as *SCA*), June 13, 1935, 355; *SCA,* January 16, 1936, 35; Willis J. King to Claude Barnett, January 6, 1936, Claude A. Barnett Papers, Archives and Manuscripts, Chicago Historical Society, Chicago, Illinois (hereinafter cited as Barnett Papers); *SCA,* April 23, 1936, 261.

the *Southwestern Christian Advocate,* "It is the business of the church to keep alive in the hearts of men a sense of the reality of God as taught and practiced by Jesus himself." Lorenzo H. King, who was minister at one of the largest African American Methodist Episcopal congregations in the country and served on the board of directors of the NAACP, argued, "This depreciation of the ideal has in it dangerous consequences for our efforts for every kind of progress." Opponents argued that the Plan of Union sacrificed the purity of the church and the advancement of racial progress for the ecumenical comfort of white Methodists.[18]

While Willis King did publicly support the plan and attempted to build support for its approval at the 1936 General Conference, Jones stayed silent. In a letter to African American newspaperman Claude A. Barnett, Jones explained his silence:

> All my public life ... I have opposed segregation in every form. . . . I realize very much, after the principles that you and I have stood for all these years, that we cannot get everything we want, but I am thoroughly disgusted with our men running to the front begging for the segregated Judicial [jurisdictional] Conference for Negroes. When it seems to me what we should have done was to accept it when it was proposed, and let the white man take the responsibility for the scheme as it stands. Because of this position of mine, I have not given out any statement and I do not care to give out one now.[19]

The Methodist Episcopal Church considered the Plan of Union at the 1936 General Conference. As if to symbolize the paternalism that existed in the northern church, African American opponents of the plan waited while two white liberals attacked the plan. Lewis O. Hartman, editor of *Zion's Herald,* criticized the plan for building a larger but no better Christian church. Ernest F. Tittle, minister of First Methodist Church in Evanston, Illinois, pointed out that the plan put the church behind secular groups working for racial justice. Tittle urged the church to wait one or two more quadrenniums when a more favorable racial climate might make union possible without segregation. But Tittle's position was labeled utopian by the next

18. *SCA,* April 30, 1936, 277; *SCA,* September 16, 1937, 589.
19. Robert E. Jones to Claude A. Barnett, March 27, 1936, Barnett Papers.

pro-union speaker, who continued: "To say that we [Methodist Episcopal Church] will not adopt the report, unless it goes farther than
we have cared to go . . . is to ask something incredible of those who
are anxious to meet us, and go forward with us."[20]

The first African American to speak was David D. Jones, Bishop
Jones's brother and president of Bennett College, a women's college
supported by the Methodist Episcopal Church. At a caucus of African
American convention delegates the night before, he was chosen to
lead the opposition to the plan. He reported that thirty-three out
of forty-four African American delegates at the caucus vowed to
oppose the plan. To describe his feelings about the Plan of Union,
he shared a story about a white lady who came to him after hearing
the Bennett College Quartette sing. She said that the beautiful music
convinced her that in heaven there would be a place for African
American people. "They are going to have a lovely mansion in
Heaven. It is going to be separate, and not quite as nice as ours, but
it is going to be lovely." Here, he implied, was the church building
its own separate structure for its African American members, a lovely
place but not equal with white Methodists.[21]

Two African American delegates spoke in favor of the plan. They
denied that it expanded segregation within Methodism and pointed
out that through constitutional amendments the jurisdictional system could change and evolve. The plan also brought southern white
Methodists into the same church as southern African American
Methodists, which to them was significant racial progress. Yet other
African American Methodists who opposed the plan answered each
of these speeches. Mary McLeod Bethune, the director of Negro
Affairs of the National Youth Administration and head of Franklin
D. Roosevelt's unofficial African American cabinet, suggested that
if every white member of the General Conference would experience
being African American for a year, there would be no doubt about
why this racial jurisdictional system was unacceptable.[22]

However, the result was never really in doubt. After just over two
hours of consideration, the General Conference approved the Plan
of Union by a vote of 470 to 83. The *Pittsburgh Courier* reported

20. *Daily Christian Advocate* [Methodist Episcopal Church], May 5, 1936, 87,
85–87.
21. Ibid., 88, 87–88.
22. Ibid., 88–92.

that of the 47 African American delegates, 11 voted for and 36 against. Delegates stood and sang "Marching to Zion," but many African American delegates did not join in. Some openly wept.[23]

Ratification of the Plan of Union by Methodist Episcopal annual conferences was the next required step. Since it was a constitutional change, voting in all annual conferences required separate votes by ministers and laity. Most annual conferences voted overwhelmingly to approve, but African American annual conferences largely voted against, although not by the often-cited margin of seventeen of nineteen conferences disapproving. Five conferences presided over by the same white bishop voted for the plan. In no other African American annual conferences did ministers and laity vote for the plan, although in six conferences ministers and lay representatives split. Eight African American annual conferences voted solidly against it. Overall, both ministers and lay delegates voted against the plan, with ministers opposing it by an 823 to 583 count and the laity opposed, 437 to 250.[24]

In the Methodist Episcopal Church, South, opposition to the Plan of Union centered on whether the jurisdictional system sufficiently separated African American and white Methodists and whether northern white Methodists could be trusted. Opponents argued that the northern church was too radical theologically and socially, and that the Plan of Union did not provide sufficient safeguards of southern interests. Yet support for union was strong in most areas of the church. In 1936, twenty-five of thirty-eight annual conferences of the southern church petitioned the College of Bishops of their church to accelerate the process of ratification. They wanted the Plan of Union submitted to the 1937 annual conference sessions in advance of the 1938 General Conference of the Methodist Episcopal Church, South. Southern bishops agreed, and the response was overwhelming. Annual conference ratification in 1937 tallied 7,650 votes for union and only 1,247 votes against it. Of all southern

23. Paul A. Carter, "The Negro and Methodist Union," 3; for another set of figures regarding African American voting on the Plan of Union, see Lawrence O. Kline, "The Negro in the Unification of American Methodism," 140.
24. Despite having two African American bishops, some annual conferences were still presided over by white bishops because two bishops could not cover nineteen annual conferences. *SCA,* January 7, 1937, 4; *SCA,* May 6, 1937, 285; *SCA,* May 20, 1937, 325; *SCA,* June 3, 1937, 349.

annual conferences, only in the Northern Mississippi Annual Conference did a majority vote against the Plan of Union. Approval at the 1938 General Conference was never in doubt, although debate lasted an entire day before delegates assented by a vote of 434 to 26. The small Methodist Protestant Church also easily approved the Plan of Union, so it too would join in the new church.

Methodists created through their Plan of Union the largest Protestant denomination in America and the largest Methodist denomination in the world with 7,336,263 members in 42,262 congregations served by 18,375 ordained ministers. However, the new church had the most segregated church structure in the country, and it hardened Jim Crow lines within the church. Nevertheless, this new church had the largest number of African Americans in a predominantly white Protestant church; a vivid reminder of how segregated worship was in the United States. African American members had more autonomy over their affairs and more leaders in the upper echelon of the institutional church than in any other predominantly white church. The Methodist Church had the largest number of African Americans and white southerners in the same church, but that unity was largely on paper.

The Plan of Union that created the Central Jurisdiction was a victory for southern white Methodists who wanted union as long as it did not violate Jim Crow. For them this was victory for sectional reconciliation without high costs. To give more in terms of race would have been an admission that the southern way of life was flawed. Here was reunion without any hint of disgrace. Northern white Methodists gained union with their southern counterparts (as well as the Methodist Protestants), which was their goal. Before union, northern white Methodists were still far from establishing racial equality in their church. Therefore, accepting the creation of a segregated system written into the church constitution was not very troubling for most northern white Methodists, especially when they bridged the chasm that had kept them apart from southern white Methodists since 1844. The few white Methodists who opposed union were reminders of how few people really contemplated what life was like for African Americans, even in an institution committed to "loving your neighbor as yourself."

The position of African American Methodists in the new church was not one of strength; instead, it was a church within a church.

The Central Jurisdiction existed as a collection of nineteen annual conferences tied together by four bishops (after its 1940 jurisdictional conference); a newspaper, the *Central Christian Advocate;* and representatives on the various boards and agencies of the Methodist Church. Geographically, the jurisdiction was immense. It stretched from New Jersey to Florida, from parts of New York to Montana, and from Georgia to New Mexico. Several annual conferences were also quite large. The Lexington Annual Conference covered the states of Kentucky, Ohio, Indiana, Michigan, Illinois, Iowa, Minnesota, North Dakota, and South Dakota. The expanse of several annual conferences was a tremendous obstacle because congregations were isolated from one another.

Demographically, the Central Jurisdiction was 4.2 percent of the members of the Methodist Episcopal Church in 1940, but its 308,557 members were spread unevenly. Three annual conferences were large, with the South Carolina conference making up 13 percent of the total jurisdiction; the Washington conference (comprised of the District of Columbia, Virginia, and parts of Maryland and Pennsylvania) 11.5 percent; and the Delaware conference (which included New Jersey and parts of Pennsylvania and New York) 10.8 percent. Yet five annual conferences each had less than 2 percent of the total jurisdictional membership, and six annual conferences had less than 5 percent each. Thus, the jurisdiction was geographically large, but its membership was diffused and disproportionately concentrated in the Southeast and Midatlantic regions.

One of the largest challenges for the Central Jurisdiction was the recruitment and training of ministers. This was not a problem peculiar to the Central Jurisdiction, but one rooted in the social and economic conditions of African Americans in the twentieth century. For all African American churches, recruiting and training African American ministers became more difficult as the twentieth century developed. While African American ministers had power and prestige in the African American community following the Civil War, the position of ministers steadily eroded in the twentieth century until the Civil Rights movement. College-educated African Americans, particularly those with postgraduate education, found increasing opportunities outside the ministry in professions that offered more lucrative salaries than the ministry.

TABLE 1

1940 Annual Conferences of the Central Jurisdiction

Central Jurisdiction Annual Conferences	Members
Atlanta	12,132
Central Alabama	13,052
Central West	12,536
Delaware	33,422
East Tennessee	5,230
Florida	4,642
Lexington	26,763
Louisiana	14,744
Mississippi	17,898
North Carolina	13,994
Savannah	5,573
South Carolina	40,461
South Florida	4,585
Southwest	5,721
Tennessee	8,238
Texas	15,668
Upper Mississippi	22,649
Washington	35,502
West Texas	15,767

Source: 1940 Minutes of the Annual Conferences of the Methodist Church.

One factor in the declining prestige of African American ministers was an image problem. Some leading African Americans feared that ministers as a group were, at worst, uneducated, immoral, greedy, and, at best, conservative figures of respectability who were out of touch with the real problems of African Americans. Booker T. Washington wrote an article in 1890 charging that the vast majority of African American ministers were unqualified. W. E. B. Du Bois's 1903 study of the Negro church concluded "We [African Americans] are passing through that critical period of religious evolution when the low moral and intellectual standard of the past and the

TABLE 2

1940 Methodist Church Membership by Jurisdictional Conference

	Members	Percent
Central	308,557	4.21
North Central	1,774,696	24.19
Northeast	1,558,017	21.24
South Central	1,307,990	17.83
Southeastern	2,010,715	27.41
Western	376,268	5.13
Total	7,336,263	100.00

curious custom of emotional fervor are not [*sic*] longer attracting the young." In 1944, Gunnar Myrdal's *An American Dilemma* charged that the African American preacher was "the typical accommodating Negro leader" and "even the Northern Negro church has remained a conservative institution with its interest directed upon otherworldly matters." The study also noted that "[i]n the Negro church the collection of money becomes of pathetic importance."[25]

Low ministerial salaries in the Central Jurisdiction occurred because of small churches. Per capita spending for ministerial support within the jurisdiction was close to the average for the Methodist Church, but the size of the average pastoral charge in the Central Jurisdiction was only about half the average for the entire church. In 1940, the Central Jurisdiction had an average of 169 members in a pastoral charge supporting a minister while the entire Methodist Church averaged 346 members supporting each minister. The problem of the enormous gap of 187 fewer members per pastoral charge did not have an easy solution, because many of the African American Methodist congregations were in rural areas.

The problem of small, rural churches was not uniquely racial, Methodist, or new. From the beginning of the twentieth century, American church leaders and rural sociologists had lamented the difficulties of the rural church and promoted reforms to make congregations larger and stronger. For both African American and white

25. Luker, *Social Gospel*, 133–34; Du Bois, *Negro Church*, 207; Gunnar Myrdal, *An American Dilemma: The Negro Problem and Modern Democracy*, 2:861, 863, 867.

rural Christians, there were too many churches dependent on the support of too few people. Denominational and ecumenical leaders recommended over and over the consolidation of congregations, particularly as transportation became more accessible. For the most part, reform activity, whether aimed at African American or white congregations, fell on deaf ears. Parishioners were extremely reluctant to leave the church where their parents were buried, where they had been married, and where their children had been baptized. The rural church might face financial problems, but for many rural Americans, both African American and white, this was nothing new. In rural areas, wherever one looked, people were poor and community institutions did not have enough money.[26]

The frequent solution to the problem of ministerial recruitment and low salaries in the Central Jurisdiction was to appoint what Methodists called a "supply pastor," who was an unordained preacher. The supply pastor was not a member of the annual conference and could not serve communion except at that particular congregation. Often he (women were not permitted to be supply pastors) served the church by conducting the worship service and preaching, but he did not perform the functions of a minister during the week. Many supply pastors in the Central Jurisdiction worked as schoolteachers, but the range of occupations among them was wide. They were encouraged to attend special training institutes for a week during the summer. Usually held at Gammon Theological Seminary in Atlanta or one of the Central Jurisdiction's colleges, these Christian leadership schools provided a simplified course of study for those ministers who did not have seminary training.

Yet as a church within a church, the Central Jurisdiction was not alone in having difficulties. African American members of other predominantly white churches experienced their own problems, some similar and some distinctly different from the Methodist experience. For example, in terms of membership and recruitment of clergy, the African American Catholic experience was quite different from that of the Methodist Church. Where Methodism was strong in the South and in rural America, Catholics enjoyed much more strength in the North and Midwest and were decidedly urban in membership. The Catholic Church in America was largely an

26. James H. Madison, "Reformers and the Rural Church, 1900–1950."

immigrant church, except in the South, where immigration lagged behind the rest of the country. Especially in the South, Catholics struggled against Protestant hegemony, church poverty, and the lack of priests. Consequently, the number of African American Catholics in the South was small compared to the number of African American Protestants. At the turn of the twentieth century, the Southeast had only ten African American Catholic parishes and sixteen African American parish schools. By 1930, these had increased to twenty-five schools and parishes and by 1960 to forty-four parishes and thirty-three schools.[27]

Being an African American Catholic was being part of a minority group within a minority group. African American Protestants were as suspicious of Catholicism as their white Protestant counterparts. Moreover, African American Catholics did not even have the comfort of a large number of African American priests. Even the liturgy was more alien than in Protestant churches because of its use of Latin and its lack of spirituals. African American Catholics had to be able to endure the continuous charge that Catholicism was a white man's religion.

The struggle to recruit and train African American Catholics for ordination was more arduous than efforts at strengthening the African American ministry generally. As head of the Josephite order, Father Joseph R. Slattery attempted to convince the Catholic hierarchy and his fellows in the order that African American priests were the key to evangelism among African Americans. However, Slattery was not free of his own apprehensions about this endeavor and became increasingly cautious about training African Americans for the priesthood. He also lost faith in the Catholic Church and ended up becoming an apostate himself. The process of training African American priests ceased under Josephites Superior Louis Pastorelli, elected to head the order in 1918. Pastorelli acted in part due to the problem that the order had in gaining positions for African American priests in the South. The Josephites did not ordain another African American priest until 1941. Officials in Rome did become concerned about the absence of African American priests in America in the 1920s, and because of this concern, American bishops

27. Michael J. McNally, "A Peculiar Institution: Catholic Parish Life and the Pastoral Mission to the Blacks in the Southeast, 1850–1980," 74.

organized a seminary in Bay St. Louis, Mississippi. The Society of the Divine Word (SDW) became the ordination path for African American priests, although it did not ordain any priests until 1934. For African American Catholics, the SDW was not a complete victory because it was a segregated seminary. Although this seminary was not the only Catholic seminary in the country opened to African American students, it was the largest and most important.[28]

African American Episcopalians faced some of the same problems as their counterparts in the Methodist and Catholic churches, particularly regarding church structure, bishops, and the training of priests. Despite the limited number of African American Episcopalians in the early twentieth century, their church status was a matter of continued dispute. Several southern dioceses did not allow African American representation, clergy or lay, at diocesan conventions. This made African American congregations virtually wards of white Episcopalians in these southern dioceses. In 1904, the Episcopal Conference of Church Workers among Colored People endorsed the creation of a separate African American missionary district as a new entity within the church structure. This would mean accepting segregation formally, but it would also mean African American autonomy rather than control by southern white bishops. African American Episcopalians accepting a missionary district was similar to African American Methodists accepting the idea of a separate jurisdictional conference in 1914. The Episcopal General Convention, however, rejected the proposal for an African American missionary district in 1907, largely because of southern white opposition. These bishops saw the missionary district plan as a threat to their control of what they saw as strictly diocesan matters.[29]

An alternative to a missionary district was the creation of a suffragan bishop, who would serve under a regular bishop, yet have no right to succession and no vote in the House of Bishops. The suffragan bishop did not have to be African American but was an aide to the regular bishop. However, in the South suffragan status was understood as a means of having an African American who would

28. Ochs, *Desegregating the Altar,* 86–132; Stephen J. Ochs, "The Ordeal of a Black Priest," 64–65.
29. Shattuck, *Episcopalians and Race,* 21–24; David M. Reimers, "Negro Bishops and Diocesan Segregation in the Protestant Episcopal Church, 1870–1954," 232–34.

supervise only African American congregations. Most African American Episcopal leaders disliked the idea. The Reverend George Bragg, editor of the African American Episcopalian church journal, termed the position "a suffering bishop." The General Convention, however, approved this idea in 1910 and the first two African American suffragan bishops were elected in 1917 and 1918, close to the time when the northern Methodist Episcopal Church elected Jones and Matthew Clair bishops. Although Jones and Clair were not suffragan bishops, their election became possible because the Methodist Episcopal Church limited their duties to African American annual conferences.[30]

The suffragan plan did not please African American Episcopalians, and agitation for an enlarged position for African Americans within the church continued. Efforts at creating a missionary district continued and some southern bishops began to waiver in their opposition. As late as 1934, there was considerable African American support for a missionary district in the South. However, the General Convention continued to support the power and responsibility of white southern bishops to supervise African American congregations. Some African American Episcopalian leaders, especially those associated with the Joint Commission on Negro Work, began to attack the missionary district plan as legalized segregation. Ironically, after years of opposition, southern white bishops decided in 1939 to endorse the missionary district plan. In 1940, the year the Central Jurisdiction in the Methodist Church was created, the missionary district plan had its most serious consideration by the Episcopalian General Convention, with strong support from southern bishops. Nevertheless, the House of Bishops voted against the plan 54 to 37 and it went no further.[31]

African American Episcopalians had supported the idea of a missionary district in the second decade of the twentieth century, at a time when African American Methodists had also supported a separate jurisdiction. Both ideas met defeat initially, in part by southern white opposition, only to return twenty years later. Southern whites then supported the missionary district plan and the jurisdictional conference system, and most African American Episcopalians and

30. Shattuck, *Episcopalians and Race,* 21–26; Reimers, "Negro Bishops," 235.
31. Shattuck, *Episcopalians and Race,* 26–29; Reimers, "Negro Bishops," 238–39.

Methodists opposed these plans. While the Methodist Church created a segregated arrangement to gain union between its northern
and southern halves, the Episcopal Church, never divided by the
Civil War, rejected it. Yet the Episcopal Church had not resolved
the question of the status of African American members, and it
stayed where it was in terms of segregation and discrimination.

After establishing the Afro-American Presbyterian Church in
1898, the PCUS continued to provide significant financial support
to this church for two decades. Then, in 1916, the southern white
Presbyterians reversed course and took these African American
churches back into their church as a separate synod, the Snedecor
Memorial Synod. Like the Central Jurisdiction, it was a segregated
church arrangement where African American and white southern
Presbyterians were officially members of the same church, but they
only came together at the General Assembly.

African American Methodists, Catholics, Episcopalians, and Presbyterians were not ignorant and nor were they martyrs. For a variety
of reasons, they had chosen to be part of a predominantly white
church, and it had become their church. They knew that the purpose of the church was to worship God and that white Americans
did not own God. While maintaining their faith in Christian fellowship, African Americans worked to bring more justice into their
churches. It was a difficult battle, but it was a battle that they did
not shrink from engaging in. Yet African American Methodists did
have a very special situation. They were part of a Jim Crow arrangement that reached over almost the entire United States. Moreover,
any change in their position in the church would require a constitutional change in a church where southern whites were powerful
enough to exercise a veto against anything threatening to them.
African American Methodists had more power and autonomy than
other African American members of predominantly white churches,
but they were also the most rigidly separated and segregated. White
Methodists sang "Marching to Zion" over the creation of a united
church, but African American Methodists may have justifiably felt
as if they were in the wilderness far from the Promised Land. While
their white counterparts celebrated union, they could have sung
"There Is a Balm in Gilead."

An instructive comparison to African Americans in the Methodist
Church at this time is the political position of African Americans

in the late 1930s. The New Deal was the most innovative and progressive set of government programs of the twentieth century, and through it African Americans received more government positions and aid than during any preceding period. Yet actual attacks on segregation were few. Most government programs accepted segregation, particularly when local officials administered the programs. Even reform programs such as the Tennessee Valley Authority maintained segregation. While Franklin Roosevelt had a cadre of mostly young, talented African American government officials, they did not occupy the top echelon of jobs and had limited power and influence. Eleanor Roosevelt was an outspoken advocate for civil rights and dared to integrate meetings even in the South, yet her only power came from her symbolic post as the first lady. Moreover, Congress passed no civil rights legislation, not even a federal anti-lynching law. The federal courts had not seriously eroded the constitutional doctrines established in *Plessy* or *Williams*.

Methodists, and other major predominantly white denominations, operated in an area defined by American society and culture regarding civil rights and race relations. Through these various racial structures they condoned, if not embraced, racial inequality. The Gospel came second to the degraded status assigned African Americans by white Americans, although most white Americans seldom juxtaposed the two in their minds. Most white Methodists accepted a Jim Crow church as easily as they accepted the Declaration of Independence and de jure discrimination. They thought little, if any, about race, whether in their religious or political life. Even if "separate but equal" troubled them, most white Americans kept their doubts to themselves and did not risk working for change. Members of the Central Jurisdiction were invisible Methodists to most church members. They existed but were out of mind and largely out of sight. African Americans in predominantly white churches, whether Methodists, Catholics, Episcopalians, or Presbyterians, praised God and worked for justice within the constraints of a discriminatory and racist economic, political, social, and religious system.

3

Methodists before and after *Brown*

O N MAY 17, 1954, in *Brown v. Board of Education,* the U.S. Supreme Court ruled that public school segregation was unconstitutional. The Court found that the doctrine of separate but equal established in the 1896 *Plessy v. Ferguson* decision violated the Fourteenth Amendment. The *Brown* decision was profound because segregated public education was so widespread in the country and the interpretation of the Constitution used by the Court threatened all de jure forms of segregation. Probably no other twentieth-century Supreme Court decision has had such enormous implications. It was a landmark decision for African Americans and gave a new meaning to equality for all Americans. Although churches were not directly affected by the ruling, it had tremendous implications regarding race relations and their own racial practices and witness to the Gospel.

The *Brown* decision was not made in a vacuum. Many changes had begun during the 1940s that made race relations more of a national issue than they had been since the end of Reconstruction. Many of the changes originated during World War II. The anticipation of entering World War II had caused a sharp increase in industrial production in 1940, but increased employment opportunities did not immediately translate into jobs for African Americans. Moreover, many companies that did employ these workers kept them in the lowest-paying jobs. For these reasons, A. Philip Randolph, an African American union organizer, organized the March on Washington Movement that in 1941 threatened a massive protest march in Washington, D.C. President Franklin D. Roosevelt wanted to avert such protest and agreed to issue an executive order against discrimination by government contractors if Randolph canceled the protest march. The deal was made, and Roosevelt issued Executive Order 8802, which established the Fair Employment Practice Committee (FEPC). Although a very weak body that could not force compliance, the FEPC brought national attention to the employment discrimination that African American workers faced.[1]

Once the United States entered the war on December 7, 1941, most African Americans rallied to the theme of a Double V: victory at home over racism as well as victory over totalitarianism in Europe and Asia. The U.S. government played up Nazi racism as a difference between the Axis and American values, but African Americans linked victory over the "Hitlers at home" with defeat of Adolph Hitler in Germany. Segregation in the U.S. armed forces particularly irritated African Americans. The army often relegated African American troops to support jobs rather than combat units, and racism convinced the Red Cross to separate blood plasma according to race. Many African American soldiers who had lived in the North experienced the Jim Crow South for the first time at southern training facilities. Some found southern white supremacy so oppressive that going overseas to engage in combat was a relief. Despite limited success in getting the armed forces to improve their use of African American soldiers, there was no victory over segregation in the armed forces during the war.

World War II also produced the most racial violence in America since 1919. The Social Science Institute of Fisk University counted 242 racial conflicts in over forty cities in 1943 alone. The full employment economy created by the war drew large numbers of African Americans from the South to the booming industries of the North and West. Most moved to large urban centers where job opportunities abounded, but where acute housing shortages intensified existing racial prejudice. The largest single occurrence of violence happened in Detroit in the summer of 1943, when a massive riot occurred before African Americans were to occupy a public housing project built next to a Polish American neighborhood. More than

1. Richard M. Dalfiume, "The 'Forgotten Years' of the Negro Revolution"; David M. Kennedy, *Freedom from Fear: The American People in Depression and War, 1929–1945*, 764–68.

thirty-four persons died and federal troops had to be called in to quell the disturbance.[2]

Several civil rights victories during the war had a significant impact in the postwar period. The NAACP experienced tremendous growth that strengthened the organization's grassroots support, particularly in the South. Its membership grew from 50,556 in 1940 to more than 450,000 in 1946. In 1944, the Supreme Court ruled in *Smith v. Allwright* that all-white primaries, a widespread means of disfranchising African American voters in southern states, violated the constitutional rights of these citizens to participate in democratic elections. This was an important victory, because the southern white monopoly on voting rights was a fundamental source of power over southern African Americans. The Supreme Court ruling did not bring immediate change, but in isolated urban areas progress did occur. African American voter registration grew rapidly in Winston-Salem, North Carolina, and in 1947, they were able to elect Kenneth Williams, a black minister, to the board of aldermen. Even in areas of the South where other suffrage restrictions kept the potential African American voters disfranchised, the *Smith v. Allwright* decision was a crack in the armor of segregation.[3]

Also, in 1944, Gunnar Myrdal, a Swedish social scientist, published his study of American race relations, *An American Dilemma*. The book's introduction, entitled "The Negro Problem as a Moral Issue," provided the ethical basis for the study, and the tome analyzed every part of African American life. Rather than focusing exclusively on the impact of segregation and discrimination upon African Americans, Myrdal emphasized the contradiction between segregation and discrimination and the American ideal of freedom and equality. At a time when the tide of the war was turning and America was establishing its place on the world stage as never before, Myrdal boldly stated, "The treatment of the Negro is America's greatest and most conspicuous scandal." Included in his book was a chapter on the African American church, which presented a

2. Harvard Sitkoff, "Racial Militancy and Interracial Violence in the Second World War," 671.

3. Robert Korstad and Nelson Lichtenstein, "Opportunities Found and Lost: Labor, Radicals, and the Early Civil Rights Movement," 793.

disquieting picture of accommodation. While acknowledging the power of particular church leaders, Myrdal concluded that the African American church was largely a conservative institution, in both the North and the Jim Crow South. Although not specifically naming any church, Myrdal noted, "There is also astonishingly little interracial cooperation between the white and Negro churches of the same denomination."[4]

The war years prompted limited reconsideration of racial policies on the part of southern churches. The southern Presbyterian Church in the United States and the Southern Baptist Convention each began to call for a more just treatment of African Americans, albeit within a segregated society. While they noted the damage done by discrimination and restrictions in employment, justice, voting, and education, neither church went so far as to condemn Jim Crow. Resolutions approved in 1945 by the Presbyterian Church in the United States (southern Presbyterians) and in 1946 by the Southern Baptist Convention endorsed improving southern racial patterns but failed to call for a new era in race relations. Additionally, both churches did not call for legislative changes to improve race relations but instead expected southern white goodwill to make the necessary adjustments.[5]

During the early 1940s, the Methodist Church did relatively little regarding civil rights. After the struggle for unification, a movement to make sweeping changes in the jurisdictional system, especially regarding its racial structure, had little prospect for success. African American delegates to the 1944 General Conference meeting in Kansas City, Missouri, found only segregated accommodations, which led the Council of Bishops to offer an official apology. The conference also adopted a resolution on conditions for peace that devoted an entire section to the issue of race. Included was a specific mention of support for the Fair Employment Practice Committee and equal protection of minorities by law enforcement officials. Further, the resolution outlined steps to avert racial conflicts

4. Myrdal, *American Dilemma*, 2:871, 1020 (Guy B. Johnson and Guion Johnson, both sociologists at the University of North Carolina who were also Methodists, conducted the research for the section on churches).

5. W. Edward Orser, "Racial Attitudes in Wartime: Protestant Churches during the Second World War," 342–45.

that emphasized that the local church had a responsibility to work to improve racial conditions and promote better communication.[6]

Other national or northern churches gave greater attention to racial problems. Both the Episcopal and northern Presbyterian churches rejected plans that would have created a racial system in their churches similar to the Central Jurisdiction. In 1944, the northern Presbyterians also decided to end all existing racially segregated synods and presbyteries "in due time," and in 1946 called for the end of segregation at its colleges and seminaries. The major national churches also became more forthright about the American racial problem and more explicit in condemning forms of discrimination. Toward the end of the war, many national churches endorsed legislative action to correct employment discrimination. Yet churches were particularly silent about housing discrimination and de facto segregation outside the South.[7]

In 1946, action by the Federal Council of Churches (FCC) contributed a more realistic stand on racial policies of churches. In March, the FCC passed a resolution that condemned segregation as "a violation of the Gospel of love and human brotherhood" and called for "a non-segregated Church and a non-segregated society." Before this statement, most churches had not categorically condemned segregation. The FCC's statement became a benchmark by which member denominations could measure themselves. Yet ironically, at the same Federal Council of Churches meeting, there was an attempt to keep African American vice president of the FCC Dr. Benjamin E. Mayes off the rostrum when President Harry Truman addressed the council.[8]

In December 1946, after a wave of racial attacks occurred in the South, particularly against returning veterans, President Truman appointed a presidential committee on civil rights. When he succeeded Franklin D. Roosevelt, Truman had no particular record of

6. *Daily Christian Advocate* May 3, 1944, 110–11; Robert M. Miller, *How Shall They Hear without a Preacher? The Life of Ernest Fremont Tittle,* 345–56; 1944 General Conference *Journal,* 729–30.

7. Orser, "Racial Attitudes," 351, 348–50; Frank S. Loescher, *The Protestant Church and the Negro,* 34–41, 125–32.

8. David W. Willis, "An Enduring Distance: Black Americans and the Establishment," 172, 181.

civil rights advocacy, but he emerged as an even more forceful leader than FDR. Truman endorsed the creation of a permanent FEPC and passage of a federal antilynching law. However, southern Democrats in Congress were so powerful that passage of such legislation was impossible regardless of who was president. Blocked by Congress, Truman appointed a presidential committee to make a series of recommendations regarding civil rights with the expectation that the report would generate more attention to the subject. Dubbed the "Noah's Ark committee," it contained two representatives from several groups, including business leaders, laborers, women, Catholics, Jews, and southerners.

The two southern members, Dorothy R. Tilly and Frank Porter Graham, were both liberals instead of segregationists. Tilly had worked closely with Jessie Daniel Ames to stop lynchings and became field secretary of the Southern Regional Conference, a new interracial group formed in 1944 to improve race relations. An influential leader among southern Methodist women in the Southeastern Jurisdiction, Tilly would play a recording of the Lord's Prayer to anonymous telephone callers trying to harass her. Frank Porter Graham was president of the University of North Carolina and had made the university a bastion of free thought in the South. Elected president of the liberal Southern Conference on Human Welfare at its creation in 1938, Graham represented southern leaders who believed that economic advance would proceed with improved race relations.[9]

The report of the presidential committee on civil rights made sweeping recommendations that included increasing the size and scope of civil rights protection within the Justice Department and Federal Bureau of Investigation. The committee urged either the states or Congress to abolish poll taxes and enact legislation protecting the right to register and vote without interference. Most important was the recommendation that segregation end in America. To accomplish this, the committee suggested that the federal government cease financial assistance to any institutions that practiced discrimination and that Congress establish a permanent FEPC.

9. Arnold Shankman, "Dorothy Tilly, Civil Rights, and the Methodist Church"; Hall, *Revolt against Chivalry*, 217, 363n13. For more on Tilly, Graham, and the Southern Regional Conference, see John Egerton, *Speak Now against the Day: The Generation before the Civil Rights Movement in the South.*

In many ways, the report, entitled *To Secure These Rights*, antici-pated most of the provisions of the 1964 Civil Rights Act and the 1965 Voting Rights Act. Truman followed up the report on Febru-ary 2, 1948, with a civil rights message to Congress that endorsed most of the committee's recommendations.[10]

In 1947, a major breakthrough against segregation occurred in a highly visible area. Americans loved baseball, and white baseball owners maintained a strict exclusion of contact between white and African American baseball players in the white major leagues, despite the existence of an African American professional baseball league. The rationale often used by baseball officials was that African Amer-ican players were not good enough to play major league ball, but this was clearly false to anyone who saw them play. However, since the white press did not cover African American baseball, there was no strong pressure from white fans to integrate baseball. Jackie Robinson broke the color barrier when Branch Rickey, owner of the Brooklyn Dodgers, recognized that the denial of African Amer-ican athletes in the major leagues was inherently inefficient and against the business interests of the owners. The public wanted to see exciting baseball, and keeping talented, explosive players out of the major leagues simply because of race hurt the game. Baseball's desegregation was significant because it was both so public and so successful. Fans did not stay away, and players did not go on strike. Soon other teams were anxious to acquire their own African Amer-ican stars. However, not all barriers within baseball fell, and it was not until 1959 that every professional baseball team had at least one African American player on its roster.[11]

In the midst of these events, the 1948 Methodist General Con-ference spoke more candidly about racial problems, but it took little action within its own house. The Episcopal Address, which outlines the concerns of the church's bishops, was given by Bishop G. Brom ley Oxnam, an outspoken liberal within the church. He asked how Christians could do anything other than condemn disfranchisement, segregation, lynchings, and discrimination in civil liberties. Yet the bishops proposed no legislative change to back up their words. The

10. President's Committee on Civil Rights, *To Secure These Rights: The Report of the President's Committee on Civil Rights*, 151–73.
11. Jules Tygiel, *Baseball's Great Experiment: Jackie Robinson and His Legacy*, 34.

commission on race relations authorized by the 1944 General Conference urged increased interracial meetings, an end to restrictive housing covenants, equal justice, voting rights, strengthened minority ministry, and establishment of a permanent office on race relations within the church bureaucracy. More candid and less optimistic was the assessment of the Women's Society of Christian Service, which stated, "Our accomplishments in inter-racial cooperation between Negro and white groups during the past quadrennium have been slight indeed."[12]

In the fall of 1948, President Truman ordered the desegregation of the armed forces, a major triumph for civil rights advocates. During World War II and after, military leaders had resisted calls for desegregation by insisting that the armed forces were no place for a social experiment and that the military should desegregate only when society as a whole desegregated. In the postwar period, civil rights leaders such as A. Philip Randolph spoke of organizing a campaign against military service in a segregated military. Truman's order signaled that another major national institution was desegregating, even though Jim Crow in the military did not immediately disappear because of foot-dragging by the military leaders, especially those in the army. Since many military facilities were in the South, desegregation of the military was another threat to segregationists.[13]

The Supreme Court also made a number of decisions in the late 1940s and early 1950s that advanced civil rights and set a legal framework for *Brown*. In *Shelly v. Kramer* (1948), the court ruled that state courts could not enforce restrictive housing covenants through which white property owners kept potential black owners from purchasing homes and property. Residential segregation concerned African Americans because it kept them from enjoying material success and limited their educational opportunities. In addition, the Court that year ruled in *Sipeul v. Board of Regents* that Oklahoma must provide truly equal education if the state opted to provide a separate law school for African American citizens rather than desegregate the University of Oklahoma law school. This did not overturn the separate but equal doctrine established in *Plessy*, but it

12. 1948 General Conference *Journal*, 183, 729, 969; 1948 *Quadrennial Reports of the Methodist Church*, 190.
13. Richard M. Dalfiume, *Desegregation of the U.S. Armed Forces: Fighting on Two Fronts, 1939–1953*, 175–200.

created a situation where southern states would have bear the expense of creating separate, very specialized institutions, or desegregate their graduate educational institutions. More ominous to segregationists, the court could apply the same standards to public education where the discrepancy between public funds for black and white education was enormous.

Two years later, the high court took the test of equality further; in *Sweatt v. Painter* and *McLaurin v. Oklahoma*, it found that the states of Texas and Oklahoma had failed to provide decent educational opportunities for black citizens seeking legal training. Texas had created a small law school with a limited faculty and inadequate library for black students instead of desegregating the University of Texas law school. In Oklahoma, George W. McLaurin was admitted to the University of Oklahoma graduate school to pursue a doctoral degree in education, but each classroom restricted his access to fellow students by limiting him to a "black only" section. In both cases, the Supreme Court ruled that southern states had made a charade of the separate but equal doctrine.[14]

It was simply the next step for the NAACP to challenge directly all separate but equal public education. A collection of legal challenges began to work their way through the federal court system in 1950. These cases represented the geographic sweep of segregated public education: Kansas, Delaware, Washington, D.C., Virginia, and South Carolina. At this time, seventeen states and the District of Columbia required segregated education, and four other states permitted local school districts to segregate. Nearly half of the forty-eight states in the union provided some segregated public education. Since public education involves so many in the population, these court cases had much more significance than did the earlier cases that focused on graduate education.

In the late 1940s and early 1950s, churches continued to widen their concern on racial policies and make some changes in their racial practices. Most significantly, in 1951, the southern Presbyterian Church dissolved its all–African American Snedecor Memorial Synod. Begun in 1916 and made up of only four small presbyteries, this synod had been administratively weak. Its congregations were

14. Mark V. Tushnet, *The NAACP's Legal Strategy against Segregated Education, 1925–1950*, 120–32.

geographically dispersed and its overall membership was small, yet the actual change to southern Presbyterian churches was slight. The presbyteries were reduced to three and transferred into geographic synods in Louisiana, Alabama, and Georgia, but they remained all–African American presbyteries until white presbyteries agreed to accept them. In addition, by 1951, all four seminaries of the southern Presbyterians had desegregated.[15]

Likewise, groups within the Central Jurisdiction began to call on the Methodist Church to begin integration of the church structure by eliminating the Central Jurisdiction. In early 1951, a national conference for urban ministers in the Central Jurisdiction unanimously endorsed a resolution condemning segregation throughout the church and calling for the 1952 General Conference to start desegregation. Later in the same year, the Delaware, East Tennessee, North Carolina, and Washington annual conferences each passed a resolution calling for the end of the entire jurisdictional system, "with particular reference to the Central Jurisdiction." The Lexington Annual Conference urged the 1952 General Conference to establish a study commission to guide the church to "a racially inclusive policy at all organization levels" and to continue its work "until its mission shall have been accomplished." Charles F. Golden, who would become a major force in Methodist desegregation, authored the resolution, and it was the first reference to racial inclusiveness as a church policy. James P. Brawley, president of Clark College in Atlanta and chair of the Central Jurisdiction's self-study committee, proposed the abolition of the jurisdiction in the areas of the country that did not require segregation while leaving it temporarily intact in areas of de jure segregation. African American Methodists outside this scaled-down Central Jurisdiction would join white Methodist annual conferences and work toward building integrated local churches.[16]

Both Golden and Brawley anticipated the day when racially separate Methodist congregations ceased to exist. The goal was not

15. Joel L. Alvis Jr., *Religion and Race: Southern Presbyterians, 1946–1983*, 22–24, 90.

16. *Central Christian Advocate*, January 31, 1952, 12; 1951 North Carolina Annual Conference (CJ) *Journal*, 15; 1951 Lexington Annual Conference (CJ) *Journal*, 54–55; James P. Brawley, "Should the Jurisdictional System Be Abolished?" *Central Christian Advocate*, March 20, 1952, 4–6, 14. Brawley was born in

simply abolition of the Central Jurisdiction and separate annual conferences; they envisioned African American and white members of the same congregation served by clergy of either race. They yearned for a church where all were truly equal before God and man. Brawley acknowledged that moving to a nonracial church system would take time, but he outlined the steps that the church might take to accelerate reaching this goal. These included the familiar suggestion for interracial meetings and end of all racial barriers in all Methodist institutions, but he also suggested "frequent test cases where Negro congregations would request to become members of white Conferences. There would be instances where individual Negroes or Negro families would seek membership in white Methodist congregations. These are types of test cases that would serve to measure progress in eliminating segregation and achieving integration."[17]

African American Methodists' expectations were increasing while the actual structure of the church was not changing. The self-study committee that Brawley chaired noted that "there has developed a growing concern regarding this segregated arrangement of the Methodist Church," but later in the report it concluded that "for the most part, the division according to the race line is just as clear today [in the Methodist Church] as it was before the Unification." Part of the rising hope of African American Methodists came from outside the church, but some came from inside as well. In areas of overlap between the Central Jurisdiction and regional jurisdictions where there was little racial tension, there were some cooperative ventures among youth, other portions of the church, and "even among ministers." African American Methodist participation in the church bureaucracy and on the boards that supervised the administration of the church had increased substantially, especially after the Great

---

Lockhart, Texas, in 1894 and served in the U.S. army in 1918. A graduate of Samuel Houston College in 1920, he later received a Ph.D. from Northwestern University. He taught at Clark College in Atlanta and became dean of the college in 1926 and president in 1941. Golden was born in 1912 in Holly Springs, Mississippi, the son of a Methodist minister. Educated at Clark College, he knew Brawley before graduating in 1936. He received a Masters of Systematic Theology degree from Boston University in 1938 and served as a U.S. army chaplain from 1942 to 1946. Beginning in 1947, he was employed by the Methodist Church Board of Missions. See *Who's Who in the Methodist Church* (1966), 140, 484.

17. Brawley, "Should the Jurisdictional System Be Abolished?" 6, 14.

Depression had ended and church staff could be increased. Nevertheless, African American Methodist staff members worked only in areas related to the Central Jurisdiction. There was greater opportunity in the church on the one hand, but walls still existed.[18]

Methodist women were also expressing themselves regarding racial policies. In 1950, the Woman's Division of Christian Service published the first comprehensive collection of state laws regarding race. Edited by Pauli Murray, who years later become one of the first ordained African American women priests in the Episcopal Church, *States' Laws on Race and Color* was both thorough and dramatic in its presentation of the magnitude of the variety of state laws relating to race. Here the Woman's Division attempted to educate the public as to the scope of de jure discrimination and segregation in America as well as legal attempts to provide equal rights. In 1952, the Woman's Division initiated a racial charter to govern its own racial practices. Divided into a statement of beliefs and specific policies, the racial charter committed all of the ratifying jurisdictional and annual conference of the Woman's Societies of Christian Service and the Wesleyan Service Guilds to practice equal employment, provide equal accommodations at all meetings. The charter also pledged that ratifying units would work for legislative change where state laws prohibited equal treatment. Although the charter was initially most important in the national office of the Woman's Division, momentum gradually built as more Methodist women's organizations adopted the charter. By 1960, each of the six jurisdictional conference women's organizations as well as eighty-eight annual conference organizations had ratified the racial charter. Although limited to Methodist women and not accepted universally, the racial charter was the most widely adopted Methodist stand against discrimination at the time.[19]

The Woman's Division was a reservoir of action regarding race relations because its leaders were unique southern women who

18. Commission to Study the Central Jurisdiction of the Methodist Church, "Report of the Commission to Study the Central Jurisdiction," April 1, 1952, James P. Brawley Papers, Atlanta University Center, Robert W. Woodruff Library, Atlanta, Georgia (hereinafter cited as Brawley Papers).

19. Alice G. Knotts, *Fellowship of Love: Methodist Women Changing American Racial Attitudes*, 195–99, 267–68; on its adoption by women's organizations, see Thelma Stevens, "A Summary... to the Commission on Interjurisdictional Relations," 2597–3–3:1, General Commission on Archives and History, United Methodist Church, Madison, New Jersey (hereinafter cited as GCAH).

came from a tradition of grassroots activism that dated back to the early twentieth century. Like the southern white women who made up the Association of Southern Women for the Prevention of Lynchings, they were indirectly liberating themselves from southern white patriarchy as they worked against de jure segregation. The Woman's Division of Christian Service was one area of the church where they had influence and control, although they did not have complete autonomy because it was part of the Methodist Board of Missions. Many of these women would still have agreed with the prayer given by Maria Gibson, president of Scarrett College, at a meeting of the executive council of the Woman's Division of the Methodist Episcopal Church, South, in 1926, when she said, "Dear Lord, we pray for the men of the Board of Missions. Thou knowest how they have troubled and worried us. They have been hard to bear sometimes, but we thank thee that they are better than they used to be."[20]

No leader among Methodist women was more important than Thelma Stevens, who grew up in Mississippi, but who, like novelist Lillian Smith, rejected segregation and dedicated herself to attacking it. Smith used her novels and Stevens used her position as executive secretary of the Department of Christian Social Relations and Local Church Activities of the Women's Division of the Board of Missions as means of pushing against the racial wall that the South had created. Both Smith and Stevens never married and therefore each remained free of traditional male authority and the frequently accompanying responsibility for raising children. Whereas Smith had been connected to the Methodist Church early, only to reject it later as too conservative, Stevens initially rejected the church only to find it provided her, despite its faults, an opportunity to work for a more just society and, consequently, a step closer to God's kingdom on earth.[21]

The 1952 General Conference met in San Francisco while the Korean War raged and McCarthyism dominated the political scene. The Council of Bishops had difficulty dealing with race relations as they drafted their Episcopal Address. Bishop Paul B. Kern of the Southeastern Jurisdiction gave the address, and he struggled to find

20. McDowell, *Social Gospel*, 119.
21. Knotts, *Fellowship of Love*, 104–7; Fred Hobson, *But Now I See: The White Southern Racial Conversion Narrative*, 18–36.

wording that would satisfy the various factions among the bishops. Bishop Oxnam described the debate in the Council of Bishops as "long and rather bitterly contested" and Kern feeling "much dispirited," by the controversy. The final wording stated that "[t]o discriminate against a person solely upon the basis of his race is both unfair and unChristian. Every child of God is entitled to that place in society which he has won by his industry, his integrity, and his character." Yet the bishops did not specifically condemn de jure segregation as evil or call for the dismantling of the Central Jurisdiction. Instead, they noted the slow growth of the Central Jurisdiction membership as a problem meriting consideration by all of the church, and they offered the opinion that the General Conference could authorize some change in jurisdictional boundaries, although they did not call it desegregation. The bishops concluded this section of the address by acknowledging that as sinners, Christians are not perfect, but faith demanded forward progress toward a more truly Christian life.[22]

Following the suggestion of the bishops, the Committee on Conferences drafted legislation to provide a means of changing the Central Jurisdiction, but the plan immediately encountered trouble with the supreme court of the church, the Judicial Council. The proposed legislation permitted transfers from the Central Jurisdiction to a regional jurisdiction if the congregations, conferences, and jurisdictional conferences directly involved approved. The Judicial Council ruled that race was indeed a boundary established in the church constitution and until a constitutional amendment modified it, the General Conference must approve each specific transfer of a congregation from the Central Jurisdiction to each regional jurisdiction. While acknowledging that times were changing, the council implicitly reiterated how vital segregation was to the creation of the Methodist Church. The Committee on Conferences consequently redrafted its legislation. The new method of transfer from the Central Jurisdiction to a regional jurisdiction required a six-step process including approval by the local congregation, by its annual conference and the receiving annual conference, by a majority of all annual conferences in both the Central Jurisdiction and the receiving re-

22. Oxnam quoted in Robert M. Miller, *Bishop G. Bromley Oxnam: Paladin of Liberal Protestantism,* 465; 1952 General Conference *Journal,* 167, 168–69.

gional jurisdiction, and by enabling legislation by the General Conference. This awkward means of desegregation did not cause any dissension because the requirements were so stiff that segregationists felt safe.[23]

The 1952 General Conference debated for the first time church racial practices in its own institutions. In the report entitled "The Methodist Church and Race," Rev. Edgar A. Love, of the Washington Annual Conference of the Central Jurisdiction, moved that Methodist institutions, including "local churches, colleges, universities, theological schools, hospitals and homes, take steps immediately to open their doors to all people alike, without distinction as to race, creed or color." Divinity schools, while only part of the motion, were feeling pressure from both sides. For instance, Perkins School of Theology, at Southern Methodist University in Dallas, Texas, had quietly desegregated by September 1952, but an effort led by Dean Harold A. Bosley to desegregate the Duke University Divinity School in 1949 met rebuff from the trustees.[24]

The Love initiative would have been a bold departure for the church and a significant challenge to segregation, but Charles C. Parlin, chair of the Committee on the State of Church, presented the report and attacked Love's amendment. He charged: "Should this amendment carry, it would require reharmonizing the whole *Discipline*. We would be completely out of order, in my opinion, if this amendment went through." Parlin, a Wall Street lawyer at the prestigious firm of Sherman and Sterling, was not the liberal that Ernest Fremont Tittle had been, but Tittle had died in 1949. Born in Wausau, Wisconsin, in 1898, Parlin received his education at the University of Pennsylvania and his legal training at Harvard University Law School. With a razor sharp mind and mastery of the church *Discipline*, he had already been active in church leadership for some time and had already served as a member of the General Conference in 1940, 1944, and 1948. He served pro bono as legal

23. 1952 General Conference *Journal,* 318–19, 398–99, 504–5, 1016–19, 1168–70.

24. 1952 General Conference *Journal,* 649; Merrimon Cuninggim, *Perkins Led the Way: The Story of Desegregation at Southern Methodist University,* 8–10; the date for desegregation at Perkins is put even earlier in Pete Daniels, *Lost Revolutions: The South in the 1950s,* 30; Dwight W. Culver, *Negro Segregation in the Methodist Church,* 131; Harold A. Bosley to A. Hollis Edens, June 4, 1949, A. Hollis Edens Papers, University Archives, Duke University (hereinafter cited as Edens Papers).

counsel for Bishop G. Bromley Oxnam when he appeared before the U.S. House of Representatives Committee on Un-American Activities. As a partner in a large law firm, Parlin had the secretarial staff and resources to devote much time and energy to the Methodist Church. Over the years, Parlin won the nickname "Mr. Methodist" for his generous service to the Methodist Church, but he was cautious regarding racial matters.[25]

The General Conference rejected Love's amendment and showed itself unwilling to move beyond exhortation and minimal change. Methodist institutions were not required to become open to all races. This was going too far for the Methodist Church in 1952. Ironically, in another memorial (or petition), the General Conference urged federal officials to desegregate the District of Columbia immediately and remove all racial barriers in the nation's capital.[26]

The desegregation of Methodist seminaries came up again the next day as the General Conference considered memorials from the students of Emory University's Candler School of Theology and Duke Divinity School to open their doors to African American students. Here was the next generation of southern white Methodist ministers expressing their disaffection with segregation. The Committee on Education presented a report that encouraged openness "except in those instances where State laws would force an undue hardship upon the institutions involved," a loophole that would exempt both the Emory and Duke seminaries. Edgar Love had moved for deletion of the exception clause from the report, but the General Conference accepted the committee's report as originally presented. The church, in effect, declined to put any pressure on these two divinity schools to open their doors to African American applicants.[27]

Methodists were not the only church wrestling with desegregation of their southern seminaries at this time. In the Episcopal Church, the small all–African American seminary in Petersburg, Virginia, was phased out, and Virginia Seminary in Alexandria, Virginia, opened its doors to African American students in 1951. However, at the University of the South in Swanee, Tennessee, the

25. 1952 General Conference *Journal*, 650; *Who's Who in the Methodist Church* (1966), 999.
26. 1952 General Conference *Journal*, 1410.
27. Ibid., 696–70, 1212.

trustees voted down a proposal to desegregate the School of Theology in 1952. This caused a furor of protest, and Rev. James Pike, dean of the cathedral at St. John's the Divine in New York, refused an honorary degree from the University of the South for this reason. Southern Episcopal bishops divided between those who insisted that their seminarians transfer out of Swanee and those who insisted seminarians stay at the school. All but one of the faculty members of the School of Theology eventually resigned rather than remain at a segregated institution. In June 1953, the trustees reversed course largely due to the exodus of theology students and support for desegregation by a majority of southern bishops.[28]

In many ways churches dealt with race relations in a manner similar to major political parties. In 1952, both the Democratic and Republican parties wrote modest civil rights platforms designed to attract black voters without offending white segregationists. Democrats balanced their ticket by nominating Governor Adlai Stevenson, a liberal, for president, and Senator John Sparksman, a segregationist from Alabama, as his running mate. Likewise, Republicans nominated General Dwight Eisenhower and Senator Richard M. Nixon, neither of whom had any particular record on civil rights, although Eisenhower had testified before Congress in 1948 against complete desegregation of the armed forces. Each party promised to take federal action in the civil rights arena. Democrats promised legislation to guarantee equal employment opportunity, equal protection of each person from bodily harm, and full protection of the rights of citizenship. Republicans proposed federal legislation in the areas of lynchings, poll taxes, and employment practices, and they even promised to end segregation in Washington, D.C.[29]

In December 1952, the Supreme Court heard the first arguments in the collection of public education cases known as *Brown v. Board of Education*. Rearguments were heard in October 1953 because the justices had some particular questions regarding the Fourteenth Amendment. The May 1954 decision was the first major decision of the Court under the leadership of Chief Justice Earl Warren, who had arrived on the Court in the fall of 1953. The decision reversed *Plessy* and the unanimity of the decision indicated that the justices

28. Shattuck, *Episcopalians and Race,* 37–40, 44–50.
29. Donald Bruce Johnson, comp., *National Party Platforms,* 1:487, 504.

were not likely to uphold any other forms of de jure segregation or discrimination. Although the Court did not rule on implementation of its decision and instead ordered more arguments on this question, the decision was a capital victory for all Americans who wanted a desegregated society.

The decision was the most momentous federal action regarding civil rights to that point. *Brown* put the judicial branch of government clearly in the forefront of federal action regarding civil rights, while both the White House and Congress lagged behind. The *Brown* decision came from the branch of the federal government most insulated from voters. However, as events would show, the legislative and executive branches of government needed to support the courts, or desegregation would proceed slowly, if at all.

Churches responded to *Brown* with a profusion of statements that affirmed the decision as an embodiment of both American democratic ideals and Christian teachings. No major denomination went on record as questioning the decision, although some individual white church leaders and congregations dissociated themselves from statements made by higher church officials and bodies. Most churches claimed that the Supreme Court's action ratified their previous racial policies, but, at the same time, they acknowledged that they needed to do more to promote equality and racial justice. Southern denominations urged their members to be calm and work for a smooth transition in this time of uncertainty.[30]

The Methodist Church found *Brown* particularly challenging since it had segregation written into its church constitution, which the Judicial Council in 1952 had reiterated. The Council of Bishops meeting in Chicago in November 1954 wrestled with how to lead the church in this new era. Conflict arose over what kind of statement, if any, to make. In the midst of the meeting, the Southeastern Jurisdiction's bishops staked out their own position:

> We, Bishops of the Southeastern Jurisdiction, have examined with care the proposed statement concerning the recent decision of the Supreme Court relative to segregation in the public schools, submitted to the Council for its consideration.

30. National Council of Churches, Department of Racial and Cultural Relations, "Statements Adopted by Religious Groups Re[garding] Segregation in the Public Schools"; *New South*, October 1956, 3–9.

We accept the Court's decision as being in harmony with the pronouncements of The Methodist Church, and in our respective Areas we are seeking to lead our people to a Christian attitude and an orderly adjustment to the changes that are involved.

We, however, call the attention of the Council to the fact that vast numbers of the people among whom we labor have not made such adjustments, and we minister in a region where acute tensions are developing. The Court in its decision recognized the healing effect of time. This principle is equally applicable to the Church. We are attempting to be shepherds of all our people, and we are convinced that any statement from the Council at this time will result in no great gain and will make our task more difficult. We therefore respectfully request that you, our colleagues, refrain from making any further statement at this time.[31]

The Council of Bishops then had what the minutes of the meeting described as "a lengthy discussion in which a number of members of the Council participated" before approving the following statement:

The historic Decision of the Supreme Court abolishing segregation in the public school system is in keeping with the attitude of The Methodist Church. In our official pronouncements, including the Social Creed and the Episcopal Address adopted by the 1952 General Conference, our position has been clearly stated. The Supreme Court itself recognized that such a ruling brought with it difficulties of enforcement, and thereby made provision for sufficient time to implement its Decision.... [T]he ultimate success of the ruling will be determined in the hearts of the people of the nation. Thus the Church is furnished with an unequaled opportunity to provide leadership during this period in support of the principles involved in the action of the Court. We accept this responsibility, for one of the foundation stones of our faith is the belief that all men are brothers, equal in the sight of God. In that faith, we declare our support of the ruling of the Supreme Court.[32]

31. Council of Bishops, Minutes, November 20, 1954, 390, Council of Bishops Papers, GCAH (hereinafter cited as CBP).
32. Ibid., 390–91.

The Council of Bishops' statement proclaimed that the Supreme Court's decision was in harmony with the church's teaching, but that the decision also created a situation where the church needed to lead society. The bishops exhorted Methodists to be active in seeking solutions when problems occurred and supportive of change rather than defenders of the status quo. However, the Southeastern Jurisdiction bishops informed their brethren that they would inform their constituents that they preferred no statement be made. This disassociation began immediately when Bishop Clare Purcell, elected the new president of the Council of Bishops, announced to the press when he returned home to Birmingham, Alabama, that the Southeastern Jurisdiction bishops did not favor the resolution. This was a powerful indication of the strength of regionalism and did not bode well for the commitment of the church to its support of the *Brown* decision.[33]

The Central Jurisdiction annual conferences had not waited for the Council of Bishops to take a stand on *Brown*. Although some conferences had already met by the time of the Court's decision, most of those meeting afterward included exuberant praise of the decision. Often the resolutions expressed the desire that the church accelerate its action instead of following change in American society. The Central Alabama Annual Conference noted,

> We know by painful experience that segregation in education or in any other area of human life is a complete evil. It has done no good and done much harm. . . .
> This is not the time for blind defense of ancient prejudices, or for spiteful schemes to circumvent the law of the land. Our nation has enough lawlessness already.[34]

33. The bishops did remove from their statement the words *gladly* and *unequal*: "Gladly" was probably in the sentence "We [gladly] accept this responsibility," and "unequal" was probably in the final sentence "In that faith, we declare our [unequal] support of the ruling of the Supreme Court." Another possible construction would have both "gladly" and "unequal" in the final sentence, so that the sentence would begin "In that faith, we [gladly] declare our [unequal] support . . ." (ibid.); Edwin L. Brock, "Methodism's Growing Cleavage," 971.

34. 1954 Central Alabama *Journal*, 47; see also 1954 Georgia Annual Conference (CJ) *Journal*, 39; 1954 North Carolina Annual Conference (CJ) *Journal*, 61; 1954 Louisiana Annual Conference (CJ) *Journal*, 81; and 1954 Mississippi Annual Conference (CJ) *Journal*, 40–41.

While the Central Jurisdiction's annual conferences praised the *Brown* decision and encouraged the church to desegregate, southern white Methodists expressed anxiety over just this possibility. On December 14, 1954, 275 white Methodist ministers and laymen gathered in Birmingham, Alabama, to form the Association of Methodist Ministers and Laymen. The association's purpose was to defend segregation within the church. As the host minister of the first meeting stated, "We note with exceeding grave concern efforts being made within our church for sudden and drastic changes in the organic structure of our church and in social relationships between the races on the congregational level." The organization declared its opposition to church literature promoting integration and stated its intention of organizing Methodists against any changes in the jurisdictional system at the 1956 General Conference. Such fear of desegregation in the church indicated how much the *Brown* decision affected even those who opposed it.[35]

The formation of an organization devoted to segregation in the church moved the Southeastern Jurisdiction's bishops to speak in February 1955, even though they had recommended leadership by silence in November 1954. Audaciously, they congratulated southern white Methodists for being leaders in racial progress in the South. They defended their record, stating:

> History records that Methodism in the South has for generations stood in the vanguard of those who labor for social justice. We have been insistent in our demands for the impartial administration of justice in the courts, equitable distribution of public school funds, larger opportunity for all in the industrial and professional fields, and the full employment by all of the privileges of citizenship.[36]

Regarding the jurisdictional system, the bishops stated, "we know of no concerted action looking toward the abolition of the Jurisdictions or any one of them." They continued by pointing out that any change in the church constitution required two-thirds approval by

35. Brock, "Methodism's Growing Cleavage," 972.
36. Southeastern Jurisdiction's Bishops, "A Statement," 1–2, Bishop William C. Martin Papers, Bridwell Library, Perkins School of Theology, Southern Methodist University, Dallas, Texas (hereinafter cited as Martin Papers).

the General Conference and annual conferences and that the Central Jurisdiction "has afforded our Negro membership opportunities and privileges they have not hitherto enjoyed."[37]

Methodist youth were not as circumspect as the Southeastern Jurisdiction's bishops were. At their national conference held in 1955 at Purdue University in Lafayette, Indiana, the next generation of Methodist leaders challenged the church to be more progressive, particularly regarding racial integration. In part, the declaration stated, "we cannot help observing an attitude on the part of the people of our church which sometimes holds back the progress we could make.... We have discovered that as we have allowed God to use us, there have been created many dynamic communities of faith in which the color of skin was forgotten in the mutual seeking for God's will. We feel that the tragic fact of segregation is a serious detriment to the witness of the world Christian community." They communicated their message directly with the Council of Bishops, and sent copies to the leaders of the Methodist Student Movement and Methodist Youth Fellowships across the country. This was a sign to church leaders that the Methodist Church already confronted a generation gap that could have potentially large ramifications for the church.[38]

The Supreme Court relieved some but not all anxiety concerning the pace of desegregation on May 31, 1955. In a ruling on the implementation of the original *Brown* decision, the justices remanded all five cases back to the federal district courts with the instruction that desegregation should occur "with all deliberate speed." The phrase curiously combined urgency with painstaking planning. Rather than establish a deadline for compliance, school boards had some latitude regarding when schools would actually desegregate. Florida attorney general Dick Erwin commented, "This is the decision that we had hoped for under the alternatives permitted by the court.... The court recognized the need ... to permit a great deal of local planning and discretion."[39]

37. Ibid.
38. National Conference of Methodist Youth Resolution, August 14–21, 1955, Purdue University, in CBP, December 1955, 540; see also Lewis F. Archer to Bishop G. Bromley Oxnam, November 10, 1955, in CBP, December 1955, 541.
39. Richard Kluger, *Simple Justice: The History of* Brown v. Board of Education *and Black America's Struggle for Equality,* 745; *Christian Century,* June 15, 1955, 702.

This optimism among southern white officials seemed justified when federal judge John J. Parker, in the South Carolina case tied to *Brown, Briggs v. Elliot,* ruled that *Brown* made state-imposed segregation illegal, but did not require state-imposed desegregation. Voluntary segregation of schools was still possible, according to what became known as the Parker doctrine. Parker's decision noted, "No violation of the Constitution is involved even though the children of different races voluntarily attend different schools, as they attend different churches." Thus the lack of interracial churches became a piece of evidence for the continuation of segregated schools. This Parker doctrine provided southern white leaders with new hope that desegregation would not come quickly.[40]

The wide latitude that the Supreme Court gave local school districts may have been influenced by the lack of support for the first *Brown* decision shown by the other two branches of the federal government. At the first presidential press conference after the decision, President Eisenhower vaguely promised that he would fulfill his constitutional duties. Congressional reaction varied according to sectional lines, but criticism of the *Brown* decision from southern members of Congress was strong, and southern governors expressed outrage. Senators James Eastland of Mississippi and Harry Byrd of Virginia rebuked the Court, Governor James Byrnes of South Carolina expressed "shock," and Governor Herman Talmadge of Georgia promised defiance. The *Brown* decision may have galvanized southern white segregationists as much as it encouraged African Americans.[41]

Churches after the second *Brown* decision operated in a period of great uncertainty. Change was afoot, but the extent and rate of change defied easy prediction. Churches were now more aware of race relations as both a challenge and an opportunity, but the questions remained: What racial policies could they form? Could these polices unite white and African American members from all sections of the country? And would church actions have any impact on society in this major issue? The message was clear that a new era of race relations had begun, although how quick and how extensive

40. Kluger, *Simple Justice,* 752.
41. Robert Fredrick Burk, *The Eisenhower Administration and Black Civil Rights,* 142, 144–45; Kluger, *Simple Justice,* 710–11; Michael J. Klarman, "How *Brown* Changed Race Relations: The Backlash Thesis," 81–91, 98–103, 116–18.

the change would be was unknown. What would replace Jim Crow was not entirely clear, but many church leaders wanted to be in the vanguard of change. They saw *Brown* as both an opportunity and a challenge. Since the decision established a legal basis for equality, churches might seize the opportunity to lead in the fulfillment of establishing brotherhood. However, churches might only follow society, which would indicate that they had little role other than as devotional institutions.

The *Brown* decision placed southern segregationists in a new position because it forced them to better define their theological stance. This was a difficult task, however, because the Bible did not lend itself to the racial conditions of the Jim Crow South. Compared to the defenders of slavery in the antebellum period, segregationists found that the Bible was far less easy to use for their purposes. They could cite nothing regarding segregation as explicit as the mention of bondage in the Ten Commandments or Paul's injunction that slaves should obey their masters.

There were many passages in the Bible used as justification for segregation, but all had interpretive problems that made the segregationist case weak. For example, segregationists cited the Tower of Babel story to justify the differences in humankind as part of God's plan (Genesis 11:1–9). However, this story did not mention race, but instead explained the differences in humanity by the myriad different languages. The account of Noah seen naked by his son Ham, and Noah's curse that Ham and his descendants would forever be servants was frequently cited, but it had numerous problems (Genesis 9:18–27). Noah was naked because of his drunkenness, the curse on Ham was by Noah rather than God, and Ham was racially a descendant of Noah just like his brothers and therefore the curse would be occupational, but not racial. The Old Testament injunctions against intermarriage were probably the most often cited biblical passages used to support segregation, but it was a prohibition of ethnic mixing and its intent was to prevent Jews from losing their religious faith by assimilating with their religiously different neighbors (Genesis 8:1; Deuteronomy 7:1–3; Ezra 10:10–11). Since African Americans were as Christian as their white neighbors were, this injunction against intermarriage was bogus. Even in ancient Israel, religion, not race, was the basis of the prohibition against intermarriage, since Jews and other peoples of the region were all Semitic.

Segregationists had even more difficulty when they confronted the New Testament. The Sermon on the Mount gave no particular mention of racial purity. The parable of the Good Samaritan acknowledged ethnic issues in the time of Jesus, but segregationists could hardly take comfort from the story. The Acts of the Apostles did make a reference to God establishing the "times of their [nations'] existence and the boundaries of the places where they would live..." (Acts 17:26). However, much of the Acts of the Apostles dealt with the issue of inclusion and exclusion in the early Christian Church, and in Acts and in many of the Epistles, the early Christian leaders explicitly reject exclusionary practices. If the early Christian Church chose inclusion of all and breaking down barriers, then how could southern white Christians justify the distinctions created by their society?

Both the Old Testament and the New Testament also included many passages that segregationists carefully ignored or avoided in their use of the Bible. In the Old Testament, God created humanity in his own image (Genesis 1:27), which implied a common ancestor for all humanity (Genesis 2:7, 22–24). The people of Israel were God's chosen people, but the mark of Israel's covenant relationship was not skin color, but circumcision (Genesis 17:12). Although segregationists often claimed that African Americans supported segregation, white segregationists did not go as far as to say they were willing to trade places with African Americans. Jesus' injunction "In everything do to others as you would have them do to you..." (Matthew 7:12) did not get much notice in segregationists' discussion of brotherhood. Jesus was also insistent about helping those in society who were in greatest need, but southern segregationists were not known for their protests against lynchings, disfranchisement, or inequality in public education. The segregationists' reading of the Bible seemed like little more than a blatant attempt to justify their own point of view through twisting the biblical text.[42]

42. David L. Chappell, "Religious Ideas of the Segregationists"; Bill J. Leonard, "A Theology of Racism: Southern Fundamentalists and the Civil Rights Movement"; Liston Pope, *The Kingdom beyond Caste*, 145–57; Everett Tilson, *Segregation and the Bible*, 18–40.

For Methodists, *Brown* undermined the legitimacy of the racial jurisdictional system because it was built around the notion of separate but equal. This meant the 1956 General Conference would inevitably wrestle with the church's structure. African American members expected concrete action by their church, while southern whites were organizing in opposition to change. The jurisdictional system was the most obvious challenge for Methodists, but *Brown* raised questions about race relations in the church that went far beyond the existence of the Central Jurisdiction.

4

The Origins of Voluntarism in
the Methodist Church

THE *BROWN* DECISION challenged the two myths maintained or
passively accepted by much of white America. First, the Great
Myth insisted that African Americans received fair treatment and
that gradual improvements were occurring in race relations; that
racial communication was clear; and that existing institutions and
organizations could handle outstanding racial issues. Believers in the
Great Myth thought African Americans would fit into American
society best by being like white people, should be grateful for the
progress made in race relations, and should be deferential to white
leaders. The Great Myth also maintained that only the Deep South
still experienced a significant racial problem.

Within the South, there existed a second and more conservative
Southern Myth that asserted that segregation was American, Christian, and natural; that any change in race relations would come
slowly and be directed by the existing white power structure working
with cautious African American leaders; and that outside agitation
was the source of all racial conflicts. Southern churches contributed
to the Southern Myth by emphasizing conversion of the individual
as virtually the sole purpose of the church. Often, white southern
churches were theologically narrow and opposed much social gospel
as leading the church away from its principal mission of making
new disciples. Southern churches also contributed to the Southern
Myth by asserting that white and African American Christians worshipped in different manners. Here was a rationale for segregation
that, at least on the surface, was more cultural than racial. Southern

white segregationists asserted that white churches worshipped in a more dignified and deliberate manner and that African Americans were more emotional and spontaneous. Some segregationists used belief in this difference to justify the separation of churches along racial lines.[1]

The Methodist Church was an institution caught between the Great Myth and the Southern Myth. On the one hand, the church's public pronouncement had called the Southern Myth inconsistent with its teachings and committed itself to eventually ending segregation. On the other hand, its structure embodied parts of the Southern Myth. Methodists had not moved beyond words, and their declarations against racial discrimination were neither pervasive nor persistent. Even less had the Methodist Church addressed the Great Myth, although a few leaders had acknowledged the presence of it and urged the church to act against all racism in American life.

Because of the *Brown* decision's challenge to the Southern Myth, the 1956 Methodist General Conference opened in late April in Minneapolis, Minnesota, with race relations and the Central Jurisdiction among its most important agenda items. Competing memorials (petitions) had come to the General Conference; some recommended no change in the jurisdictional system, and some requested the abolition of the Central Jurisdiction. Still other memorials had suggested ending the entire jurisdictional system and transferring power to the General Conference. The nearly seven hundred delegates faced the most significant decisions regarding the structure of the church since unification of the Methodist Episcopal Church, Methodist Episcopal Church, South, and the Methodist Protestant Church in 1939.

Events outside the church reinforced the urgency of these issues and illustrated the polarization going on in American society. In December 1955, African Americans in Montgomery, Alabama, began a boycott of city buses in protest of the rigid system of bus

1. For the cultural difference behind church segregation, see Methodist Layman's Union, "A Pronouncement," February 12, 1959, 1642–6–2:22, GCAH; "Dear Friends" [Woman's Division of Christian Service] from Woman's Society of Christian Service, First Methodist Church, Monroe, Louisiana, May 6, 1958, General Board of Global Ministries, Women's Division, GCAH (hereinafter cited as GBGM-WD); and Samuel S. Hill, *Southern Churches in Crisis Revisited*, 76–84, 103–15.

segregation, the rudeness of drivers, and hiring discrimination by the bus company. The bus boycott had already united African Americans in Montgomery and inspired others across the nation. Although the initial demands of the Montgomery Improvement Association (MIA) did not call for complete desegregation of the buses, white city officials in Montgomery had refused to make any concessions. Adding to the strife, the home of the MIA's young leader, Rev. Martin Luther King Jr., a young Baptist minister who had just completed his Ph.D. at Boston University, had already been bombed. Another indication of the racial tension building in the country occurred on March 12, 1956, six weeks before the beginning of the General Conference. Southern members of Congress from the states that had made up the Confederacy issued the "Southern Manifesto," a sharp attack on the *Brown* decision. Even though the Supreme Court had given federal judges wide latitude in implementation of desegregation, the statement announced: "We regard the decision of the Supreme Court in the school cases as a clear abuse of judicial power." The ninety-six signing Congressmen went on to exhibit several maxims of the Southern Myth by accusing the Court of disrupting "the amicable relations between the white and Negro races that have been created" and charging that "outside agitators are threatening immediate and revolutionary changes in our public school systems." The Southern Manifesto was part of a campaign called "Massive Resistance" that attempted to keep Jim Crow alive by altering their laws so that localities, or a state itself, might cease public education rather than desegregate.[2]

In many parts of the Deep South, white Citizens' Councils had already formed and used economic coercion as a means of preventing desegregation. They pressured African Americans to withdraw support for desegregation or face loss of jobs, insurance, or loans. These Citizens' Councils, also called the "uptown Klan," opposed all desegregation. Their flexing of economic power was a reminder that white southerners meant to keep African Americans under their control. In a bold move, the white South Carolina Annual Conference of the Southeastern Jurisdiction condemned Citizens'

---

2. David J. Garrow, *Bearing the Cross: Martin Luther King, Jr., and the Southern Christian Leadership Conference*, 58–62; Henry Steele Commager, ed., *Documents of American History*, 2:618.

Councils, but this was hardly the typical southern white Methodist reaction to these developments. Events like the Southern Manifesto and the formation of white Citizens' Councils showed that resistance to desegregation was strong across a broad spectrum of the South and was not limited to the political arena.[3]

General Conference delegates in Minneapolis heard an Episcopal Address that repeated the bishops' 1952 statement that racial discrimination was "both unfair and unChristian." The bishops recommended that a commission representing all parts of the church examine the jurisdictional system and race relations in the church over the next quadrennium and recommend action to the 1960 General Conference. In view of *Brown* and the situation in Montgomery, the Episcopal Address dealt lightly with the subject of segregation specifically and race relations generally. Bishop Oxnam speculated in his diary that Bishop Fred Pierce Corson had made a deal with white southern bishops to go easy on race in return for their support in choosing him to give the Episcopal Address. Whether or not a deal was struck, the bishops preferred a study commission to any hastily conceived action from the floor of the General Conference. This proposal for a commission presented the appearance of action regarding the Methodist racial structure without moving rapidly.[4]

As in every General Conference, much of the early work was done in committees. The Committee on the State of the Church began earnest consideration of racial issues and presented the General Conference with a report entitled "The Methodist Church and

3. 1955 South Carolina (SEJ) Annual Conference *Journal*, 159; Numan V. Bartley, *The New South, 1945–1980*, 187–222.

4. Bishop G. Bromley Oxnam's diary, May 1, 1956, Bishop G. Bromley Oxnam Papers, Manuscript Division, Library of Congress (hereinafter cited as Oxnam Papers); see also "Methodist Bishops Evade the Big Issue," *Christian Century*, May 9, 1956, 573; and Waldo Beach, "The Methodist General Conference," *Christianity and Crisis*, June 11, 1956, 73. In an undated interview with James P. Brawley, Bishop Arthur J. Moore said that he and Bishop Oxnam agreed that on the jurisdictional system "the two extremes must not be allowed to come together in a clash at the General Conference" ("Interview with Bishop Moore," Brawley Papers). For an account of the bishops' decisions about the creation of a commission, see Bishop Costen J. Harrell to Nolan B. Harmon, March 23, 1956, Bishop Costen J. Harrell Papers, Special Collections and Archives, Robert W. Woodruff Library, Emory University, Atlanta, Georgia (hereinafter cited as Harrell Papers).

Race." Included in the report was the statement "There must be no place in The Methodist Church for racial discrimination or enforced segregation. Recognizing that we shall not have attained this goal we rejoice in the progress made." This was too much rejoicing and too little confessing for many delegates. W. Sproule Boyd, a minister from the Northeastern Jurisdiction, moved to change the second sentence to state:

> Recognizing that we shall not have attained this goal so long as we have within the organizational structure of our Church a Jurisdictional Conference based on race, rather than geography, we nevertheless rejoice in the progress that has been made.[5]

This proposed amendment did not move the church forward, but it did illustrate the fixation on the Central Jurisdiction as the embodiment of racial problems in the church. Even if the Central Jurisdiction disappeared overnight, segregated annual conferences and racial discrimination in church policies and in church-related institutions would still exist. Racial policies below the jurisdictional level would actually be more difficult to resolve since they touched people more directly, but it was easy to see the Central Jurisdiction as the embodiment of church failure. Yet Boyd's motion made explicit the church's failure to combat racism.

Opponents of Boyd's amendment attempted to refer the motion to the Committee on Conferences since this committee would actually propose any structural changes in the jurisdictional system. Southern white opponents objected to the church confessing to a sin that many members in their region did not consider a sin. Like the Southeastern Jurisdiction's bishops after the *Brown* decision, these delegates preferred the church to be silent on the subject of race relations. Other delegates from outside the South also joined in objecting to Boyd's motion as going too far. However, supporters of Boyd's motion were more numerous and they reiterated several points to the General Conference. First, the church needed to confess its sin because the structure of the church was not consistent with its principles. Second, integrity required that action be immediate instead

5. 1956 General Conference *Journal,* 412.

of delayed. Several speakers noted that society was changing quickly and that the church needed to keep pace. Finally, segregation in the church hurt efforts to evangelize in other parts the world. The church in America was not separate from the church in the world.[6]

Time in the morning session expired before the General Conference voted on referral. At the next session of the conference, Boyd presented a substitute for his original amendment. The substitute read:

> Recognizing that we have not attained this goal [ending racial discrimination and segregation in the Methodist Church], yet rejoicing in the progress made, we recommend that discrimination or segregation by any method or practice, whether by Conference structure or otherwise in The Methodist Church, be abolished with reasonable speed.[7]

This motion broadened the thrust of the original motion, but at the same time it clearly set the church's pace of desegregation according to the timetable set by the Supreme Court in the second *Brown* decision. "All deliberate speed" and "with reasonable speed" were similar enough in phrasing for everyone to know that the church was willing to move with society. The new phrasing pleased the conference and won approval without any opposition. Given the white southern clamor against *Brown*, the lack of opposition was itself noteworthy.[8]

The General Conference still faced the more difficult task of adjusting the church's structure in a way that would allow desegregation. The General Conference wrote and submitted to annual conferences for ratification a constitutional amendment called Amendment IX that had three major parts. The first part permitted local churches of the Central Jurisdiction to transfer into annual conferences of regional jurisdictions. The second part streamlined desegregation by permitting entire annual conferences of the Central Jurisdiction to transfer into the regional jurisdiction. By either method, desegregation required approval by two-thirds majority votes of each of the involved bodies so that transfer occurred because

6. Ibid., 412–23.
7. Ibid., 449.
8. Ibid., 450–55.

of a consensus of African American and white Methodists. The amendment also specified that whenever 25 percent of the Central Jurisdiction's membership had transferred into regional jurisdictions, one Central Jurisdiction bishop would transfer into the regional jurisdiction that had received the most members of Central Jurisdiction. The amendment concluded with the statement that the Central Jurisdiction would officially dissolve when all its annual conferences and bishops had transferred into regional jurisdictions.[9]

Amendment IX broke ground in three ways. The existing procedure for transfer from one jurisdiction to another required a General Conference enabling act in each specific case, in addition to approving votes at each level in the church. This was a slow process, and only six Central Jurisdiction churches had used this procedure between 1952 and 1956 in order to transfer out of the Central Jurisdiction into regional jurisdictions. The amendment would change the church constitution so that enabling legislation would no longer be required. Second, Amendment IX permitted the transfer of entire Central Jurisdiction annual conferences, which might enable the rapid abolition of the Central Jurisdiction. Third, the amendment would put into the church constitution a commitment to abolish the Central Jurisdiction.[10]

The General Conference reaction to Amendment IX was quite favorable since it permitted desegregation without threatening any region of the church, although limited opposition came from members of the Central Jurisdiction and liberal white delegates. Rev. C. Anderson Davis of the Central Jurisdiction pointed out that the amendment attacked only the problem of the Central Jurisdiction without desegregating any other portion of the church, and that it might permit a smaller, weaker Central Jurisdiction to continue indefinitely in areas where transfer approvals did not come. However, several other members of the Central Jurisdiction took issue with Davis. Thurman Dodson, who had been president of the National Bar Association, told the conference:

> [W]e appreciate all of the shortcomings of this Resolution [Amendment IX], as far as it goes. We are not being fooled

9. Ibid., 1403–5.
10. Ibid., 1496–97.

at all by it. We realize that this Amendment does not abolish segregation in The Methodist Church. But it does move in a direction toward which this great Church of ours ought to move.[11]

Supporters of Amendment IX also pointed out with pride that it was not coercive. One delegate proclaimed that under Amendment IX "there will neither be forced segregation as in the past, nor forced integration as there would be if we were right now to abolish the Central Jurisdiction." Leonard D. Slutz, a Cincinnati lawyer and member of the committee that drafted Amendment IX, assured the conference that segregation did not really exist in the church, because African American Methodists were represented in all portions of the church, but that Amendment IX would end an image problem.[12]

Chester A. Smith, a white liberal from New York, offered a substitute for Amendment IX that would have abolished the Central Jurisdiction immediately with its annual conferences joining regional jurisdictions "as will be agreeable to those Jurisdictions and to the Annual Conferences of the former Central Jurisdiction." Smith's amendment was so vague that it was more a gesture toward cleansing liberal guilt over segregation than a viable alternative to Amendment IX. The uncertainty about what would replace the Central Jurisdiction kept any African American Methodists from endorsing Smith's proposal, and it was soundly defeated by the General Conference. Then the body approved Amendment IX with well above the two-thirds majority needed for sending a constitutional amendment to the annual conferences for their ratification. The word "voluntary" only appeared once in Amendment IX, but Methodists put special emphasis on this word in subsequent years and the amendment was the genesis of the Methodist faith in "voluntarism."[13]

The General Conference quickly authorized a study commission that would review both the jurisdictional system and church race relations during the next quadrennium and report to the 1960 General Conference. The commission was specifically charged to study the effectiveness and weaknesses of the jurisdictional system and to hold public hearings in all jurisdictions "on racial segregation in

11. Ibid., 471.
12. Ibid., 464, 459, 465–69.
13. Ibid., 475.

The Methodist Church and all other problems related to the Jurisdictional System." So that the commission would represent a cross section of the church, the commission's membership was unusually large, with seventy members. Although the official name of the commission was "The Commission to Study and Recommend Action Regarding Interjurisdictional Relations," it was widely referred to as the Commission of Seventy. The commission held an organizational meeting before the General Conference concluded so that it could begin work without delay.[14]

By forming the commission and submitting a constitutional amendment permitting voluntary desegregation, the 1956 General Conference devised a means of taking limited action without developing a comprehensive plan of desegregation. The annual conferences would probably approve Amendment IX and it might start desegregation before the end of the new quadrennium. The study commission would have four years to measure the church's mood and to decide on legislation to propose to the 1960 General Conference. The church, like American society, was willing to acknowledge that a new era in race relations had begun, but Methodists needed more time to decide how rapidly and extensively to change. Delay bought time for Methodists to see how quickly American society implemented new racial practices.

The last major discussion of church policy regarding church racial policies that the 1956 General Conference addressed dealt with working conditions at the Methodist Publishing House. The largest religious publisher in America, the Methodist Publishing House was one of the biggest employers in Nashville, Tennessee. Responding to reports of segregation and discrimination among workers at the Methodist Publishing House, the General Conference approved actions begun by the Publishing House to rectify the situation and urged the publisher to become a leader in providing equal employment opportunity among all workers.[15]

The anxiety within the church regarding racial policies especially

14. Representation on the commission was distributed partly on jurisdictional membership, although each jurisdiction had an additional two bishops and two lay members. The Southeastern Jurisdiction had fourteen members; the North Central, Northeastern, and South Central jurisdictions had twelve members; the Central and Western jurisdictions each had ten members (ibid., 497–503, 1406–8).
15. Ibid., 975–76, 1672–73.

relating to the jurisdictional system became readily apparent at jurisdictional conferences during the summer of 1956. The Central Jurisdiction received a self-study report that emphasized that church segregation was the fundamental problem and that the Central Jurisdiction was not the only form of segregation among Methodists. Yet the report also indicated a new awareness of the complexity of desegregation, for it noted that the Central Jurisdiction had given African American Methodists certain advantages that they had not had before, particularly in electing their own leaders and increased representation in the denomination. These advantages did not outweigh the immorality of segregation, but change might endanger some of these advantages. The report noted:

> We should remember that there is a philosophy in the majority group of our population which supports an all-Catholic group, or an all-Jewish group, or an all-labor group. If there are valid considerations which make such groupings logical, effective and desirable among those in the majority who are not under the physical disadvantages of a different color, we submit with a minority as distinguishable as ours, we would be less than pragmatic if we should discard the advantages of a separate grouping before the disappearance of all the badges and incidents of our second-class status in the mistaken belief that the dissolution of such special grouping was tantamount to integration.[16]

The report also urged Central Jurisdiction congregations not to transfer into white annual conferences unless there was going to be a fully integrated church created by the transfer. Otherwise, the Central Jurisdiction's annual conferences would be weaker. African American Methodists needed to be wary of proposals that would end the Central Jurisdiction by simple semantics, dispersal of segregated annual conferences, or a slow process of attrition. The report explicitly stated, "The transfer of churches should envisage interracial congregations or integration," something not addressed in Amendment IX.[17]

16. 1956 Central Jurisdiction Conference *Journal,* 192, 161–201.
17. Ibid., 200.

While race relations remained a principal focus for the Central Jurisdiction, several other jurisdictional conferences devoted significant time to the jurisdictional system itself. In the Northeastern Jurisdiction, Bishop G. Bromley Oxnam spelled out the reasons for scrapping the entire jurisdictional system. He condemned it for producing six churches within a church, promoting regional and parochial leadership, and serving no useful purpose in evangelism. In a style that was typical for Oxnam, he was bold and hard-hitting. Without specifically identifying the Southeastern Jurisdiction's College of Bishops, he castigated a jurisdiction's bishops for issuing a statement contrary to that of the Council of Bishops. Oxnam may have been preaching to the converted, for the Northeastern Jurisdictional Conference passed a resolution that called for the abolition of the entire jurisdictional system.[18]

Yet, just as ardently, the Southeastern Jurisdiction's bishops extolled the virtue of regionalism at its jurisdictional conference. They remained convinced that the jurisdictional system was the heart of unification and integral to the unity of the church. The Southeastern Jurisdictional Conference agreed and passed a resolution calling for continuation of the jurisdictional system.[19]

The bishops of the Southeastern Jurisdiction also sought to reassure their members that Amendment IX was going to work in their favor. The Southeastern Jurisdiction's bishops recommended Amendment IX because:

> Believing as we do in regional self-determination and in the liberty that leaves men free to work out their problems in the places where the problems exist and as an enlightened conscience and the Spirit of God may lead, we commend the proposed Amendment to the Annual Conferences of this Jurisdiction for their favorable consideration.[20]

The conference also went on record regarding the jurisdictional system itself, supporting a resolution that concluded, "We look with

18. 1956 Northeastern Jurisdiction Conference *Journal,* 255–67, 207–8.
19. Ibid.; 1956 Southeastern Jurisdiction Conference *Journal,* 127–29, 152, 212–13.
20. 1956 Southeastern Jurisdiction Conference *Journal,* 156, 152–56.

disfavor on any proposal that would radically change our Jurisdiction Plan."[21]

The South Central Jurisdiction—after its bishops had reiterated that the General Conference had done nothing to harm the present jurisdiction system and had expressed confidence in the study commission created by the General Conference—also passed a resolution urging annual conferences to ratify Amendment IX. The bishops also stressed that emotional reactions regarding church racial policies fed rumors that distorted what the church had done. They implored conference delegates to dispel those fears.[22]

Ironically, the southern jurisdictional conferences seemed to support Oxnam's charge of a church within a church. At neither conference did the bishops nor the conferences openly say that the Methodist Church was eliminating segregation with "reasonable speed" because the church found segregation evil. Amendment IX received praise precisely because it did not force any forward movement regarding race in these sections of the church. The fear that the bishops expressed regarding rumors indicated a real fear of possible schism or mass defection should the church move too quickly. Rather than point out how change would improve the church and that segregation was an embarrassment to the proclamation of the Gospel, leaders simply expressed the faith that the national church would not thrust integration upon southern white Methodists. This was not the rousing, race-baiting defense of segregation some southern politicians were making, but it encouraged inaction. Southern white leaders aimed to soothe their own members rather than promote closer relationship with African American members.

The Commission of Seventy spent the remainder of 1956 and early 1957 planning its activities, but the composition of the commission revealed one weakness of the church, for the commission had only eleven women members. This gender gap was most evident in the Southeastern Jurisdiction, which had the largest number of jurisdictional members at fourteen, but among these only one woman. None of the other jurisdictions, including the Central Jurisdiction, were significantly more equitable towards women. Each of the remaining five jurisdictions had two women members. Like other

21. Ibid., 213.
22. 1956 South Central Jurisdiction Conference *Journal*, 205, 78–80.

major American churches in the twentieth century (and even earlier), women comprised over half of the membership but were very poorly represented in church leadership. Most women with major church positions tended to be in all-women church organizations such as the Methodist Woman's Society of Christian Service.[23]

Patriarchy pervaded more than just churches during this time, and Methodists at the 1956 General Conference did take a giant step toward reform by approving the ordination of women as elders (full members of annual conferences). Nevertheless, on issues such as race relations, there was a crucial difference between the leadership of men and women in the South. The Woman's Society of Christian Service was far more likely to have interracial contact and meetings than were Methodist men. Although these meetings were infrequent and scattered across the South, they showed that many southern Methodist women did not place nearly as much emphasis upon segregation as white southern men did. With only one woman member of fourteen total members, the Southeastern Jurisdiction effectively nullified any significant dissension within its delegation on the commission.[24]

The Commission of Seventy was not the only part of the church working on race relations. The Board of Social and Economic Concerns, led by Rev. A. Dudley Ward, organized nearly twenty interracial workshops in various cities across the country. Carefully coordinated between the regional white annual conference and the African American annual conference, these workshops served as a model of racial dialogue and information regarding local racial problems. Begun in 1956 and stretching through 1959, the workshops included all bishops of the area, some sociological or demographic

23. The membership of the Commission of Seventy provided for a minimum of three ministers and three laypersons from each jurisdiction but provided an additional minister and layperson for each five hundred thousand members in each jurisdiction. It also included two bishops and two additional laypersons from each jurisdiction. The Southeastern Jurisdiction had fourteen members, the Northeastern, North Central, and South Central jurisdictions each had twelve members, and the Central and Western jurisdictions had ten members each.
24. Original sources or documents of Methodist women, especially of African American women, are difficult to find. How much richer would be knowledge of Methodism if women were proportionately represented in archives and manuscripts is beyond my poor ability to estimate. For secondary sources, see Thelma Stevens, *Legacy for the Future: The History of Christian Social Relations in the Woman's Division of Christian Service, 1940–1968.*

information about changing conditions, and small group discussions regarding race. These workshops brought many local church leaders—especially male laity, African American and white—together to learn about each other and have conversations about local conditions.[25]

In northern cities, the meetings discussed the changing housing market as more African Americans moved into neighborhoods that were previously all-white and as more white residents fled to the suburbs. In many cases, local Methodist congregations were either apathetic or terrified about the changes and had done little to welcome African Americans moving into new neighborhoods. Cooperation between congregations of the Central Jurisdiction and regional jurisdictions in the same cities were tentative and weak. The opportunity of reaching African Americans moving into northern cities was largely unmet by the Methodist Church. Church leaders often felt overwhelmed by the enormity of the task compared to their limited time and financial resources.

These workshops created needed dialogue between African American and white Methodists, but there were few follow-up conferences. A majority of these interracial Methodist meetings were solitary experiences rather than annual or semiannual events to build bridges between Methodists. Another problem with these conferences was that the Southeastern Jurisdiction was poorly represented. While it hosted conferences in Atlanta, Georgia, Morristown, Tennessee, and Daytona Beach, Florida, there were no conferences in Mississippi, Alabama, or South Carolina. This lack of dialogue between Methodists in the Deep South hardly inspired trust between leaders of the Central and Southeastern jurisdictions.

In the spring of 1957, the Commission of Seventy began its own hearings in each jurisdiction regarding the jurisdictional system and race relations within the church. The hearings were an attempt to

25. Interracial Conferences sponsored by the Board of Social and Economic Concerns were in Milwaukee, Wis., February 1956; Jamaica, N.Y., September 1956; Kansas City, Mo., October 1956; Baltimore, Md., December 1956; Atlanta, Ga., January 1957; Detroit, Mich., April 1957; Indianapolis, Ind., May 1957; St. Louis, Mo., May 1957; Daytona Beach, Fla., September 1957; Houston, Tex., September 1957; Pittsburgh, Pa., December 1957; Glendale, Calif., February 1958; Milwaukee, Wisc. (follow-up conference), April 1958; Phoenix, Ariz., January 1959; and Morristown, Tenn., February 1959.

open dialogue across sectional lines within the commission, but they also created fear among some members. Edwin L. Jones, executive committee member from the Southeastern Jurisdiction, worried that there was too much focus on race relations within the church and confided to retired Bishop Costen J. Harrell that he "was worried to death about this commission." Jones elaborated,

> It is a matter of history, well known to everyone who can read, that the Yankees forced the Civil War on us as they were more interested in forcing immediate freedom for the slaves than they were in progressive liberation from slavery. They were willing to shed the blood of Southerners as well as their own soldiers in order to bring this about. I detect the same intolerance and determination on the part of the same sort of people outside of the South to force integration on us before we are ready for it and against our wishes.[26]

Jones was as an important figure among Southeastern Jurisdiction laymen, as were Parlin in the Northeastern and Brawley in the Central jurisdictions. Born in 1891, educated at Duke University, he was a highly successful businessman in the construction firm started by his father, a firm that built the Atomic Gaseous Diffusion Plant in Oak Ridge, Tennessee, in the middle of World War II. A philanthropist for Methodist causes, he served on the national church General Council of World Service and Finance from 1952 to 1964. He was deeply conservative politically and socially, and he represented the antithesis of Thelma Stevens, who also came from the Southeastern Jurisdiction. Where Stevens was liberated and committed to the social gospel, Jones was patriarchal and pietistic.

If the Commission of Seventy worried Jones, it also raised anxiety in the Council of Bishops. The bishops realized that division within their own ranks was not constructive and might endanger the commission's ability to form a consensus. Therefore, the Council of Bishops approved a meeting of the twelve bishops on the commission to discuss privately the role of the jurisdictional system. This group of bishops would report to the full council at a special

26. Edwin L. Jones to Bishop Costen J. Harrell, November 2, 1956, Harrell Papers.

meeting devoted solely to discussing the jurisdictional system. The bishops did not want to dictate a plan to the commission, but they wanted to put forth a united position.[27]

The special meeting of the twelve bishops on the Commission of Seventy occurred in New York in September 1957. The sketchy records of the meeting indicate that the bishops reported widely varying experiences regarding the jurisdictional system. Bishops Paul N. Garber and Arthur J. Moore of the Southeastern Jurisdiction insisted that the jurisdictional system was definitely part of the Plan of Union and that dropping the jurisdictional system would seriously undermine the credibility of the church with the probable loss of large numbers of Southeastern Jurisdiction members. They did not use the word *schism*, but the specter was raised. One other jurisdiction, presumably the South Central Jurisdiction, represented by Bishops William C. Martin and A. Frank Smith, had used the jurisdictional system favorably; three reported no benefit and reservations about its continuance; and one jurisdiction, probably the Northeastern Jurisdiction, represented by Bishop Oxnam, found the jurisdictional system divisive and harmful to the work of the church.[28]

After much discussion, the bishops agreed to maintain the jurisdictional system, but to make much of the structure optional. Their plan envisioned a larger General Conference that included all jurisdictional conferences meeting together. The General Conference would meet, complete most of its work, and adjourn, at which time the jurisdictional conferences, meeting in the same city, would do their work. With new bishops elected and jurisdictional representation on church boards and agencies settled, the General Conference would reconvene and consecrate the new bishops. The General Conference committee on the episcopacy would appoint bishops as it saw fit, but each jurisdictional conference had veto power if its committee on the episcopacy felt a bishop was inappropriate for its region. This plan would effectively make the jurisdictional conferences subcommittees of the General Conference for the purpose of electing bishops and representatives, but it would allow jurisdictions

27. Council of Biships, Minutes, Cincinnati, Ohio, April 25, 1957, 171, CBP.
28. Minutes, "Informal Meeting of Bishops Serving on the Commission to Study and Recommend Action Concerning the Jurisdictional System," September 26 and 27 [1957], New York, Oxnam Papers.

to go beyond this function. Oxnam commented in his diary that while the meeting was at times tense, he felt that the outcome was quite productive and would eventually end the harmful effects of the jurisdictional system. The twelve bishops, including the Central Jurisdiction's Edgar Love and Willis King, apparently decided not to make a specific recommendation regarding continuation of the Central Jurisdiction.[29]

As the twelve bishops met, national attention again focused on the issue of school desegregation. In Little Rock, Arkansas, a federal judge had ordered the desegregation of Central High School due to a suit by the parents of nine African American students. This was just the sequence of events permitted under the second *Brown* decision, should parents find a school board not moving with "all deliberate speed." The school board indicated it would comply with the judge's order, but Governor Orval Faubus ordered the Arkansas National Guard to prevent the African American students' entry into the school. When threatened with a citation for contempt of court, Faubus withdrew the National Guard and allowed desegregation to take place, but a mob forced evacuation of the school. President Eisenhower decided to restore order and enforce the court's ruling by seizing control of the Arkansas National Guard and sending U.S. Army paratroopers to Little Rock to protect students in the desegregated Central High.

The crisis in Little Rock made Faubus a successful regional politician and secured his reelection. Overnight he went from an obscure state politician to a regional hero. School desegregation actually slowed after the Little Rock incident as more southern politicians found it advantageous to resist federal authority. President Eisenhower's use of federal troops in Little Rock rekindled memories of what white southerners believed about Reconstruction: that the federal government had attempted to impose its own ideas about race relations on a prostrate South. Although this was a flawed interpretation of Reconstruction, it was strongly held, especially among conservative white southerners. The fear of federal intervention in southern affairs also resonated with some southern white Methodists who feared that "Yankee" Methodists might also try to coerce integration within the Methodist Church.

29. Ibid.; Oxnam diary, September 26, 1957, Oxnam Papers.

Possibly because of the Little Rock crisis, the two southern regional jurisdictions attracted far more Methodists to their hearings than all other jurisdictions. In both jurisdictions, the panels heard southern white Methodists defend segregation and the southern way of life and heard the threat that major change within the jurisdictional system would produce mass defections. Speakers defended the jurisdictional system as an integral part of the Plan of Union that should not be altered. However, also in both jurisdictions, some called segregation sinful and wanted the church to move forward regarding race relations. The chair of the Commission of Seventy panel visiting the Southeastern Jurisdiction reported that he had received several confidential appeals for the church to take more decisive action. Reports of support for desegregation from within the Southeastern Jurisdiction prompted Edwin L. Jones, a Duke University trustee, to write Dr. Hollins Edens, president of Duke University, complaining about a "communistically minded person" at the Duke Divinity School. He charged: "Desegregation will never save our church, our church people, or our non-church people. What gives me most concern is why the non-essentials are overemphasized at Duke ... in place of the saving gospel of Jesus Christ for which the church is organized."[30]

Within the Central Jurisdiction, the Commission of Seventy's panel heard a plethora of reasons for abolishing the jurisdiction, but the most consistent theme heard was that church segregation was morally indefensible. African American Methodist speakers did not have strong feelings regarding the jurisdictional system besides abolition of the Central Jurisdiction. When pressed by the panel, a majority of speakers believed that it was best to abolish the entire jurisdictional system. Most speakers felt that the church was not doing nearly enough to build racial brotherhood and that it lagged behind secular society. African American Methodists wanted more interracial activity to build trust and understanding. Some on the panel detected that African American Methodists had not thought much beyond the abolition of the Central Jurisdiction in terms of what should follow on the annual conference and congregational

30. Reports of all regional jurisdictions are in the Lawrence Riggs Papers, DePauw University Archives and Special Collections, Greencastle, Indiana (hereinafter cited as Riggs Papers); Edwin L. Jones to Hollis Edens, November 4, 1957, Edens Papers.

levels. Most speakers supported Amendment IX, but there was also a feeling that it was not enough. The panel concluded that African American Methodists did not fear losing positions of power designated for them by the existence of the Central Jurisdiction, if the church really made merit and ability the criteria for positions. However, the panel also felt this view was stronger among lay African American Methodists who worked outside the church than among African American ministers.[31]

In the three northern regional jurisdictions, the Commission of Seventy panels discovered there was strong sentiment for the abolition of the Central Jurisdiction, but no unanimity regarding the geographic jurisdictions. Sentiment for ending the entire jurisdictional system was strongest in the Northeastern Jurisdiction, but even in this section, the Woman's Society of Christian Service found the jurisdictional system helpful. Most speakers felt that Amendment IX was a good means to desegregate the church, but they did not have specific steps regarding what to do beyond the abolition of the Central Jurisdiction.

In January 1958, the Council of Bishops devoted a special three-day meeting to consider the jurisdictional system. Oxnam, who was secretary of the council, wrote little about the discussion in the minutes, but in his diary, he described the debate as "long and at times intense." Retired Southeastern Jurisdiction bishop Costen J. Harrell argued that the jurisdictional system was a covenant that could not be altered without betraying the Plan of Union, which had brought the separate Methodist denominations together in 1939. Oxnam refuted that idea and asserted that the jurisdictional system was only a part of the Plan of Union, one that had an amendment process so the church could make changes in it. He noted that in approving Amendment IX, southern white Methodists had already consented to change in the jurisdictional system. Any suggestion that the jurisdictional system was a solemn covenant that could not be changed was bogus.[32]

At the meeting, the Central Jurisdiction's bishops read to the Council a joint statement regarding use of Amendment IX. The

31. Report of the Findings of the Panel Assigned to Hold Hearings in the Central Jurisdiction, February 6, 1958, 1–8, Charles Coolidge Parlin Papers, GCAH (hereinafter cited as Parlin Papers).
32. Oxnam diary, January 7, 1958, Oxnam Papers.

statement began with the bishops affirming their desire to abolish the Central Jurisdiction and pointing out that their annual conferences had enthusiastically approved Amendment IX. The bishops then recommended more emphasis on preparing the church for desegregation so that transfers into regional jurisdictions would be based on mutual trust and respect. Then the bishops concluded that until such time that "the majority of our churches will be welcomed into other Jurisdictions," the Central Jurisdiction should remain as is "with a reasonable degree of strength." Amendment IX could be used in isolated instances where African American Methodist congregations were far from other parts of the Central Jurisdiction, but otherwise delay was preferable to the piecemeal action that could occur under Amendment IX. The bishops' statement was consistent with the Central Jurisdiction's 1956 self-study commission, chaired by James P. Brawley, which warned against moving Central Jurisdiction congregations into regional jurisdictions before sufficient change in racial attitudes had transpired:

> We are likely to delude ourselves when we think that merely shifting a Negro church from a Negro conference to a white conference removes segregation. This procedure merely shifts segregation from one conference to another; it provides no real solution to the problem and reduces the membership of the Negro conference that is heavily dependent upon the membership of the conference to give larger representation and to give potency to the group that might fight segregation and help to bring about reform.[33]

The Central Jurisdiction's bishops' statement irritated some allies of the Central Jurisdiction. Oxnam characterized the statement as "unintelligible and evasive." He felt betrayed in working for desegregation and then having African American leaders say the time and the method for it were not right. The Central Jurisdiction bishops' statement led some Methodists to conclude that African American Methodist leaders were more concerned with positions of power than desegregation and that foot-dragging was preferred over not

---

33. Statement of the College of Bishops of the Central Jurisdiction, Minutes, Council of Bishops, Gatlinburg, Tenn., November 1957, CBP; Report of the Commission to Study the Central Jurisdiction, April 15, 1956, 51, Brawley Papers.

having their own jurisdiction. Yet the Central Jurisdiction's bishops wanted their colleagues to know that Amendment IX left much to be desired as a means of desegregation. It was a nucleus for further action, but it was also flawed. As leaders of their people, the bishops wanted to go on record as opposing an action that would permit the best and brightest of their churches and pastors to transfer and leave smaller, weaker churches and less trained ministers behind. Amendment IX allowed for desegregation, but it really did not provide an organized and clear mechanism for going from a segregated church to a desegregated church. Furthermore, desegregation of only part of the church was not very appealing to African American bishops who knew very well that most of their members lived in areas where Amendment IX had little chance of use in the near future.[34]

As the Commission of Seventy wrestled with race relations in both the church and the jurisdictional system, Christian charity was at times in short supply. Harold A. Bosley, minister of the First Methodist Church in Evanston, Illinois, responded to a proposal of southern bishop Arthur J. Moore by saying, "I had thought we were commissioned to make a careful study of the Jurisdictional system, not to find excuses for maintaining it as it is now." Bishop Oxnam expressed his feelings about a meeting of the commission in his diary: "I think we made real progress although our southern friends are utterly impossible. . . . A generation has to die before we really reach a solution." Late in 1957, Edwin Jones wrote Bishop Harrell about the hostility towards the South he perceived on the Commission of Seventy and lamented, "Why we ever united with these folks is beyond me."[35]

The tension within the Commission of Seventy reflected the tension mounting over desegregation in society as a whole, especially in the Deep South. "Massive Resistance" became the slogan among state legislatures as states passed a plethora of legislation to thwart or minimize efforts at school desegregation. By the end of the 1956–1957 school year, the states of Alabama, Florida, Georgia, Louisiana,

34. Oxnam diary, January 7, 1958, Oxnam Papers.
35. Harold A. Bosley to Bishop Arthur J. Moore, January 24, 1958, Arthur J. Moore Papers, Arthur J. Moore Methodist Museum, South Georgia Conference Archives, Epworth by the Sea, St. Simons Island, Georgia (hereinafter cited as Moore Papers); Oxnam diary, September 23, 1958, Oxnam Papers; Edwin L. Jones to Harrell, December 26, 1957, Harrell Papers.

Mississippi, North Carolina, South Carolina, and Virginia still had completely segregated public education systems. Also, southern states, led by Alabama, passed legislation that basically outlawed the operation of the NAACP or required it to turn over to the state its membership lists. By 1957, the NAACP reported being under attack in Alabama, Arkansas, Florida, Georgia, Louisiana, Tennessee, Texas, South Carolina, and Virginia. After the Supreme Court decision in 1954 and before the fall of 1957, 750 school districts had desegregated, but over the next three years, only 49 additional districts began integration. After Little Rock, the Eisenhower administration largely attempted to avoid another confrontation while continuing to quietly uphold federal courts. It was a policy that left to the Supreme Court and lower federal courts the burden of decision making regarding school desegregation.[36]

White church leaders were not completely quiet during the growing controversy over school desegregation. A few pastors risked their personal safety by confronting angry mobs. For instance, a Clinton, Tennessee, Baptist minister, Paul Turner, received injuries as he protected an African American student desegregating a public school, and an Episcopal minister in Mansfield, Texas, had to be rescued by Texas Rangers as irate racists attempted to take out their anger on him as he defended desegregation. Two white ministers escorted African American high school students in Little Rock in their first attempt at desegregating Central High School. More numerous were ministers who spoke out from the pulpit in defense of desegregation or civil rights only to be driven from their pulpits. In November 1957, eighty Protestant ministers in Atlanta, Georgia, including twenty Methodist ministers, issued a statement supporting public school desegregation as politicians talked of shutting down the school system rather than allowing desegregation. Even evangelist Billy Graham was not silent. Challenged by Reinhold Niebuhr in the *Christian Century*, Graham responded with a general statement in *Life* magazine that called on southern Christians to live in harmony and with respect for one another and pointed out that in his crusades there was no longer any segregation. It was hardly

36. Aldon D. Morris, *The Origins of the Civil Rights Movement: Black Communities Organizing for Change*, 30–35; Burk, *Eisenhower Administration*, 192–230.

an attack on all segregation, but it did not support a reactionary position.[37]

Despite the tensions among Methodists, a consensus emerged within the Commission of Seventy regarding basic points. The jurisdictional system itself would be retained, but changes would be made in the timing and location of jurisdictional conferences to combine these conferences with the General Conference. This would in effect make jurisdictional conferences more like subcommittees of the General Conference rather than separate entities. Under discussion was an arrangement whereby jurisdictions would still elect bishops, but consecration would occur at the General Conference. Appointments of bishops would be by a committee of the General Conference, but jurisdictional committees could veto the appointment of a bishop to their jurisdictions. The changes, if approved by the 1960 General Conference and the annual conferences, would give the church a national character while maintaining the jurisdictional system with enough power to allow jurisdictions to pursue their own activities if they desired. These changes paralleled those arrived at the meeting of the bishops on the Commission of Seventy in the fall of 1957.[38]

Debate over the fate of the Central Jurisdiction focused on whether to establish a target date for abolishing the jurisdiction, an idea mentioned in several hearings. Usually the suggested date was either 1964 or 1968, but sometimes later. Within the commission, the target date proposal cut across both racial and geographic lines but had little, if any, episcopal support. Advocates of a target date felt strongly that setting such a date strengthened those who supported integration by giving specificity to the church's efforts at overcoming racial discrimination. A target date committed the church to desegregation in a concrete way and yet provided time for opponents of

37. *Atlanta Journal and Constitution,* November 3, 1957; Reinhold Niebuhr, "Proposal to Billy Graham," *Christian Century,* August 8, 1956, 921–22; Billy Graham, "Billy Graham Makes Plea for an End to Intolerance," *Life,* October 1956, 138, 140–44, 146, 151; Ernest Q. Campbell and Thomas F. Pettigrew, "Men of God in Racial Crisis," *Christian Century,* June 4, 1958, 663–65; Colbert S. Cartwright, "What Can Southern Ministers Do?" *Christian Century,* December 26, 1956, 1505–6.

38. Commission to Study the Jurisdictional System, Minutes, February 6–7, 1958, 7–8, Parlin Papers.

desegregation to come around. Advocates of a target date believed that the church had already decided to abolish the Central Jurisdiction through Amendment IX and there was nothing gained by dragging the process out.

Among the Central Jurisdiction's members on the Commission of Seventy, the target date was divisive. Bishop Willis King and Dr. Brawley argued against a target date. King feared that the church would not be ready in 1968 for the abolition of the Central Jurisdiction and that ending it too quickly might spark an exodus to the AME, AMEZ, and CME churches. Brawley felt that the target date put too much emphasis upon ending the Central Jurisdiction and not enough on ending all forms of segregation in the church. He also did not believe that a target date would prove beneficial or realistic. Looking at school desegregation, he asked the commission, "If you can't enforce decisions of the Supreme Court in the Deep South, how can you enforce a decree of The Methodist Church where you do not have such law?" Supporting the target date from within the Central Jurisdiction were Charles F. Golden and Thurman Dodson. Dodson admitted that he had doubts about whether the church would be ready to abolish the Central Jurisdiction by 1968, but he also believed that the church needed an explicit goal. A target date was, after all, pretty innocuous, he added.[39]

Some of the white members of the commission from the Northeastern, North Central, and Western jurisdictions supported a target date, but many influential members of the commission were opposed. Rev. Bosley and Rev. John R. Wilkins, prominent ministers from the North Central and Western jurisdictions, respectively, felt that a target date would not help. Parlin turned over the chair of a meeting so that he could speak against a target date, and most members of the Southeastern Jurisdiction's delegation urged rejection of a target date. With the Central Jurisdiction split, the Southeastern Jurisdiction solidly opposed, and lacking any episcopal support, the Commission of Seventy rejected a target date for ending the Central Jurisdiction. Instead, the commission urged continued reliance on Amendment IX and the establishment of a smaller commis-

39. Ibid., 12, 9–13; Commission to Study the Jurisdictional System, Minutes, December 10, 1958, 4, Parlin Papers.

sion to focus on promoting racial brotherhood and use of Amendment IX.[40]

The Commission of Seventy considered how to further racial inclusiveness through a study of Methodist-related institutions to determine what racial policies and practices existed. This study showed that among fifty-eight Methodist-related hospitals across the country, none excluded African American doctors in their by-laws, but forty had none on their staff. Although thirty-two hospitals did not separate patients by race, twenty-five reported separating patients by race, usually by rooms rather than by wards or floors. One hospital refused to accept any African American patients. Two of forty-one schools of nursing refused African American students, although only twenty-one had ever had an African American student. Four Methodist homes for the aged had policies of denying African American residents, while thirty-four others replied they had never received an application from an African American. Eleven homes for children refused to accept African American children, fourteen others had none, and only six had African American children. Among Methodist-related colleges and universities, forty-one of eighty-two responding institutions had interracial faculties, and eighty of eighty-two institutions reported interracial student bodies. Of this latter figure, however, seventy included Asian students. Only forty-eight of eighty-two colleges and universities reported having African American students in their student population. These figures showed modest improvement over an earlier study of Methodist institutions conducted by sociologist Dwight Culver in 1953.[41]

A study of the use of Amendment IX made by Charles F. Golden for the Commission of Seventy revealed great reluctance in the Central Jurisdiction to transferring into regional jurisdictions. Local churches found that financial assessments made of each congregation, referred to by Methodists as "apportionments," were far higher

40. Commission to Study the Jurisdictional System, Minutes, February 6–7, 1958, 10–14, Parlin Papers; Commission to Study the Jurisdictional System, Minutes, December 10, 1958, 4, Parlin Papers.

41. C. A. McPheeters to Members of the Sub-Committee, February 23, 1959, 4–5, Peter C. Murray Central Jurisdiction Collection, GCAH (hereinafter cited as Murray Collection); Dr. Keyser's Report to the Sub-Committee on Integration, not dated, 1–2, Murray Collection; A Survey of Methodist Colleges and Universities, February 1959, Riggs Papers; Culver, *Negro Segregation*, 128–41.

in white annual conferences than in the Central Jurisdiction. This was partly a result of much higher pensions and minimum salaries for ministers. There was also a fear among African American ministers that if they transferred into a conference with few African American congregations, then they would be effectively frozen at their present church. They believed they would lose any opportunity to advance because white congregations were unlikely to accept an African American minister. For these reasons, efforts at using Amendment IX had virtually ended within the Central Jurisdiction after only nine churches had transferred into Western, North Central, and Northeastern jurisdictions. Another thirty-six churches had begun the process but then ceased action, indicating that the Central Jurisdiction's bishops had disseminated their trepidation about Amendment IX.[42]

The commission decided to recommend that the Board of Social and Economic Concerns or its successor (there was a movement afoot to combine this Board with the corresponding agencies for temperance and world peace) establish a special agency to continue the work of the Commission of Seventy. Specifically, it would work with annual conference committees of interracial brotherhood to build a meaningful communication between regional annual conferences and overlapping conferences of the Central Jurisdiction. In addition, this agency would work with church leaders to form and to promote integrated churches. Last, this agency would report to the 1964 General Conference regarding the progress made toward ending the Central Jurisdiction and all segregation in the Methodist Church. Like the decision to continue use of Amendment IX, the Commission of Seventy recommended further efforts that depended upon voluntary cooperation for success. Annual conferences or congregations could simply take this action as an exhortation. Yet by the very nature of being a voluntary body, the commission saw very little else that the church could do.

Bishop Moore and Edwin Jones began congratulating themselves on persuading the commission to accept the continuation of

42. C. A. McPheeters to Members of the Sub-Committee, February 23, 1959, 2, Murray Collection; A Survey of Methodist Colleges and Universities, February 1959, Riggs Papers.

the jurisdictional system and make no major change regarding race relations in the church. In one letter Moore once estimated that, on a hundred-point scale, white southerners had scored eighty-five points. He wrote another bishop in the Southeastern Jurisdiction that "we are going to the General Conference with very great gains and a few losses in the Southern viewpoint." In another letter, Moore congratulated Jones for proposing the abolition of the Central Jurisdiction at the April 1959 meeting of the Commission of Seventy. Moore saw it as a brilliant tactical move that silenced critics on the commission who felt that the report was not doing enough to end the jurisdiction. By a large majority, the commission voted down Jones's motion. Jones also assessed the report's section on race relations as "not legislation; they [the recommendations] are exhortations. It will give some people ammunition to 'pop-off' with, but if each local church keeps its head it will not affect any local church that doesn't want to be affected."[43]

Ironically, just as a victory in the Commission of Seventy seemed assured, southern white laymen were threatening to bolt out of the Methodist Church because of possible integration. In Birmingham, Alabama, over fifteen hundred laymen of the Southeastern Jurisdiction met again to organize resistance to any change in the jurisdictional system. Similar organizations formed in Mississippi and Louisiana. Bishop Purcell noted that the leaders were capable men who could raise plenty of funds to finance their activities. Even more threatening, Methodists and others in Alabama pushed a law through the state legislature that would allow 65 percent of the membership of a congregation to withdraw from a national church and take the church property with it. Technically, the denomination rather than local congregations owned all Methodist, Episcopal, Catholic, and Presbyterian church properties. Although Methodist church officials suspected that the Alabama law was unconstitutional, the law reflected widespread anxiety regarding church desegregation among southern white Methodists. Both Jones and Moore went to Birm-

43. Moore to Bishop Clare Purcell, April 6, 1959, Moore Papers; Jones to R. Laurence Dill, November 20, 1959, Harrell Papers. See also Moore to Jones, December 16, 1958, Moore Papers; Moore to Bishop Bachman G. Hodge, April 9, 1956, Moore Papers; and Bishop Costen J. Harrell to Edwin L. Jones, June 5, 1959, Harrell Papers.

ingham to talk with angry laymen and wrote letters trying to reassure them that rumors regarding integration in the Methodist Church and abolition of the Central Jurisdiction or the entire jurisdictional system were unfounded.[44]

The Methodist segregationists believed that change from rigid segregation was likely to produce a complete end of all racial barriers and result in integration in all parts of life, including their churches. The use of troops in Little Rock, Arkansas, conjured up fears of an unreasonable North furiously oppressing the South by imposing its racial policies. Talk of changing the jurisdictional system or of ending the Central Jurisdiction excited these fears within the church. M. B. Grace, a white lawyer in Birmingham, communicated the fears of many in the Methodist Laymen's Union when he told Bishop Moore that rumors circulated that Moore and Bishop Marvin Franklin in Mississippi could not be trusted to defend the South and that northern Methodists were pressing integration within the church. Describing the ideas of the organization, Grace continued:

> We believe the northern bishops and churchmen are deter-
> mined that the Methodist churches in the South be integrated,
> and we are just as determined it shall never be integrated. . . .
> The negro people will not appreciate white people coming
> into their churches, and we white people will not appreciate
> negro people coming into white churches and attempt[ing] to
> take part in the running or management of white churches. If
> the negroes should ever be integrated in the white Methodist
> churches, there will be nothing but confusion, ill will and
> chaos.[45]

The fears of racial change represented in the Methodist Laymen's Union consumed these white southerners. They were used to dominating the lives of African Americans and had never related to them

44. Bishop Clare Purcell to Bishops Arthur J. Moore and Paul N. Garber, April 2, 1959; Bishop Hodge to Southeastern Jurisdiction Bishops, April 3, 1959; Bishop Moore to Purcell, April 6, 1959; Bishop Moore to Bishop Hodge, April 9, 1959; Moore to Purcell, July 31, 1959; M. B. Grace to Moore, August 17, 1959; Moore to M. D. Grace, August 19, 1959; Edwin Jones to Judge Whit Windham, August 31, 1959; Jones to Hodge, August 31, 1959; Jones to Judge Windham, December 14, 1959, all in the Moore Papers.
45. M. B. Grace to Bishop Arthur J. Moore, August 17, 1959, Moore Papers.

as equals. There were no Methodist rules against African American Methodists attending a white congregation, but all the laws of southern society said clearly they were not welcome. However, these white southerners felt that if society's restrictions ended, then African American Methodists might assume that they indeed were welcome or had the right to go wherever they pleased. These segregationists clearly wanted out of a church that might approve or legitimize this view in any way.

Besides organizing to oppose any change in the jurisdictional systems, Methodist segregationists took aim at church school literature. A number of Mississippi Methodist churches wrote to Henry M. Bullock, General Secretary of the Editorial Division, Board of Education, to protest articles that the petition said promoted integration and attacked segregation. These petitions argued that devotional literature was being replaced by political advocacy, that the material was particularly unsuited for young people, and therefore that Methodist churches in the area were no longer using church school literature because of the biased contents. The Woman's Division of Christian Service received similar protests about its literature. One Monroe, Louisiana, Woman's Society of Christian Service voted forty-two to one to send a letter of protest that charged, among other things, that agitation regarding race relations came from psychological misfits, the uninformed, and the Communist party.[46]

When the Commission of Seventy released its report in early January 1960, press accounts seized upon the recommendation to retain the Central Jurisdiction, and on two statements regarding the church's failure. One emphasized the limited progress to obtain true brotherhood, and the other admitted the inability to legislate an immediate end to segregation. The NAACP criticized the report for not making the church "a positive example of equality, democracy, and brotherhood within its own ranks" and noted that segregationists would derive comfort from the report. *The Christian Century* accepted the commission's recommendations as prudent, given the

46. "Resolution Concerning Methodist Church School Literature," General Board of Church and Society, GCAH (hereinafter cited as GBCS); Henry M. Bullock to Dudley Ward, October 15, 1957, GBCS; "Dear Friends" [Woman's Division of Christian Service] from Woman's Society of Christian Service, First Methodist Church, Monroe, Louisiana, May 6, 1958, 3, GBGM-WD.

current state of race relations in the South, but it criticized the lack of a target date. The *Central Christian Advocate*, the biweekly newspaper of the Central Jurisdiction, reviewed the report in its March 1, 1960, issue in a defensive manner. It pointed out that the Commission of Seventy was not condoning segregation and that the report recognized that the racial problems of the church were not confined to jurisdictional and annual conference structures. Two issues later, it reprinted a blistering attack on the report made by the theological school faculty at Drew University, a Methodist seminary in the Northeastern Jurisdiction.[47]

Less than a month after release of the report, four college students at North Carolina A&T University changed the pace of the Civil Rights movement by sitting in at a lunch counter and refusing to leave. Although this was not the first use of sit-ins, this one ignited a fire that quickly spread. Across the South, African American communities, especially in their churches, rallied behind the youths, who were willing to risk jail to assert their rights. Although the NAACP was initially reluctant to endorse civil disobedience because it represented law breaking, sit-ins flourished. Racial tension escalated to new heights as police filled jails with these students and when, in some instances, gangs of angry white southerners attacked nonviolent sit-in participants. In parts of the upper South and in several major southern cities such as Atlanta and New Orleans, sit-ins were successful. Sit-ins also produced a new civil rights organization, the Student Non-violent Coordinating Committee (SNCC).

Sit-ins upset segregationists not just because they attacked Jim Crow, but because they also had theological implications. Most segregationists were pietistic Christians who believed that Christians should respect the law and established authority. Often segregationists cited St. Paul's Letter to the Romans 13:1–7, where the apostle said that rulers are appointed by God, and Christians should be obedient. In addition, southern white Christians largely rejected the

47. "Methodists Favor Segregated Church," *New York Times*, January 8, 1960, 1, 12; "N.A.A.C.P. Deplores Methodists' Stand," *New York Times*, January 9, 1960, 23; "Methodists Told to Retain Racial Setup," *Washington Post*, January 8, 1960, B6; "Methodists Recommend Keeping Status Quo," *Christian Century*, January 20, 1960, 69; "The Commission of Seventy," *Central Christian Advocate*, March 1, 1960, 11; "A Theological Point-of-View," *Central Christian Advocate*, April 1, 1960, 9–10.

belief that Christians could be God's kingdom on earth before the Second Coming. However, while willing to condemn sit-in participants for breaking laws, segregationists conveniently saw Massive Resistance campaigns against the Supreme Court's *Brown* decision as lawful attempts to maintain Jim Crow.[48]

Liberal Christians believed that sit-ins were religious as well as political protest. To them, here was a rejection of evil that uplifted all of society. Thelma Stevens and A. Dudley Ward mobilized their connections within the church to support students and particularly to defend them from expulsion from colleges, a very real threat at some Methodist-related institutions. In Washington, D.C., American University's chair of the Board of the Trustees reportedly wanted all students who participated in sit-ins expelled, whether they were arrested or not. Stevens wrote to Mrs. A. Paul Hartz in Virginia to rally support for students at Randolph-Macon College outside of Richmond so that the administration would not take punitive action against those involved in sit-ins. For Methodists, sit-ins were a new point of fracture; often the dividing line was generational as well as theological.[49]

Methodists gathering in late April for the 1960 General Conference held in Denver, Colorado, knew that much of their time and energy would center on the report of the Commission of Seventy and church racial policy. The Episcopal Address urged caution and patience in consideration of the report so that delegates would preserve what they perceived as the inclusiveness that existed already within the Methodist Church. Regarding racial matters, the bishops repeated their 1952 and 1956 statements that racial discrimination was "unfair and unChristian" and that the church had an obligation to end all segregation or discrimination. The bishops recommended that Methodists find a moderate path between inaction, which would "stultify our Christian profession," and radical change, which might end all discrimination swiftly but destroy the unity of the church.[50]

The first real test of how the General Conference walked this path came early in the consideration of the Commission of Seventy's

48. For a succinct discussion of segregationist pietistic theology, see Charles Marsh, *God's Long Summer: Stories of Faith and Civil Rights*, 89–115.

49. Thelma Stevens to Mrs. A. Paul Hartz, December 28, 1960, 2597–3–3:1, GCAH; interoffice memo to [A. Dudley] Ward from "J." 10/20/60, GBCS.

50. 1960 General Conference *Journal*, 205–7.

report. The second recommendation stated that "the General Conference of 1960 undertake no basic change in the Central Jurisdiction." This wording appealed to southern white Methodist leaders since it allowed them to say that nothing significant had been done beyond the already approved Amendment IX. The text went on to encourage use of Amendment IX during the quadrennium, but critics argued that the sentence conveyed to the uninformed an unwillingness to abolish the jurisdiction. Roy H. Nichols, an African American Methodist minister from the Western Jurisdiction and one of the few African American leaders from a regional jurisdiction, explained that the church should not confuse or misrepresent its position regarding elimination of the racial jurisdiction. The General Conference agreed that the commission's recommendation did not adequately express the church's commitment and inserted a new introduction that spelled out that the church remained committed to abolition of the Central Jurisdiction by Amendment IX.[51]

Harold C. Case, president of Boston University, offered an amendment establishing 1968 as a target date for the elimination of the Central Jurisdiction by Amendment IX. Case argued that 1964 was too early and that 1972 was too far in the future, but 1968 allowed sufficient time for details to be worked out and for all Methodists to prepare for the change. Case's amendment produced heated debate, including the observation from a southern white delegate that Christ had never established a target date for the coming of God's Kingdom. Opponents argued that a target date would only stir up fears among southern white Methodists thus slowing down real progress, while target date supporters believed that it would energize the process of desegregation.[52]

Before voting on Case's amendment, Jones proposed a substitute amendment in the form of a constitutional amendment that would dissolve the Central Jurisdiction immediately, instead of in 1968, by having it absorbed by the Northeastern, North Central, and Western jurisdictions, essentially to put all African American Methodists back into the "mother" church. This clever tactic put supporters of the target date on the defensive. Here was a southern white leader

51. Ibid., 311, 311–21.
52. Ibid., 322–33.

proposing the elimination of the Central Jurisdiction immediately, but on terms that went back to before 1940 when African Americans in the Methodist Church were only part of the northern church. Not surprisingly, the General Conference rejected it. Parlin, as chair of the Commission of Seventy, then closed out the debate on the Case amendment, saying that nothing took more of the commission's time than discussion over a target date, but that it was an unproductive emotional issue. He insisted that Amendment IX provided a means of eliminating the Central Jurisdiction and a target date did not significantly strengthen it. The General Conference narrowly voted down the Case amendment.[53]

Settling the target date question did not end all attempts to speed the dissolution of the Central Jurisdiction. Lloyd F. Worley, leader of the liberal Methodist Federation for Social Action, proposed that the General Conference recommend to the Northeastern, North Central, and Western jurisdictions that they invite the Central Jurisdiction's annual conferences to join them. Worley was only proposing that the General Conference recommend to the three other regional jurisdictions that they accept responsibility for moving the church forward. His motion offered a means of quickly eliminating racial segregation on the jurisdictional level. Again, Parlin was given the opportunity to comment before the vote, and he confessed that he was inclined to accept this proposal but that African American Methodist leaders urged him to oppose the Worley amendment. They feared that the Worley amendment might actually backfire on all concerned and might heighten expectations while not improving the mechanism for transfers. It would also have four jurisdictional conferences work out the racial problems of the entire church and excuse from the process the two regional jurisdictions that overlapped a majority of all African American Methodists. The conference agreed to Parlin's hesitant recommendation to defeat the Worley amendment. Then the General Conference ended debate regarding abolition of the Central Jurisdiction by approving the slightly rewritten recommendation to continue using Amendment IX to end the racial jurisdictional conference.[54]

53. Ibid.
54. Ibid., 334–35, 351–60.

The opposition to the Worley amendment by African American Methodist leaders reflected several important considerations. First, African American Methodist leaders were willing to disappoint white liberals who wanted to end segregation by any means as soon as possible. African American Methodists were determined not to rush the process if it jeopardized their ultimate goal of a truly racially inclusive church. Second, like the white Methodists in the Deep South, they felt that change in race relations was accelerating and the old walls were coming down. Where many southern white Methodists had great fear regarding integration reaching their local churches, African American Methodist leaders were optimistic. Third, lack of planning was dangerous, since African American Methodists were such a minority in the church, and good intentions would not necessarily create a colorblind church. They wanted to be sure of the actual procedures of desegregation so that they would not create a new system of racial exclusion at a lower level in the church.

The 1960 General Conference also considered the recommendations of the Commission of Seventy that would promote racial brotherhood in the church. Here, Chester A. Smith set off a firestorm when he proposed amending the commission's recommendation urging Methodist institutions to examine their racial practices and policies so that they complied with the church's stand against discrimination. He specifically proposed that no money from the church go to support Duke University's Divinity School as long as that seminary continued to admit only white students. Raymond E. Balcomb, a minister who served on the Commission of Seventy, moved as a substitute that each Methodist-related institution receiving World Service funds be required to report annually regarding their racial policies and practices. The debate again centered on whether the general church should be coercive or allow each section to move as quickly as it found possible. Thurman Dodson, a lay leader in the Central Jurisdiction, pointed out that the church was coercive in creating and maintaining the racial jurisdiction, but again the General Conference refused to implement a more stringent action. Both the Smith amendment and the Balcomb substitute were defeated. Instead, the General Conference accepted the Commission of Seventy's recommendations for achieving a more inclusive church, which included the exhortation that Methodist-related institutions examine their racial policies and practices and bring them in line with that of the church itself.[55]

Where the 1960 General Conference deviated from the Commission of Seventy's report in a substantial way was over the next step, involving the entire church in working towards inclusiveness. Rather than giving the work of desegregating the church to the new Board of Christian Social Concerns, the conference established a new commission, named the Commission on Interjurisdictional Relations. The new commission would have six members from each jurisdiction: one bishop, two clergy, and three lay members. The new Commission of Thirty-Six, as it would be called, would promote use of Amendment IX, investigate problems in desegregation, communicate with the Council of Bishops and church press regarding progress, and present to the 1964 General Conference a new list of recommendations based on the experience of the next quadrennium.[56]

In reference to the jurisdictional system and efforts at making the church more unified, the 1960 General Conference accepted the recommendations of the Commission of Seventy. A constitutional amendment was approved and sent to annual conferences for ratification that would encourage, but not require, jurisdictional conferences to meet at the time and place of the General Conference. If a jurisdictional conference chose not to meet with the General Conference, then it would be required to meet before rather than after the General Conference so that consecration and assignment of bishops would occur at the General Conference. These changes would make the jurisdictional system much weaker while still permitting a jurisdictional conference to be more vigorous if it so desired. This constitutional amendment would have created a stronger national church, but annual conferences subsequently failed to ratify the amendment, and the jurisdictional system remained unaltered.[57]

In sum, the 1960 General Conference maintained the work of the Commission of Seventy and faith in Amendment IX as a means of desegregation. In rejecting a target date, the church relied on what its defenders called voluntarism, desegregation that occurred by

55. Ibid., 480–89.
56. Ibid., 690–95, 697–703, 1694–97.
57. Ibid., 363–68, 413–30, 1682–85.

consensus. The General Conference was not alarmed that so little desegregation had actually occurred during the last quadrennium or that African American Methodist leaders had resisted invitations to dismantle quickly the Central Jurisdiction. The expectation existed that the new Commission of Thirty-Six would iron out the problems with Amendment IX and Methodist desegregation would go forward. The General Conference had clearly avoided any action that would provide ammunition for a mass exit by any part of the church. Particularly for leaders in the Southeastern Jurisdiction, they could return home to say that General Conference action was temperate and that white southern Methodists were still in control of their own destiny.

African American Methodist leaders had less to cheer about, but they were not without hope. Since African American Methodists were themselves divided regarding a target date, its defeat was not a slap in the face. In voting down the Worley amendment, the General Conference decided that desegregation would not be thrust upon reluctant African American Methodists as segregation had been in the creation of the Central Jurisdiction. Most of all, African American Methodists knew that the church had not moved very quickly on desegregation before and was not so far behind society as to feel compelled to move more rapidly. The Civil Rights movement was still young and growing, and the walls of de jure segregation were under great pressure. This was the greatest factor giving African American Methodists reason for hope.

The Great Myth had come under increasing scrutiny, but the Methodist Church had not rejected it. Amendment IX had committed the church to ending the most glaring example of the Southern Myth, but in a manner that was consistent with the tenet of the Great Myth that change should come slowly and be controlled by responsible white and African American leaders. During the quadrennium, many white Methodists had characterized the guiding principle of church desegregation as voluntarism. This meant that the church would not coerce members or institutions, but instead rely on persuasion and time to bring about change. Voluntarism as a concept was inherently a double standard, since African American Methodists had not volunteered for the Central Jurisdiction; nevertheless, supporters of voluntarism maintained that the policy would desegregate the church with reasonable speed and without causing a mass exodus. This was Christianity tempered by caution.

Acceptance of the Case amendment by the 1960 General Conference would have required more Christian faith both among most southern white Methodists and some African American Methodists. Experts in leadership recommended setting specific goals and target dates, and acceptance of a target date might have convinced youths that the church was changing meaningfully and quickly. It may have also emboldened support for change among southern white clergy.

The target date of 1968 would have also directly challenged the Great Myth that race relations were basically good and slowly getting better. It would have said more emphatically than could Amendment IX alone that the church was confessing the failure of its structure and urgently sought to change. This would be a stronger repudiation of segregation and discrimination. Yet a target date would have surely fed the distrust of the national church in parts of the Deep South and may have produced a significant defection. Establishing an eight-year transitional period was only a guess at what was prudent and possible. No one could have accurately predicted in 1960 where the Civil Rights movement would be by 1968. Although the last meeting of the Central Jurisdiction would take place in August 1967, this was not a certainty even in the fall of 1966. The target date of ending the Central Jurisdiction by 1968 was for Methodists a road not taken.

5

The Central Jurisdiction Speaks

B ETWEEN 1960 AND 1964, much of the South was a battleground
between forces demanding an end to de jure segregation and
those committed to preserving the Southern Myth. Through rallies,
marches, and one-to-one conversations, supporters of civil rights
worked at breaking down the barriers that had been erected over
years of segregation. Through violence and control of political and
economic power, white racists attempted to hold back the flood of
change and maintain white supremacy. As this conflict raged across
the South and in parts of other sections of the United States, the
Kennedy and Johnson administrations wrestled with strategies for
dealing with civil rights. More white Americans slowly recognized
the injustice and brutality of the southern system, and some moderate white southerners lost their willingness to preserve the status
quo. Methodists, in and out of the South, increasingly found themselves drawn into the vortex of the conflict.

John F. Kennedy entered the presidency in January 1961 and proclaimed in his inaugural address that the torch had been passed to a
new generation. Yet if Kennedy wanted to declare a new age and
new beginning, he did not want to focus upon civil rights. Although
African American voters had provided a key segment of his slim
electoral margin, Kennedy knew that many groups could claim they
had elected him. Moreover, southern Democrats so dominated key
congressional committees that Kennedy was obliged to work with
them if his legislative agenda were to succeed. At the beginning of
his presidency, Kennedy wanted civil rights leaders to control their
followers and to support his economic program so that he could
avoid use of federal troops in the South. Sadly, his plan was a sce-

nario that ignored conditions in the South, overrated the control of civil rights leaders over their followers, and underestimated the force segregationists would use in order to preserve their privilege. By the middle of 1963, Kennedy would abandon entirely his early strategy regarding civil rights and view civil rights as a great moral issue that the nation could no longer afford to ignore. Unfortunately, he would reach this conclusion only after much strife and upheaval.[1]

For African American and white Methodists, the years 1960–1964 would be a quadrennium that focused upon ending the Central Jurisdiction and improving race relations in and out of the church. The Commission of Thirty-Six, which had been established by the 1960 General Conference in Denver, Colorado, produced excitement within church circles in April 1961 by devising a plan to end the Central Jurisdiction. The plan used Amendment IX to parcel out the Central Jurisdiction's annual conferences to regional jurisdictions. Yet African American Methodists found problems with this approach and called a conclave in March 1962 that decided against the plan and any transfers into regional jurisdictions until after they had the opportunity to realign their annual conference boundaries so they did not straddle regional jurisdictions. More importantly, African American Methodists wanted their white counterparts to commit themselves more concretely to ending racism in the church rather than simply removing the Central Jurisdiction. Just ending legal segregation was no longer enough. As in American society, Methodists found that racial tensions were not easily resolved.

The Central Jurisdiction's 1960 conference met in Cleveland, Ohio, where its bishops reminded the assembled delegates that the church's racial problems started in local congregations, where church segregation had begun, but they also acknowledged that African American Methodists had no desire to force their way into white Methodist churches. The College of Bishops of the Central Jurisdiction stated "We do not wish to take over churches; we do not wish to visit in churches unless invited; but, if invited we feel that there should not be reprisals; we want to be men in our country and in our churches."

1. The most comprehensive account of the civil rights policies and actions of President John F. Kennedy is Carl M. Brauer, *John F. Kennedy and the Second Reconstruction.* Brief accounts that are particularly helpful are Allen J. Matusow, *The Unraveling of America: A History of Liberalism in the 1960s,* 60–93; and James T. Patterson, *Grand Expectations: The United States, 1945–1974,* 468–85.

To monitor proposals from the Commission of Thirty-Six and to advise the Central Jurisdiction on desegregation, the conference created the Committee of Five to evaluate any plan of desegregation and to consult with the Central Jurisdiction's bishops.[2]

The Committee of Five brought to the jurisdiction new leadership and experience with desegregation. Attorney Richard Erwin, a layman from North Carolina, was a graduate of Howard University's law school, where Charles H. Houston had created a cadre of civil rights lawyers. Rev. John J. Hicks, of St. Louis, had served on the school board of that city when it desegregated local schools. W. Astor Kirk had been among the first African American students at the University of Texas–Austin, where he received a Ph.D. in political science. The Methodist Board of Social and Economic Concerns employed him as an assistant secretary. Rev. John H. Graham, a member of the Upper Mississippi Annual Conference, worked as an assistant secretary on the Board of Missions in New York City. Rev. James S. Thomas also had a Ph.D. and was an assistant secretary on the church's Board of Education. All five members were relatively young; their average age was only forty-one. All had grown up in the South but had lived outside of it for some time during their adult life. They had excellent connections to the boards and agencies of the church. This committee was well equipped to lead the jurisdiction in uncharted waters, but it also had a large task because the Commission of Thirty-Six had a great potential to act.[3]

Within the annual conferences of the Central Jurisdiction there was a vast reservoir of ideas and concerns. For example, the 1960 Louisiana Annual Conference had expressed its conviction that it should merge with the overlapping white annual conference and that open itinerancy should prevail in this integrated annual conference. Likewise, the 1960 Tennessee Annual Conference had complained of the persistence of job discrimination at the Methodist Publishing House in Nashville. Furthermore, the 1961 Central West Annual Conference called for interracial pulpit exchanges for four weeks a year so that African American and white Methodists could become

2. 1960 Central Jurisdiction Conference *Journal,* 138, 68.
3. Ibid., 115, 117–19; *Who's Who in the Methodist Church* (1966), 400, 494, 729, 1304; *Who's Who in Methodism* (1952), 327.

acquainted. Other Central Jurisdiction annual conferences requested meetings with their overlapping white annual conferences so that they could end what the 1960 North Carolina Annual Conference called "the vast chasm which exists between the two conferences."[4]

Some regional jurisdictions were also anxious to see desegregation move more quickly. The 1960 North Central Jurisdictional Conference invited the churches of the Central Jurisdiction within its bounds to transfer into the North Central Jurisdiction by the end of the 1960–1964 quadrennium. The 1960 Northeastern Jurisdictional Conference passed a similar resolution after a long debate over whether it would be better to invite all of the Central Jurisdiction to transfer into the Northeastern Jurisdiction or just the annual conferences in or near the Northeastern Jurisdiction. Both sides of this debate wanted a rapid end to the Central Jurisdiction but differed over what method would bring the best results. In the West, Bishop Donald Tippett reiterated that African American Methodists were already part of the Western Jurisdiction and that the church would only benefit when all regional jurisdictions were likewise unified. However, in the Southeastern and South Central jurisdictional conferences, there was only modest mention of civil rights, with little discussion of abolition of the Central Jurisdiction or church desegregation. This silence was striking given the number of the sit-ins and the rise of civil rights activity throughout the South. This lack of engagement reflected the region's denial of the problem and complacency within the status quo built around the Southern Myth.[5]

The willingness to explore race relations honestly among Methodists was evident in the Quadrennial Program on Race led by the Woman's Division of Christian Service, Board of Missions, and the Division of Human Relations and Economic Affairs, Board of Christian Social Concerns. Thelma Stevens and A. Dudley Ward, who directed these church agencies, strove to involve all annual

4. 1960 Louisiana Annual Conference (CJ) *Journal,* 25–26; 1960 Tennessee Annual Conference (CJ) *Journal,* 59–60; 1960 Central Alabama Annual Conference (CJ) *Journal,* 40–41; 1960 North Carolina Annual Conference (CJ) *Journal,* 47.
5. 1960 North Central Jurisdiction Conference *Journal,* 111–15, 142, 151–52; 1960 Northeastern Jurisdiction Conference *Journal,* 311–28; 1960 Western Jurisdiction Conference *Journal,* 40–42; 1960 Southeastern Jurisdiction Conference *Journal,* 122–25, 298; 1960 South Central Jurisdiction Conference *Journal,* 117–21.

conferences in a dialogue regarding both national and local racial issues. Both leaders and their small staffs were idealistic and wanted to energize the church to become a liberal force for change in American society.

The planning conference for the quadrennial emphasis program met in Louisville, Kentucky, in March 1961, and brought together over two hundred Methodist leaders representing thirty-nine regions across the country. The vision for the program was that the regional committees would eventually see one hundred local committees created so that by 1964 "several million Methodists might be seriously at work in local churches [on improving race relations]." The conference outlined ways for the regional committees to support the Commission of Thirty-Six in its efforts at desegregating the church and to spearhead activities to promote civil rights in the areas of education, housing, voting, employment, and public facilities. The meeting reflected a more progressive view than did most church gatherings, but the participants who were attracted were also the Methodists most interested in social justice.[6]

The Commission of Thirty-Six was clearly a continuation of the Commission of Seventy. Nearly half of the members of the Commission of Thirty-Six had served on the Commission of Seventy, and the election of Charles C. Parlin as chair of the commission reinforced the continuity between the two commissions. The commission was clearly male-dominated and largely led by the lay members. There were no bishops on the executive committee, and laypersons on it outnumbered clergy by a two-to-one ratio, eight laypersons to four ministers. In many ways, the composition was a testament to the power of the laity in the Methodist Church. Bishops obviously were still influential in the commission, and ministers were equal in number to laymen in the full commission, but this amount of lay power on a churchwide commission of such crucial importance was markedly different from more hierarchical churches. Although national church leaders, especially lay leaders, were often unknown by the vast majority of people in the pews, these individuals embodied the values and spirit of the organization.

6. Report of the Orientation Conference for the Quadrennial Program on Race Relations, Louisville, Kentucky, March 20–24, 1961, 4, GBGM-WD.

The commission also reflected continued patriarchal power within the church. There were only two women on the commission and only one of them served on the twelve-member executive committee, which did most of the commission's work, meeting ten times while the full commission met only six times in the four years. The Commission of Seventy had had eleven women members, so the new commission actually concentrated male influence. There is no evidence that this was intentional, but it was hardly surprising, since there were no women bishops and very few women ministers, leaving only eighteen lay positions on the commission open to women. (There were one bishop, two clergy, and three lay members from each of the six jurisdictions.) Still, having only two women in eighteen possible positions vastly underrepresented women in terms of their total membership and participation in the church. There may have been some awareness that the beliefs of men and women diverged at times, but the assumption still prevailed that men were church leaders except in women's organizations. Gender inequality was not a consideration to most Methodists at this time.[7]

Setting right to work, the Commission of Thirty-Six produced in late April 1961 a plan to abolish the Central Jurisdiction by moving blocks of its annual conferences, called episcopal areas, into the four overlapping regional jurisdictional conferences. (The Western Jurisdiction was not included, since there were so few Central Jurisdiction churches in its bounds.) The plan required no constitutional changes or General Conference action because implementation could be accomplished via Amendment IX. The plan had several voluntary steps and no final date for completion, but in the introduction to the plan, Chairman Parlin noted that it could produce the transfer of three annual conferences of the Central Jurisdiction into the Northeastern Jurisdiction in just one year. Other transfers could also take place just as quickly. The plan offered the hope of a rapid dissolution of the Central Jurisdiction and eventually the abolition of all racial bodies, including racial congregations.[8]

The first step would be approval of transfer of Central Jurisdiction

7. The 1956 General Conference authorized for the first time the ordination of women in the Methodist Church.

8. First Report of the Commission on Interjurisdictional Relations, Washington, D.C., April 28–29, 1961, 1–3, Parlin Papers.

annual conferences into regional jurisdictions. The Northeastern, North Central, and South Central jurisdictions would each receive three annual conferences of the Central Jurisdiction overlapping or near the boundaries of each of these regional jurisdictions. Because most of the membership of the Central Jurisdiction lay within the bounds of the Southeastern Jurisdiction, it would receive eight annual conferences. The Central Jurisdiction's bishops would transfer into regional jurisdictions with blocks of annual conferences so that one bishop would join the Northeastern, North Central, and South Central jurisdictions, and two would join the Southeastern Jurisdiction. As soon as the transfers were complete, the Central Jurisdiction would cease to exist. The order in which votes were taken by the various annual conferences and jurisdictional conferences did not matter so long as each transferring annual conference approved by a two-thirds vote, the entire Central Jurisdiction approved by a two-thirds vote, and the receiving regional jurisdiction approved by a two-thirds vote.[9]

Yet the plan did not stop with the abolition of the Central Jurisdiction. It also aspired to desegregate the church from within. First was the desegregation of annual conferences. Once a block of Central Jurisdiction annual conferences relocated into one of the regional jurisdictions, that jurisdiction could proceed to merge annual conferences so that there would no longer be separate African American and white annual conferences in the Methodist Church within that jurisdiction. Once this was accomplished, the next logical step would be to integrate local churches. On this subject the plan stated, "Ultimately—depending on the desires of the members concerned—it is hoped and expected that the final merger of individual congregations will become possible." In this brief statement was a vision of Methodists moving from a segregated structure to a nonracial church at the level of the local congregation. The plan cryptically recognized that racially organized local churches had no place in a Christian organization and only existed as a cultural contradiction of the teachings of Jesus. Methodist leaders seemed to accept that ultimately a fully racially inclusive church would melt down all racial characteristics of local congregations.[10]

9. Ibid.
10. Ibid, 2.

The plan also recognized that abolition of the Central Jurisdiction would require some financial adjustments. The annual conferences of the Central Jurisdiction could not immediately meet all the financial requirements of minimum ministerial salaries and pensions that mergers of annual conferences would entail, because the seventeen conferences of the Central Jurisdiction had the lowest salaries and pensions in the church. The plan noted, "Since the achievement of a fully inclusive Church is the concern of the whole Church, we recognize that the ultimate responsibilities for solving financial inequities must be assumed by the whole Church." The plan was sketchy and brief, but it presented a way to desegregate quickly and to end the Central Jurisdiction without undue financial burden on the local churches or annual conferences.[11]

Voluntary agreement was at the heart of the Commission of Thirty-Six's plan. Commission members recognized that the transfer of Central Jurisdiction annual conferences into the South Central and especially the Southeastern jurisdictions might take some time and acknowledged that this would leave a smaller, weaker Central Jurisdiction for some time while support for desegregation among southern white Methodists grew. Voluntary action was also central to the merger of annual conferences. The plan acknowledged that racial conferences would continue until "all Conferences affected are ready for this move." The lack of a timetable meant that the merger of African American and white annual conferences, like the abolition of the Central Jurisdiction, would not be coercive, but would be completed when the parties involved agreed to merge. The plan urged all Methodist institutions to comply with all facets of the church's policy on race, yet this was also voluntary.[12]

The plan was hastily conceived and actually had only mixed support within the Commission of Thirty-Six, although this became apparent only later. The commission did not hold hearings on the plan before it disseminated the plan to the church. At the meeting to vote on approval, only twenty-four of the thirty-six members were present. Nineteen voted for the plan, three opposed, and two abstained. Thus, the plan, which did boldly envision a means of rapid desegregation, gained approval of only slightly more than half of

11. Ibid.
12. Ibid.

the entire Commission of Thirty-Six. However, in the cover letter sent to bishops and to the church press, Parlin noted that the plan had the unanimous support of commission members from the Central Jurisdiction. This provoked an angry letter from Bishop Charles Golden of the Central Jurisdiction, who argued that Parlin's letter was misleading, since at least one member of the commission from the Central Jurisdiction was absent. More importantly, Golden argued that it was unfair to single out the voting of the Central Jurisdiction. Golden concluded, "I trust that none of us may resort to unfair tactics to accomplish desired ends. I would like to feel that you did not deliberately plan to mislead those to whom your communication was addressed"—the Council of Bishops and all annual conferences of the church.[13]

Golden's letter produced some controversy within the Commission of Thirty-Six. Dennis Fletcher, another member of the Commission from the Central Jurisdiction, wrote Parlin to agree with Golden that the singling out of the Central Jurisdiction was "unfortunate, whether it was intentional or unintentional." Yet Rev. Harold Bosley of the North Central Jurisdiction wrote to all commission members that he could not see what was wrong with Parlin's introduction to the plan. He then speculated that Golden's letter might be "an attempt to cast a shadow of suspicion over the Commission's support of the first report...," and he urged: "let us 'close ranks' behind the first report and see that it is presented with vigor and pushed with real effort throughout the entire Church." Edwin Jones, a member of the Southeastern Jurisdiction's commission, reacted caustically to Golden's letter, writing privately to Parlin that "I believe that you Yankees are beginning to learn something about what we have all been knowing for some time. You can't satisfy them [African Americans] and there is no need in trying."[14]

If the Commission of Thirty-Six went to work quickly to desegregate the Methodist Church, so did other groups working at the time for desegregation in American society. The Congress of Racial Equality (CORE), led by James Farmer, quickly put pressure on the Kennedy administration regarding civil rights issues. Committed

13. Charles F. Golden to Charles C. Parlin, May 16, 1961, Parlin Papers.
14. Dennis R. Fletcher to Charles C. Parlin, May 26, 1961, Parlin Papers; Harold A. Bosley to Charles C. Parlin, May 29, 1961, Parlin Papers; Edwin L. Jones to Charles C. Parlin, May 26, 1961, Parlin Papers.

to interracial, nonviolent protest, CORE had been founded in 1947, but it had remained a relatively small organization with activity limited largely to northern and border states until the spring 1961 Freedom Rides. In this campaign, two busloads of civil rights activists left Washington, D.C., to show that the 1960 Supreme Court's decision in *Boynton v. Virginia,* which desegregated interstate transportation facilities, especially bus terminals, was widely ignored across the South. The trip was relatively uneventful until the buses were just outside Anniston, Alabama. There, a mob attacked and firebombed one of the buses. Fortunately, there were no fatalities; CORE members hurried off the bus, and Rev. Fred Shuttlesworth of Birmingham, Alabama, organized a caravan to rescue the displaced Freedom Riders. Then the other bus arrived at the Birmingham bus terminal, but there it was met by a mob that set upon the Freedom Riders. By arrangements made with Public Safety Commissioner Eugene "Bull" Connor, the mob had fifteen minutes to savagely assault the Freedom Riders before the police arrived.

Many southern whites saw Freedom Riders as provocateurs who got what they deserved. Alabama governor John Patterson said, "The state of Alabama can't guarantee the safety of fools, and that's what they are." It seemed to those committed to segregation a confirmation of the Southern Myth that trouble came from the outside, ignoring that many of the Freedom Riders were native southerners. However, to other southern whites, the violence used against the Freedom Riders was disturbing, for it exposed the violent roots of segregation.[15]

The bravery of the Freedom Riders and their commitment to nonviolence inspired others within the Civil Rights movement to action. New recruits quickly stepped forward to continue the journey to Jackson, Mississippi. The Kennedy administration worked behind the scenes to gain security for the Freedom Riders, but another attack in Montgomery, Alabama, again shocked the nation. After more arm twisting by the Kennedy administration, federal marshals and National Guard units in Alabama and Mississippi provided security for the Freedom Riders until they reached Jackson, Mississippi, where

15. Bartley, *New South,* 308. The most comprehensive scholarly account of the Freedom Rides is Catherine A. Barnes, *Journey from Jim Crow: The Desegregation of Southern Transit.*

they were promptly arrested by local authorities in a deal worked out between Attorney General Robert Kennedy and local officials.

While Methodists read the headlines and followed news of the Freedom Rides, initial reaction to the Commission of Thirty-Six's first report was favorable. The annual conferences of the Northeastern Jurisdiction voted overwhelmingly to accept the transfer of the Delaware, Washington, and North Carolina annual conferences of the Central Jurisdiction. Each of these three annual conferences also voted to approve their transfer into the Northeastern Jurisdiction by the necessary two-thirds majority required by Amendment IX. All that remained under Amendment IX to complete the process was approval by the other Central Jurisdiction annual conferences. Some other African American annual conferences also gave early signs of approval to the plan. Two of three annual conferences of the St. Louis episcopal area presided over by Bishop Matthew Clair Jr. voted to approve in principle their transfer into the North Central Jurisdiction, but these conferences failed to take a count vote as required by Amendment IX. The Louisiana Annual Conference passed a resolution endorsing the Commission of Thirty-Six's first report and pledged to vote on transfers as requests came to the annual conference. The Georgia and the South Carolina annual conferences voted in principle to approve the transfer of annual conferences of the Central Jurisdiction to regional jurisdictions.[16]

Despite these initially favorable responses, there were signs of trouble as well. One apparent problem was that Methodist leaders were either unfamiliar with Amendment IX or unsure of what action to take on the Commission of Thirty-Six's plan. Not only did Central Jurisdiction annual conferences fail to fulfill the count vote requirement of Amendment IX, but some annual conferences in the North Central and South Central jurisdictions also voted approval without taking the required two-thirds count vote. This meant that favorable signals were sent, but another year would go by before official action might take place. A second sign of trouble

16. Charles C. Parlin to Members of the Commission on Interjurisdictional Relations and to Members of the Council of Bishops, June 29, 1961, Parlin Papers. For samples of consideration by Central Jurisdiction annual conferences, see 1961 *Florida Annual Conference Journal,* 29; 1961 Louisiana Annual Conference *Journal,* 24–25; and 1961 North Carolina Annual Conference *Journal,* 18.

was that none of the five annual conferences presided over by Bishop Golden responded favorably, with four referring the plan to committee and another taking no action. Also taking no action were the annual conferences of the Southeastern Jurisdiction. Since Golden's annual conferences lay within the bounds of the Southeastern Jurisdiction, and they could expect to be the last annual conferences to transfer into a regional jurisdiction, their inaction reflected the lack of communication between African American and white Methodists in that area. However, the Georgia and South Carolina annual conferences of the Central Jurisdiction presided over by Bishop M. L. Harris responded favorably to the Commission of Thirty-Six's first report. This indicates that episcopal leadership was crucial to acceptance of the plan and that the Central Jurisdiction's bishops were not united.[17]

The Commission of Thirty-Six's first report was fundamentally flawed because it failed to align African American and white Methodists geographically. The plan transferred portions of some annual conferences of the Central Jurisdiction into regional jurisdictions that these annual conferences did not overlap. To recommend that the North Carolina Annual Conference of the Central Jurisdiction transfer into the Northeastern Jurisdiction made no geographic sense, because none of the churches in the North Carolina conference were within the bounds of the Northeastern Jurisdiction. African American and white Methodist congregations in North Carolina would be in separate "regional" jurisdictions and have different bishops even though they might be located in the same town. This was not a plan for desegregation that maintained regional integrity, and the problem was not isolated to the North Carolina Annual Conference. In fact, 60 percent of the Central Jurisdiction's churches in the Lexington, Central West, and Southwest annual conferences, which under the plan would transfer into the North Central Jurisdiction, were outside of the bounds of that regional jurisdiction. Bishop Roy H. Short of the Southeastern Jurisdiction wrote to several colleagues, "[I]t is proposed that the Negro work in Virginia and North Carolina be related to the Northeastern Jurisdiction, whereas the rest of the Negro work in the other Southeastern states would be related to

17. Ibid.

the Southeastern Jurisdiction. That does not look like careful thinking to me."[18]

The plan heightened the pressure on the Central Jurisdiction because it opened the door to rapid action and it raised expectations. To reject the plan without a clear rationale as to how to remedy its inadequacies would increase the charge that African American Methodists were not wholeheartedly opposed to segregation. African American Methodists did not want to play into the Southern Myth. Because of both the initial positive reaction of parts of the Central Jurisdiction and the realization that serious problems remained, the Committee of Five, the Central Jurisdiction's think tank regarding desegregation, organized a special jurisdictional meeting to confer over church desegregation. Called by the bishops of the Central Jurisdiction, over two hundred delegates gathered in Cincinnati, Ohio, in March 1962. Since there were no bishops to elect or other business to conduct, this meeting focused exclusively on Methodist racial policies and practices. It was a time to unite the jurisdiction as never before behind specific and comprehensive goals for a racially inclusive church.

Although some civil rights successes had come in the Deep South by spring 1962, and public opinion showed that a growing number of southern whites accepted the inevitability of desegregation, African American Methodist leaders coming together in Cincinnati could not risk overconfidence. The Civil Rights movement was not yet toppling Jim Crow institutions across the South, and the Kennedy administration was still far more interested in foreign affairs than in civil rights. An example of the resilience of white supremacy confronted African Americans in Albany, Georgia. Here, a community-wide campaign to desegregate this southern Georgia community bogged down in conflicts between the Southern Christian Leadership Council and the Student Non-violent Coordinating Committee regarding tactics. The Albany white power structure, especially under the leadership of Police Chief Laurie Prichett, was able to thwart the impact of nonviolent, mass civil disobedience even though

18. For exact location of congregations, see the Central Jurisdiction map for April 1961 in the front of this book. Bishop Roy Short to Bishop Walter Gum, May 16, 1961, GCAH; W. Astor Kirk, "An Approach to the Central Jurisdiction Problem of the Methodist Church," undated, 5–7, Murray Collection, GCAH.

Martin Luther King Jr. at times joined the campaign and went to jail in Albany. After carefully studying nonviolence and prior civil rights campaigns, Prichett prevented police brutality and transferred those arrested to jails across southern Georgia. Albany never ran out of jail space and African Americans could not pressure the white government leaders to desegregate.[19]

Position papers prepared for the Cincinnati conference by Revs. Ernest T. Dixon, Major J. Jones, and Joseph E. Lowery and layman W. Astor Kirk outlined two basic options before the Central Jurisdiction. Kirk, an assistant secretary on the church's Board of Social and Economic Concerns and a member of the Committee of Five, suggested using Amendment IX to transfer local churches into the regional jurisdiction they lay within. This would avoid the geographic discrepancies created by the Commission of Thirty-Six's plan and might be done en masse rather than as individual actions. A second option, proposed by both Dixon and Lowery, recommended realigning annual conference boundaries so that Central Jurisdiction annual conference boundaries did not cross the boundaries of regional jurisdictions. This would mean no transfers until after the 1964 Central Jurisdiction meeting unless the Central Jurisdiction's bishops called a special session, but it would allow transfers by episcopal areas as outlined by the Commission of Thirty-Six.[20]

One area of common agreement between the various papers presented was that too many white Methodists were advocating abolition of the Central Jurisdiction without considering other forms of racism in the church. This criticism noted that the church's problem was the impatience of white liberals as much as southern white intransigence. These papers answered that the Central Jurisdiction was committed to rapid movement toward an inclusive church, but that little discussion had gone beyond elimination of the Central

19. Adam Fairclough, *To Redeem the Soul of America: The Southern Christian Leadership Conference and Martin Luther King, Jr.,* 85–109; Garrow, *Bearing the Cross,* 17–230; Clayborne Carson, *In Struggle: SNCC and the Black Awakening of the 1960s,* 56–65.

20. W. Astor Kirk, "An Approach to the Central Jurisdiction Problem of the Methodist Church," undated, 9–13; Ernest T. Dixon Jr., "A Proposed Solution to the Central Jurisdiction Problem," undated, 4–10; Joseph E. Lowery, untitled paper, March 1962, 3–9, Murray Collection; Major J. Jones, "Pre-Conference Reflections of the Jurisdictional Problem of the Methodist Church," undated, 5.

Jurisdiction. Kirk asserted, "no plan for dissolving the Central Jurisdiction as a racially segregated unit within The Methodist Church
can be accepted as adequate unless it is designed—consciously, deliberately, calculatedly—to achieve ultimately an inclusive church."[21]

One problem not considered by the Commission of Thirty-Six
was the status and opportunity for African American ministers. The
Methodist Church had a long tradition of an open itinerancy where
all ministers (ordained elders) were equal members of an annual
conference and, in theory, any minister could serve at any church.
African American Methodists, especially ministers, wanted to be
sure that they would be accepted as full members of merged annual
conferences and that there would be an open itinerancy system.
Outside portions of the South, African American ministers might
join an annual conference in a regional jurisdiction where there were
very few African American churches. Unless there was an open itinerancy where these ministers could serve white churches as well as
African American congregations, their opportunity to serve within
that annual conference would be quite limited, especially compared
to white ministers in the same annual conference. Unless there were
cross-racial appointments in all annual conferences, the church would
perpetuate a racial system on the local church level, with African
American ministers for African American congregations and white
ministers for white congregations. If America was entering into a
new era of race relations where African American and white lawyers,
doctors, and teachers worked alongside each other and served African
American and white Americans alike, why should Methodist ministers continue to be bound by race? Yet, even in the North, interracial churches were usually only transitional, as when a neighborhood
changed from all-white to mixed and then all–African American.[22]

James P. Brawley, president of Clark College in Atlanta, Georgia,
gave the keynote address at the Cincinnati conference. He emphasized that white Methodists, like white Americans generally, did
not see African Americans as equals. This was especially true in the
South, but other parts of the country were as guilty even if they
were not explicitly committed to white supremacy. He asserted that

21. Kirk, "An Approach," 8; Jones, "Pre-Conference Reflections," 3; Dixon,
"A Proposed Solution," 3–4, Murray Collection.
22. Jones, "Pre-Conference Reflections," 4–5; Lowery, untitled, 2; Murray
Collection.

until the church made brotherhood its first priority, its racial problem had no solution. A paternalistic attitude toward African American Methodists often came across as the idea that the church was de-segregating for them, rather than desegregating for the benefit of all Methodists. In highlighting the failure of the entire church, not just the two southern jurisdictions, Brawley noted the lack of racial in-clusiveness on the local level in the areas of the New England and the West that did not overlap the Central Jurisdiction. Here were two areas that could be models for the entire church, but instead traditional patterns of separation and paternalism prevailed.[23]

The solution to the church's problem was not simply the dissolu-tion of the Central Jurisdiction, Brawley asserted. The church must come up with a comprehensive plan that did not leave African Ameri-can Methodists stranded in new, smaller units of segregation or subject to paternalism. First, the church at the 1964 General Con-ference must declare "in unequivocal terms that the entire Church and all of its institutions . . . shall be desegregated and no one shall be denied admission because of color or racial identity." This policy of inclusiveness would reach from local churches to all Methodist-related institutions. Brawley recommended creation of racially inclu-sive churches, cross-racial appointment of ministers, and desegrega-tion of women's, ministerial, and youth groups.[24]

Although not specifically mentioned at the Cincinnati confer-ence, an example of just this lack of commitment to inclusiveness among Methodists was being played out at the Southeastern Juris-diction's retreat center at Lake Junaluska, North Carolina. Ironically, it deeply involved Edwin Jones, who served on the Commission of Thirty-Six's executive committee with Brawley. As chair of the board of trustees of Junaluska, Jones orchestrated a rearguard attempt to maintain as closely as possible a segregated facility, even question-ing the superintendent about how many African Americans worked in any capacity of the staff and encouraging him to keep the num-ber as small as possible. The assembly's efforts to resist integration caused a number of protests from Methodist youth organizations from across the country. Jones and the board also found themselves

23. James P. Brawley, "The Problem of the Central Jurisdiction and the Meth-odist Church," undated, 11–21, Murray Collection.
24. Ibid. 26, 26–30.

attacked by segregationists, who charged that African Americans were being allowed broad access to the retreat center's facilities, a charge that Jones categorically denied.[25]

After the conclusion of the Cincinnati conference, an eighteen-member committee wrote recommendations to the Central Jurisdiction's annual conferences, published as *The Central Jurisdiction Speaks*. These recommendations noted that the Central Jurisdiction "is only one of a number of unmistakable manifestations of racialism within the fellowship and policy of The Methodist Church."[26] This was the first time that leaders of the Central Jurisdiction had called the church racist, although the term was politely changed to "racialism." The committee then took issue with the first report of the Commission of Thirty-Six because of the geographical inconsistencies in the plan. The committee also urged annual conferences of the Central Jurisdiction not to transfer into regional jurisdictions until after the 1964 Central Jurisdiction's meeting, where annual conference boundaries could be realigned so that none overlapped two regional jurisdictions. Since the jurisdiction's conference followed the meeting of the General Conference, this recommendation effectively told the Commission of Thirty-Six that no transfers would occur during the quadrennium. Regarding transfers in the next quadrennium, the committee recommended that they occur "with all deliberate speed; and wherever possible, the transfer of Central Jurisdiction churches, conferences, institutions, etc., be consummated in terms of merger with the existing geographic units." The suggestion that transfers occur simultaneously with or be followed rapidly by

25. J. W. Fowler Jr., the superintendent of the Junaluska Assembly, wrote to Edwin Jones: "You will recall talking to me on many occasions about the various operations here, among which was the large number of negroes present on the grounds some years ago, and we have, in accordance with your suggestions, reduced the number under the employment of the Assembly" (Fowler to Jones, August 10, 1962, Lake Junaluska Board of Trustees Papers, Lake Junaluska Assembly, Heritage Center, Commission on Archives and History, Lake Junaluska, North Carolina; hereinafter cited as Lake Junaluska Papers); regarding the number of African Americans present at Junaluska, see Jones to Fowler, August 14, 1962, and Fowler to Jones, August 17, 1962; for youth protests, see Norton E. Wey to Jones, July 17, 1962, Gayle Graham Yates to Jones, June 26, 1962, and Jones to Bishop Walter Gum, July 28, 1962, Lake Junaluska Papers.

26. Finding-Steering Committee, *The Central Jurisdiction Speaks*, published by the Central Jurisdiction Study Committee (Committee of Five), not dated, 7, Murray Collection.

complete merger indicated a desire to have a guarantee that transfers into regional jurisdictions would not start a new phase of segregated existence.[27]

The committee did pledge to cooperate with the Commission of Thirty-Six to develop a comprehensive plan of action prior to the 1964 General Conference. Such a plan could address many of the problems that occurred on the lower levels of the church, but at a minimum it needed to have the 1964 General Conference insert into the *Discipline* that the entire church and all church-related institutions were open to all, regardless of color or racial identity. In addition, a new commission should succeed the Commission of Thirty-Six to monitor and promote integration on the local levels of the church during the next quadrennium.

One significant and new recommendation from the Cincinnati conference was that the successor commission to the Commission of Thirty-Six should "protect minority rights." Here African American Methodists expressed concern about their future in a desegregated church. Those African American Methodists gathered in Cincinnati realized that a racially inclusive church would not be easy to build in a racist society. De facto discrimination was deeper than de jure segregation, and in the near future African American Methodists needed to protect their interests even as they worked toward a color-blind church. In his keynote speech, Brawley gave as an example the need for continued financial support of the historically African American colleges supported by the annual conferences of the Central Jurisdiction. Church desegregation should not include the abandonment of institutions that had historically served African Americans. Here, African American Methodists acknowledged a desire for institutional guarantees for their interests after abolition of the Central Jurisdiction.[28]

The Cincinnati conference clarified the position of African American Methodists, but it set the Central Jurisdiction on a collision course with the Commission of Thirty-Six. The Cincinnati conference's recommendations meant rejection of the first report of the Commission of Thirty-Six and raised the specter of little progress

27. Use of the phrase "with all deliberate speed" reflected more the influence of the *Brown* decision in the minds of African American Methodists than a desire to have church desegregation proceed as slowly as school desegregation (ibid., 8–9).

28. Ibid., 9; Brawley, "The Problem," 25, Murray Collection.

on desegregation until after both the 1964 General Conference and the 1964 Central Jurisdiction conference.

The Central Jurisdiction was not alone in refining its goals and policies. The Woman's Division chose the spring of 1962 to renew and revise its decade-old racial charter. Reflecting the changes in race relations, the new charter policy statement focused more on how women could influence society's view on race rather than simply opening up their own employment opportunities and other activities for women in the church. It explicitly called for an end to segregation in all levels of the Methodist Church, including "the local churches." Additionally, the charter called for Methodist women to bring about an end to discrimination in their communities in "education, housing, voting, employment and public facilities." The charter was a step forward, but leaders of the Woman's Division knew the challenge would be getting local chapters of the Woman's Society of Christian Service to take it seriously in their communities.[29]

In part because of the strengthening of the charter and the Woman's Division's open championing of civil rights activities, criticism of the leadership and publications of the division was at times heavy. Methodist women in the South, especially in Mississippi and Alabama, berated Thelma Stevens, the head of the Woman's Division Department of Christian Social Relations and Local Church Activities—sometimes personally. Critics accused the Woman's Division of being one-sided and too political. Stevens challenged her critics to go back to the Bible that they claimed to defend. She was confident they could not find a defense of segregation and denial of equal rights in the teachings of Jesus.[30]

By the summer of 1962, the Quadrennial Program on Race was also well under way in the church. Reports from the various thirty-nine regional committees exhibited inspiring success stories in some areas as well as frustrating inaction in other regions. Much depended upon the industry and commitment of annual conference leaders—episcopal, ministerial, and lay. Many areas reported that their largest problem remained a sense of purpose or direction. About one-third of the regions reported focusing upon desegregation of the church

29. Knotts, *Fellowship of Love*, 244–45, 273–74.
30. There are a number of letters to the Woman's Division regarding civil rights activity with replies from Thelma Stevens and her staff in GBGM-WD.

structure in their areas, while a few attempted to work on issues such as employment and housing. Many of the regional committees placed their efforts in education via the church publication *We Can and We Will*, written for the two sponsoring church agencies by sociologist Dwight Culver. The hundred-page workbook was a survey of the issues facing both the Methodist Church and American society in race relations.[31]

In advance of the first meeting of the Commission of Thirty-Six after the Cincinnati conference, Parlin prepared a fourteen-page memo that outlined the areas of disagreement between the Central Jurisdiction and the Commission of Thirty-Six, suggesting some avenues for further work. The major point of difference was the timing of transfers of annual conferences from the Central Jurisdiction into regional jurisdictions. The Commission of Thirty-Six wanted as many transfers as possible to precede the 1964 General Conference, while the Cincinnati conference supported transfers only after the realignment of annual conferences. Connected to this question was the Cincinnati conference's recommendation that transfers also include merger of annual conferences as an integral process, with transfer and merger occurring simultaneously rather than as two distinct stages of desegregation. Parlin judged the one-step transfer and merger process as impractical because African American and white annual conferences needed more time to negotiate merger agreements. Parlin's memo also suggested that the Commission of Thirty-Six devote more time to the financial problems that the entire church had to face in desegregation.[32]

In May 1962, the Commission of Thirty-Six met, with many of its white commission members still hoping to salvage the first report. A resolution made by Rev. Dean Richardson of the Northeastern Jurisdiction and Edwin Jones, two members who were usually at odds with one another, sparked an excited exchange between members. The motion initially called on the Central Jurisdiction's annual conferences to "release" the Delaware, Washington, and North Carolina annual conferences, but the commission changed the wording to request that African American annual conferences "give special

31. "Summary of Pertinent Data Found in Reports Received from 38 Regional Consultative Committees on Race as of July 1, 1962," 1–2, GBCS.
32. Parlin, "Statement to the Interjurisdictional Commission," May 2, 1962, 613, Parlin Papers.

consideration to approving the transfer of" these three annual conferences to the Northeastern Jurisdiction. The commission defeated an amendment to delete the North Carolina Annual Conference from the motion because it was entirely outside the bounds of the Northeastern Jurisdiction. The commission then approved the Richardson-Jones motion and another one that requested that the bishops of the Central Jurisdiction call a special session of the jurisdictional conference to consider changes in the boundaries of annual conferences in order to facilitate transfers via Amendment IX. The latter motion included the offer of financial aid from the commission's budget to make such a meeting possible. The commission also passed a motion to petition the 1964 General Conference to call upon all Methodist-related institutions to desegregate and end all forms of racial discrimination. However, an amendment to this resolution that specifically included all local congregations failed to win approval. This was a sign that the issue of local church desegregation was too explosive. However, this was a glaring omission and showed that the commission members, like the entire church, were struggling to fully understand the church's racial problem.[33]

The Committee of Five and the Central Jurisdiction's bishops responded to the Commission of Thirty-Six's motions with a joint statement in September 1962. It pledged that the Committee of Five would plan the realignment of the Central Jurisdiction's annual conferences so that no conference crossed over the bounds of any regional jurisdiction. The jurisdiction would act upon this plan at its regularly scheduled 1964 session, not at a special session. This would lead the way for use of Amendment IX during 1964, but since jurisdictional conferences meet after the General Conference, this plan meant in the minds of African American Methodist leaders that desegregation was dead until after the 1964 General Conference. The leaders of the Central Jurisdiction believed that too much emphasis was being put on what African American Methodists could do to desegregate the church and not enough on what the entire church needed to change. Before going beyond realignment of annual conference boundaries, African American Methodists wanted to see how much of the burden white Methodists were willing to

33. Commission of Thirty-Six, Minutes, May 4, 1962, 3, 6, Parlin Papers.

assume. These were questions that only the 1964 General Conference could answer.[34]

In September 1962, the Kennedy administration also suffered a defeat in its own efforts at staying out of the civil rights struggle in the South. James Meredith, an air force veteran and native of Mississippi, applied for admission to the University of Mississippi, popularly called "Ole Miss." Ole Miss was the flagship university of the white power structure in the Magnolia State, and Meredith's application was an audacious act of defiance against segregation in Mississippi. Governor Ross Barnett promised not to let Meredith enroll and was backed in his defiance by nearly all state politicians. The Kennedy administration negotiated behind the scenes to achieve a peaceful desegregation of Ole Miss. They believed that they had assurances from Barnett, despite his overheated rhetoric, that Meredith would receive the necessary protection from state officials, augmented by federal marshals. However, just before Meredith began attending classes, Barnett reneged on his pledge. State law enforcement withdrew just as a mob besieged federal marshals holed up in the Lyceum Building on the Ole Miss campus. In order to protect the marshals and restore order to the campus, President Kennedy sent in federal troops just as Eisenhower had done in Little Rock, Arkansas, in 1957. As with the Freedom Rides, efforts at winning southern white political cooperation failed miserably, to the embarrassment of the Kennedy administration. The desegregation of Ole Miss was also demoralizing to moderate whites who wanted stability over defiance. At Ole Miss, many professors and more students left—not in protest to Meredith's presence, but in protest to the mishandling of the entire affair.[35]

In the area of civil rights, there were some parallels between the Kennedy administration and the Methodist Church in 1961–1962. Rising expectations among African Americans meant that token gestures and hopeful words would not be satisfying. Kennedy had hoped to focus not on civil rights but on foreign policy and economic issues, but events in the South demanded much of his and Attorney

34. Central Jurisdiction Study Committee, "The Central Jurisdiction Speaks," 11–14, Murray Collection.
35. John Dittmer, *Local People: The Struggle for Civil Rights*, 138–42.

General Robert Kennedy's time. In the process, the president and his advisers learned more about the depth of the problem, something they had not understood before. Despite this, they had little concrete change to show for their actions. The South at the end of 1962 was still a bastion of segregation despite some ground gained by the sit-ins and Freedom Rides.

For the Methodist Church, many of these same features were true in late 1962. African American Methodists expected a more vigorous and thorough program against racism in the church. The first report of the Commission of Thirty-Six had devised a plan that had some important features, but it placed too large of a burden on African American Methodists and inadequately spelled out the timetable for concluding desegregation. The plan had serious geographic flaws that could not be addressed until the Central Jurisdiction realigned its annual conference borders. Issues that Methodists needed to address beyond the abolition of the Central Jurisdiction were not included, so African American Methodists said no to the plan and instead prepared for a more comprehensive church action.

During the early 1960s, there was a convergence of events in American society and the Methodist Church. Civil rights became such a powerful issue that national and local officials were forced to pay attention to their policies and practices. Methodist leaders, like the Kennedy administration, found that civil rights was an issue that could not easily be solved. Methodists discovered that concrete proposals for change did not ensure progress. No easy solution was evident, and African American Methodists were not going to accept a whitewashing of the church's problems.

6

Open the Church Doors!

WHITE MISSISSIPPI METHODISTS heard a surprising message from twenty-eight of their ministers on January 2, 1963. These ministers wrote a manifesto for the *Mississippi Christian Advocate* entitled "Born of Conviction." It started:

> Confronted with the grave crises precipitated by racial discord within our state in recent months, and the genuine dilemma facing persons of Christian conscience, we are compelled to voice publicly our convictions. Indeed, as Christian ministers and native Mississippians, sharing the anguish of all our people, we have a particular obligation to speak. Thus understanding our mental involvement in these issues, we bind ourselves together in this expression of our Christian commitment. We speak only for ourselves, though mindful that many others share these affirmations.[1]

The manifesto stressed four points. First, all Methodist ministers must have the freedom to preach the Gospel as they understood it. Second, Methodist Church policy permitted no racial discrimination. Third, the church supported public schools and they should remain open in Mississippi. Finally, the twenty-eight ministers stressed that support for integration was not support for communism. The manifesto also rebuked several articles of segregationist doctrine. The twenty-eight ministers argued that Methodist ministers needed to preach the Gospel without any constraints so that, like Jesus of

1. Ellis R. Branch, *Born of Conviction: Racial Conflict and Change in Mississippi Methodism, 1945–1983*, 98–99.

139

Nazareth, they could proclaim the Gospel regardless of the receptivity of the audience. In endorsing desegregation by the national church, the ministers affirmed Methodist unity over the Southern Myth, particularly the belief that the South alone understood its race relations and that all outside pressure on southerners was illegitimate and harmful. The commitment to public schools was a signal that integration was practical, probably inevitable, and preferable to absolute defiance.[2]

The bold statement deeply divided white Mississippi Methodists. Bishop Marvin Franklin, who had served in Mississippi since his election to the episcopacy in 1948, refused to either support the statement or criticize it. He only said it was consistent with the teachings of the church. Some Mississippi Methodist ministers, such as Rev. William B. Selah, minister at Galloway Methodist Church, which was the largest Methodist congregation in the state, publicly endorsed the statement. Yet the Mississippi Methodist Ministers and Laymen Association denounced the statement. Many of the signers came under pressure, at times physically, to leave their pulpits. Most left their churches, and by March 1963, the Methodist Board of Social Concerns had established a fund to aid the displaced signers of the manifesto. Mississippi white Methodists had finally come face-to-face with the sharp division over race and civil rights.[3]

Such division was not evident among the African American Methodists who were part of the 1963 Central Jurisdiction annual conferences, because they clearly backed their jurisdictional leadership by endorsing the principles outlined at the Cincinnati conference. The disarray over the first report of the Commission of Thirty-Six was finished by early 1963. Although annual conference resolutions were not identical with one another, most provided that before transferring into regional jurisdictional conferences there must be some assurance that the merger of African American and white annual conferences would quickly follow. Members of the Central Jurisdiction did not want separate African American annual conferences in regional jurisdictions for an extended period. Their resolutions typically sought assurances that the Central Jurisdiction's laity would be

2. Ibid., 99–100; see also *New York Times,* January 19, 1963, 4; and Bartley, *New South,* 244–60.
3. A. Dudley Ward to Chairmen of the Committees on Human Relations and Economic Affairs, March 1963, GCAH.

able to participate in all aspects of their new jurisdictional and annual conferences and that the Central Jurisdiction's bishops would transfer into regional jurisdictions with their annual conferences with full episcopal responsibilities. These comprehensive resolutions indicated that Central Jurisdiction annual conferences anticipated trouble unless they explicitly stated their concerns. Just as important, the overwhelming support for these resolutions showed that jurisdictional leaders had considerable grassroots support.[4]

In July 1963, in response to a request from an executive committee of the Commission of Thirty-Six, James P. Brawley explained why desegregation was proceeding slowly. Amendment IX was simply a means of abolishing the Central Jurisdiction by transferring either churches or annual conferences into white annual conferences or jurisdictional conferences. This would not end segregation within the institutional church. African American Methodists were concerned about the election of bishops and other high church officials, and this was only a natural concern based upon their experience of discrimination within the church. He accused the Commission of Thirty-Six of failing to develop an overall plan, "(a) to desegregate all churches and institutions of The Methodist Church; (b) to outline procedures and specific programs for developing a racially inclusive fellowship at all levels; and (c) to bring the Negro membership and institutions fully into the mainstream of the total program of the Church at all levels."[5]

A few months before Brawley's memo, Rev. Martin Luther King Jr. wrote his "Letter from a Birmingham Jail" in response to eight local white clergymen, two of whom were Methodists, who condemned his presence in Birmingham as "unwise and untimely." Both statements made similar points, although Brawley's explained why the Central Jurisdiction was not moving more quickly, while King's was a defense against the charge of expecting change too quickly. Brawley surely would have agreed with King when King wrote,

4. 1963 Central Alabama Annual Conference *Journal*, 38–40; 1963 Central West Annual Conference *Journal*, 78–84; 1963 Delaware Annual Conference *Journal*, 49, 139–44; 1963 East Tennessee Annual Conference *Journal*, 73–74; 1963 Florida Annual Conference *Journal*, 59–60; 1963 Georgia Annual Conference *Journal*, 61–62; 1963 Mississippi Annual Conference *Journal*, 33–34; 1963 South Carolina Annual Conference *Journal*, 105–6; 1963 Upper Mississippi Annual Conference *Journal*, 21, 68–69 (all Central Jurisdiction).
5. Brawley, "Reluctance of the Central Jurisdiction," 9, Parlin Papers.

"Shallow understanding from people of good will is more frustrating than absolute misunderstanding from people of ill will." Likewise, King would have certainly agreed with Brawley, who noted,

> The Christian Church in America, The Methodist Church not excepted, has been a party to all that has been inflicted upon the Negro, either by practice or by silence[,] and [by] endorsement of community patterns and practices. The Methodist Church has failed to take a definite and uncompromising stand beyond pronouncements. It has failed to take a stand as a church and become deeply involved in the racial problems of the community in a changing order. The Negro in his soul has cried out for help which he did not get when the Church could have been his bulwark of strength in all of the trying situations of segregation, exploitation and denial of opportunities that are the inherent rights of every citizen and every child of God.[6]

In fact, Brawley may have been inspired to be so bold by King's acknowledgment that "Though there are some notable exceptions, I have also been disappointed with the white church and its leadership." King continued, "In the midst of blatant injustices inflicted upon the Negro I have watched white churchmen stand on the sidelines and mouth pious irrelevancies and sanctimonious trivialities." Both King and Brawley were saying that this was the time for action rather than rhetoric. Inaction had prevailed for too long. The American church must come firmly down on the side of justice.[7]

The Birmingham campaign in the spring of 1963 also forced the Kennedy administration to change radically its civil rights strategy. Known as "Bombingham" for the numerous bombs set off against civil rights activists and as the most segregated of American cities, the choice of Birmingham for a major Southern Christian Leadership Conference campaign was fraught with dangers. In addition,

6. Martin Luther King Jr., "Letter from a Birmingham Jail," *Christian Century*, June 12, 1963, 767, 770; Brawley, "Reluctance of the Central Jurisdiction," 12–13, Parlin Papers.

7. King, "Letter from a Birmingham Jail," 769–75; for a thorough study of Birmingham leaders, see S. Jonathan Bass, *Blessed Are the Peacemakers: Martin Luther King, Jr., Eight White Religious Leaders, and the "Letter from Birmingham Jail,"* 110–30, 238–56.

the SCLC campaign did not start well. White community leaders criticized King's timing because they believed city government reforms were underway that would likely remove from power Public Safety Commissioner Eugene "Bull" Connor, a Methodist, who was notorious for his use of force against civil rights activists. Moreover, though SCLC's point man in Birmingham, Rev. Fred Shuttlesworth, was a civil rights champion and close ally of Martin Luther King Jr., his dictatorial style alienated elite Birmingham African American leaders.[8]

The campaign ran into difficulty because early marches did not draw as many African Americans as expected and Connor displayed uncharacteristic restraint. King and his lieutenants knew that they needed more media attention to build public pressure on Birmingham leaders, so they took the audacious step of allowing African American high school students and older children to march. Soon Birmingham was a tinderbox ready to explode after Connor had used police dogs and water cannons to drive back marchers. Tensions were so high that it appeared that anarchy and racial warfare might break out. Hurriedly, in early May 1963, Birmingham business and city leaders reached an agreement with King to initiate desegregation. Despite a wave of bombings after the agreement and criticism of it by Shuttlesworth, nonviolence and the agreement held.

President Kennedy had closely monitored events in Birmingham and wanted to avoid both an international public relations disaster and an outbreak of violence. The crisis in Birmingham convinced Kennedy to make a major shift in civil rights strategy, and he endorsed comprehensive federal civil rights legislation that would end de jure segregation. He knew the struggle in Congress would be difficult, especially in the Senate. Nevertheless, Kennedy believed it was necessary to end the racial strife in the South and to improve the world's image of the United State. The president addressed the nation in June 1963 to outline his new approach to civil rights, using rhetoric that emphasized morality and the Golden Rule. President Kennedy said in part:

> We are confronted primarily with a moral issue. It is
> as old as the scriptures and is as clear as the American
> Constitution.... [I]f, in short, he [African Americans]

8. Garrow, *Bearing the Cross*, 231–64.

144 / METHODISTS AND THE CRUCIBLE OF RACE

can not enjoy the full and free life which all of us want, then
who among us would be content to have the color of his skin
changed and stand in his place? Who among us would then
be content with the counsels of patience and delay?[9]

Kennedy's change represented a significant break from his previous tack of urging civil rights leaders to be patient. The desegregation of Birmingham, Alabama, and President Kennedy's policy shift were also signs to moderate white southerners that segregation was dying fast.[10]

A shift in attitudes in the Methodist Church was evident in late August at the Second Methodist Human Relations Conference, held in Chicago. Organized jointly by the Board of Christian Social Concerns under A. Dudley Ward and the Department of Christian Social Relations, and the Woman's Division of the Board of Missions under Thelma Stevens, it brought together more than eleven hundred Methodists to discuss race relations. Conference speakers included activist James Meredith, comedian and activist Dick Gregory, New Orleans federal judge J. Skelly Wright, and Martin Luther King Jr. However, King's address to the conference brought protests from segregationists. The committee of Christian Social Concerns of a Methodist church in Dorchester, South Carolina, complained so vehemently that conference chair Bishop Raymond Grant wrote Ward, "That protest from a South Carolina church was a gem. They must have a commission that is neither Christian, social, or concerned." Bishops Nolan Harmon and Paul Hardin, two of the eight clergy addressed by Martin Luther King Jr.'s "Letter from a Birmingham Jail," complained about distribution of a copy of the letter to conference attendees. Bishop Harmon accused the Board of Christian Social Concerns of heading "toward a deplorable irresponsibility" because there was no mention of the contexts in Birmingham when the eight clergymen wrote to King. Harmon continued, "I stand at the bar of my Jurisdictional Conference to which alone I must report."[11]

9. Matusow, *Unraveling of America*, 90.
10. Ibid.; Patterson, *Grand Expectations*, 480–81; David R. Goldfield, *Black, White, and Southern: Race Relations and Southern Culture, 1940 to the Present*, 141.
11. Bishop Raymond Grant to A. Dudley Ward, August 8, 1963, Board of Christian Social Concerns, GCAH; Claude Keathley, "Bishop Harmon Defends State Churchmen," August 28, 1963, *Birmingham (Alabama) News*, 72.

The Human Relations Conference produced a list of the most advanced recommendations thus far from a national cross section of the Methodist Church. The conference approved several memorials (petitions) to the 1964 General Conference. First among the recommendations was that the transfers and mergers to abolish the Central Jurisdiction should be completed by 1968. This was a stepped-up timetable for completion and more definite than what was being discussed in the Commission of Thirty-Six. Second, the conference members urged that the Council on World Services and Finance establish a special fund to equalize pension and minimum salaries between the Central Jurisdiction and overlapping annual conferences. This fund would eliminate a financial burden on merging annual conferences, especially in annual conferences where merger involved a large number of African American Methodist congregations. Third, the assembled Methodists recommended that all Methodist ministers should be assigned churches without regard to race. This would create a new level of church openness. Fourth, all Methodist schools and colleges should open their doors to students and faculty on a nondiscriminatory basis, or the church should withdraw its institutional affiliation and funds from those schools or colleges. Similarly, a nondiscrimination policy should be part of all Methodist hospitals, homes for children or the aged, and all church agencies and boards. The Board of Pensions and other church agencies should insure that the companies in which they invest or with whom they do business practice nondiscrimination in employment. Finally, the conference members urged all Methodists to become more directly involved in their local communities to obtain integration of public schools, registration of voters, and equal access to public accommodations. The conference sent a special delegation of leaders as emissaries to participate in the March on Washington. The Methodist conference dates had been set long before the March on Washington but coincided with the march.[12]

The conference's resolutions may have been more liberal than any previous national Methodist meeting because the attendees were already involved in their conference or women's organization social

12. Dolores McCahill, "Human Relations Unit Asks Methodist Integration Now," *Chicago Sun-Times*, August 31, 1963, 14; see also "The Message of the Second Methodist Conference on Human Relations," adopted August 30, 1963, Chicago, 1441–5–3: 14, GCAH.

concerns ministry. There was some southern opposition at the conference to the completion of church desegregation by 1968, but support for tougher church standards was broad. However, civil rights activity in American society was convincing more Methodists that they needed to be increasingly involved in demanding equal rights as more white Americans realized that de jure discrimination could not continue to have a place in American life.

The peak of the 1963 civil rights activity came on August 28 at the March on Washington, when more than 250,000 American citizens gathered in the nation's capital to support the comprehensive civil rights bill then before Congress. Methodist bishops John Wesley Lord and Edgar A. Love, who presided over the annual conferences that included the District of Columbia, wrote to a number of ministers in the surrounding area urging them to join the march. At least seven Methodist bishops, as well as a specially deputized group of representatives from the Second Human Relations Conference in Chicago participated in the march. In addition, the National Conference of the Methodist Student Movement and the National Conference of Methodist Youth Fellowship had delegations. Although Malcolm X dismissed the protest as meaningless and the SNCC's John Lewis was pressured behind the scenes to tone down his criticism of the Kennedy administration, the march projected a united image of Civil Rights organizations and goals. It was more successful than organizers had hoped. The large interracial crowd was orderly and peaceful. From the perspective of church leaders trying to get wary members committed to civil rights legislation, nothing could have been more powerful. The most memorable speech of the event, Martin Luther King Jr.'s "I Have a Dream" speech, emphasized a vision of American society where race was of no consequence and harmony replaced discord. It was an eloquent statement of Christian principles that could reach moderate white Americans, North and South.[13]

However, the euphoria of the March on Washington did not translate into immediate legislative action, nor did Methodists experience any respite from their internal struggles. During the late summer and fall of 1963, the issue of open public accommodations came to

13. Methodist News Release, 1441–4–1:23, GCAH; Knotts, *Fellowship of Love*, 245–46.

the Methodist Church in a graphic manner in Mississippi. Although churches were not public businesses such as restaurants, theaters, or hotels, churches often proclaimed their doors open to all. Moreover, there would be considerable irony if the federal government made businesses more open than churches. The 1960 sit-ins had been accompanied by a number of attempts to integrate churches, often called "kneel-ins," because civil rights activists often linked southern churches with upholding segregation. Kneel-ins occurred across the South and often met resistance. Two of the largest white Methodist congregations in Jackson, Mississippi, the Galloway and the Capitol Street Methodist churches, became the focus of interracial groups attending worship services. Both congregations decided to turn away African American worshippers. (Ironically, Galloway was named for a bishop who was a southern liberal during the early years of the twentieth century.)

Rev. Ed King, a white Methodist minister who was the chaplain at the historically African American Tougaloo College, organized student interracial teams to visit these churches. A native Mississippian, King became very involved in the Civil Rights movement with a particular passion for challenging church leaders to recover a more authentic Christianity. Starting in October 1963, Jackson police began making arrests, charging the students with attempting to disrupt public worship. Soon other Methodists, from as far away as Chicago and Detroit, arrived on subsequent Sundays to press the churches to desegregate, only to meet the same fate. The national headquarters of the Woman's Society of Christian Service paid bail for those arrested, upsetting many Mississippi Methodist women.[14]

For Methodists in and outside of Mississippi, this vital issue went to the heart of their faith. For segregationists, worship was an intimate time with their God separated from the cares of the outside world. In their view, states' rights applied to the church organization,

14. W. J. Cunningham, *Agony at Galloway: One Church's Struggle with Social Change*, 13; Arthur M. North and Barry Shaw, "To the Council of Bishops of the Methodist Church," November 8, 1963, 1–4, Bishop Nolan B. Harmon Papers, MSS 134, Archives and Manuscripts Department, Pitts Theology Library, Emory University, Atlanta, Georgia; Nicholas von Hoffman, "Church Integration Effort in Mississippi," *Chicago Daily News*, October 26, 1963, 28. See also accounts of attempts to integrate Jackson churches in *New York Times*, June 10, 1963, 19; *New York Times*, June 12, 1963, 22; *New York Times*, July 17, 1963, 12; *New York Times*, October 7, 1963, 77; and *New York Times*, October 21, 1963, 62.

and no bishop or General Conference had the power to tell them how to run their congregation. The racial separation of churches that intensified after the Civil War was to segregationists a Godsend, because it contributed to their myth that separation could be beneficial to all and was not inherently discriminatory. Although some segregationists openly advocated white supremacy, separate worship allowed others to maintain comfortably the Southern Myth that racial relations were amiable and characterized by choice rather than coercion. The arrival of interracial teams was a tremendous affront. In blocking these teams at the church door, the ushers were defending a myth that was as deep as their professed faith in God. To admit these interracial teams was to admit also that their values of racial purity and separation were without merit.[15]

For those trying to integrate such congregations, this was also a critical faith issue. For these believers, the vitality of Christianity came from both its reconciliation of God with humanity and its reconciliation of human with human. Worship of God while maintaining a strict wall of intolerance at the church doors seemed a complete denial of Jesus' call for utter devotion to God and love of thy neighbor. To these Methodists, breaking through the sinful barriers created by prejudice was a way of bringing God back into the worship at these churches. This was also a redemptive act for the national Methodist Church because it had erected its own racial walls. Just as Jesus drove the money changers out of the temple in Jerusalem for defiling the worship of God, these Methodists saw themselves as restoring the authentic worship of God in these congregations and beyond. They wanted reconciliation between whites and African Americans even in Jackson's Methodist churches, and they were willing to go to jail for their faith.

The confrontations within these congregations and on the church steps between ushers and interracial teams were dramatic. Although a majority in these congregations wanted to keep the church doors closed, there were vocal critics within. In fact, in 1963, when Galloway officials first rejected a group of five African American students, its minister of nineteen years, Dr. W. B. Selah, announced to the congregation that he would not continue and immediately requested that Bishop Franklin reassign him. The first arrests occurred

15. Marsh, *God's Long Summer*, 88–115.

in October 1963, when three Tougaloo College students came to Capitol Street Methodist Church on World Wide Communion Sunday, a day that celebrated the unity of Christian fellowship. Their arrest led to an exchange between the students and the police where one of the students pointed out that the church-offering envelope for this Sunday actually portrayed hands of different hues reaching for the communion chalice. On another Sunday, an arresting police officer avoided a theological discussion with a student by commenting, "Just leave Jesus out of this." The most dramatic of the arrests was of John Garner, a member at Galloway who was part of the faction that wanted to open the church to all visitors. He was a white physics teacher at Tougaloo who decided to support the desegregation attempts. He and his wife invited one of his African American students and two visiting Methodist ministers to attend Sunday school class with them. They entered the class without trouble, but soon thereafter police arrived and arrested them. His efforts to explain that he was a member of the church and that this was his Sunday school class went for naught. The student, the two ministers, and John Garner were arrested just the same.[16]

These arrests led the Council of Bishops to issue a statement in November 1963 that reiterated that all Methodist churches should be open to whomever wanted to worship. The bishops endorsed the end of segregation and discrimination in "education, housing, voting, employment and public facilities." Then they noted that equal treatment necessarily extended to churches, and to not do so would be "to be guilty of absurdity as well as sin." Methodist pastors should receive all persons into membership in their churches, and they felt that to arrest "any persons attempting to worship is to us an outrage." The bishops hoped their statement would quell the conflict brewing on the steps of churches on Sunday mornings. But it changed nothing. The local churches denied that the interracial teams were attempting to worship and maintained that their primary purpose was publicity. Police in Jackson continued to make arrests on Sunday mornings, and thirty-seven people, mostly but not entirely Methodists, eventually faced charges in Jackson.[17]

16. Ibid., 127–41.
17. Council of Bishops, "Statement Adopted November 13, 1963, Detroit, Michigan," in CBP, 1013–14; *New York Times,* November 18, 1963, 14; *New York Times,* December 14, 1963, 16; *New York Times,* December 16, 1963, 15.

These arrests raised the issue of how much autonomy a local church or a church institution should have within a national denomination. If, in the words of St. Paul, the body of Christ has many members, what standards should those members accept, and who sets those standards? This dilemma was as old as the Christian church, but it was sharply focused for Methodists by events in Mississippi. Was the issue of racial brotherhood one on which the national church could insist upon unity, or could there be local or regional variations of how far inclusiveness extended? The continuing arrests, despite church pronouncements, generated more pressure for establishing norms.

For many Methodist ministers the issue ran far deeper. The Methodist Church had a tradition of open communion, meaning that the communion table was open to all persons who had been baptized and made a profession of Christian faith, whether they were Methodists or not. Open communion affirmed the unity of all Christians and was an integral part of an ecumenical spirit. This idea contrasted with other churches, particularly Southern Baptists, who practiced closed communion, which is open only to church members of that denomination in good standing. Racial segregation made a mockery of Methodist open communion, for if a person literally could not get in the church door, then there was no way the church could uphold the tradition of open communion; it excluded African American Methodists from the communion rail when white Christians of other denominations were included.[18]

As events in Jackson, Mississippi, developed, the Commission of Thirty-Six wrote its report and created the Plan of Action for the 1964 General Conference. Dissension within the commission was still quite evident. The commission proposed the creation of a new commission, of twenty-four members, to facilitate transfers of annual conferences once the boundaries of Central Jurisdiction annual conferences were realigned; a general church fund to assist merging African American and white annual conferences with pension adjustments; and a fall 1967 deadline for the succeeding commission to propose a means of ending whatever might remain of the Central Jurisdiction. This draft of the commission's report and its Plan of Action received twenty votes in favor and four against, with all the

18. Mathews, "Evangelical America," 25.

opposition coming from members of the Southeastern Jurisdiction. Several Southeastern Jurisdiction delegates felt that the plan abandoned voluntarism because the fall 1967 deadline, in their minds, constituted a mandate to eliminate the Central Jurisdiction before the 1968 General Conference. The final report and the Plan of Action of the Commission of Thirty-Six retained voluntarism as its central theme, but they also placed more responsibility on the entire church to end institutional obstacles to desegregation. The final version even italicized the statement: *"Voluntarism is basic in the Commission's proposal."*[19]

The Central Jurisdiction's study committee, the Committee of Five, wrote its own set of memorials to the 1964 General Conference. Their proposals, called "Creative Pursuit of an Inclusive Church," sought to strengthen the Plan of Action proposed by the Commission of Thirty-Six, pointing out that "the Central Jurisdiction cannot be dissolved in a *Christian* manner without fundamental changes in the main body of church law." The Committee of Five asked the General Conference to make the *Discipline* explicit that all Methodist churches were open to everyone regardless of race or ethnic background. Further, the Committee of Five urged the General Conference to restrict jurisdictional conferences from doing anything that would perpetuate any form of racial separation. Specifically, the committee objected to the Plan of Action because it envisioned the transfer of Central Jurisdiction annual conferences into regional jurisdictions without any provision for a merger of African American and white annual conferences beyond the stipulation that mergers were "to be worked out when such merger is mutually agreeable." The Committee of Five feared that in the Southeastern Jurisdiction no agreement could be made for quite some time and that African American annual conferences there would slip back in time to when white bishops presided over African American annual conferences. The Committee of Five's memorials also called for withdrawal of

19. Amendment to the Report and Plan of Action, Approved by the Executive Committee of the Commission on Interjurisdictional Relations, April 26, 1964, 14, Parlin Papers; 1964 General Conference *Journal,* 1855; Commission of Thirty-Six, Minutes, October 17–18, 1963, Chicago, 3–6, Parlin Papers; Commission of Thirty-Six Executive Committee, Minutes, November 26, 1963, Chicago, 1–7, Parlin Papers; Commission of Thirty-Six, "Report and Plan of Action," January 3, 1964, 24–32, Parlin Papers.

Methodist funds from any church-related institution that did not provide written certification of its nondiscrimination in admission and employment practices.[20]

The Committee of Five's memorials created deep fear among members of the Southeastern Jurisdiction on the Commission of Thirty-Six. Edwin Jones wrote to Parlin, charging, "There does not seem to be any limit to which our Central Jurisdiction folks want to go in order to force their views on the Church." Another particular fear among southern white Methodists raised by the Committee of Five's memorials was, again, integration of local churches. Bishop Harmon wrote to Bishop Paul Garber, "This group is not asking for legislation so much as all sorts of resolutions to try to force immediate integration in the local churches.... I do not think we can win in any General Conference fight on the floor over any type of resolution which strongly favors pressured integration in our southern churches."[21]

On Easter Sunday, March 29, 1964, only three weeks before the General Conference convened, Bishops Golden of the Central Jurisdiction and James K. Mathews of the Northeastern Jurisdiction came to Galloway Methodist Church in Jackson to worship. The duo introduced themselves and asked to enter and worship with the congregation. The ushers, known in the congregation as "bouncers" or "color guards," informed them that it was against the congregation's policy to allow African American people to enter Galloway and that Bishop Golden could not enter. At approximately the same time ten blocks away, another interracial group of Methodist ministers was arrested for attempting to worship at Capitol Street Methodist Church. Golden and Mathews were not arrested and left to

20. Dr. Brawley, John King, and Bishop Golden produced a similar set of amendments that they proposed to the executive committee of the Commission of Thirty-Six days before the start of the General Conference. The Committee of Five, "Creative Pursuit of an Inclusive Church," February 1964, 2, 5–6, 12–13, Parlin Papers (emphasis in the original); Proposed Amendments to "[The] Report and Plan of Action for the Elimination of the Central Jurisdiction," January 3, 1964, Charles F. Golden, John T. King, and James P. Brawley, Parlin Papers; Report and Plan of Action, 30, Parlin Papers.

21. Edwin Jones to Parlin, February 20, 1964, Parlin Papers; Bishop Nolan Harmon to Bishop Paul Garber, February 24, 1964, Paul Neff Garber Papers, Special Collections and Archives, McGraw-Page Library, Randolph-Macon College, Ashland, Virginia (hereinafter cited as Garber Papers); Memorandum To: The Southeastern Delegates [attached statement], 7–8, Parlin Papers.

attend Easter services at a Central Jurisdiction church within the city. Methodists could hardly experience a more gripping image of the racial division within their church than having bishops turned away while trying to worship on Easter Sunday. Clearly, the bishops' statement had not improved the situation. Much work remained for the church's leadership.[22]

Although the timing may have been a surprise, some Methodist leaders had anticipated Mathews's going with Golden to Jackson. There were press reports back in December 1963 indicating that such a trip was a possibility. Bishop Nolan Harmon wrote to Bishop Roy Short that "I think that it would be very terrible if Mathews does yield to pressure—and he will have to in time—and comes to Jackson with Golden, and then gets arrested." Harmon also wrote directly to Bishop Franklin urging him to try to negotiate an arrangement with Mathews and Golden. He continued,

> [Y]ou will have to get your men together there and tell them
> exactly how things are, and that you will expect these two
> men to be given a place in the church if and as they come to
> worship. I think even the hardest-boiled layman will admit
> that our churches ought to be open for worship. Certainly we
> can never have two Methodist Bishops arrested for going into
> a Methodist church.

Possibly, Golden and Mathews were not arrested because of pressure placed on the local congregation not to arrest bishops.[23]

The event was also an example of Bishop Charles Golden's leadership style, one not averse to confrontation. He had persuaded Mathews that they needed to do this because the issue affected all Methodists, not just African American Methodists. Golden also convinced Mathews that local church officials had been given enough time and still had failed to open their doors. This was a dramatic event in the life of the church, just as the Cincinnati conference, of

22. James K. Mathews, "Easter in Jackson" [unpublished statement], Garber Papers; Cunningham, *Agony at Galloway,* 13, 55–60.
23. Bishop Nolan Harmon to Bishop Roy Short, December 19, 1963, Roy H. Short Papers, GCAH (hereinafter cited as Short Papers, GCAH); Bishop Nolan Harmon to Bishop Marvin Franklin, December 19, 1963, Short Papers, GCAH; regarding the report of Bishop Mathews traveling to Mississippi, see *New York Times,* December 14, 1963, 16.

which Bishop Golden was the program director, had been a defining moment for the Central Jurisdiction. He was the most militant of Central Jurisdiction bishops, and for a generation of young African American ministers, Golden was a prophet calling the church to repent and change.

The 1964 General Conference opened in Pittsburgh, Pennsylvania, with the Episcopal Address given by Bishop Gerald Kennedy to over 850 delegates. Still relatively young as a bishop at fifty-two years old, Kennedy was known as a powerful orator, and his picture appeared on the cover of *Time* magazine, an unusual honor for a Methodist bishop. As spokesperson for the council, Bishop Kennedy decried barring anyone entry into Methodist churches because of race and rejected any attempt to square segregation with Scriptures. Noting that past church actions "have brought nothing but shame to us," the bishops' address called upon the General Conference to "insist upon the removal from its structure of any mark of racial segregation and we should do it without wasting time." The council wanted a resolution of racial problems within the church and an end to negative publicity regarding both the Central Jurisdiction and arrests at churches in Jackson, Mississippi.[24]

On the issue of a Methodist congregation's right to bar participation in worship based on race, the General Conference was emphatic. Methodist churches were to be completely open to all. The General Conference adopted the report from the Committee on Membership and Evangelism that emphasized the inclusive nature of membership, which pointed out that the Methodist Church was part of the universal Christian Church. "Therefore, all persons, without regard to race, color, national origin, or economic condition, shall be eligible to attend its worship services, to participate in its programs." It explicitly stated that both attendance and membership at "any local church" was open to all after "the appropriate vows" of baptism and profession of faith. This was a clear victory for Methodists outraged by the arrests and rebukes that had gone on in Jackson, Mississippi, and it was a resounding statement that the church was national, not a collection of autonomous local entities. No Meth-

24. The Council of Bishops could not agree on whether to "encourage" or "insist" upon removal racial structures and finally left the wording to Bishop Kennedy, who chose the stronger wording. See Council of Biships, Minutes, April 18, 1964, 1148, CBP; 1964 General Conference *Journal*, 204–5.

odist congregation could pretend that it had the authority to determine its membership according to race. Not to be outdone, the first report of the Christian Social Concerns Committee again stated that membership, Holy Communion, and all church activities were open to all persons. Further, it pointed out that "[t]o read a racial qualification into these statements [in the *Discipline*] is to ignore both the plain meaning of words as well as the plain meaning of the Gospel."[25]

The Committee on Social Concerns also emphasized the church's responsibility to open all its institutions, agencies, and bodies to all persons upon the basis of full equality. In language that was more explicit and detailed than before, the church went on record as encouraging all Methodists to defend equal rights throughout their communities. These rights included voting rights, equal treatment and respect by law enforcement officials, integrated public education (including even where segregation was de facto as well as de jure), fair employment opportunities, open housing, equal treatment in public facilities, and the right to protest and demonstrate against violation of rights. The defense of protests included the right to practice civil disobedience against laws that clearly violated God's laws and where legal redress had failed to produce reform. In addition, the General Conference endorsed the pending civil rights bill with specific instructions that the conference secretary send a copy of the resolution endorsing the legislation to every U.S. senator, where at that time a southern filibuster was delaying action. The national church was now fully on board with ending de jure segregation.[26]

When the General Conference began to consider the Commission of Thirty-Six's report and Plan of Action as amended by the Executive Committee, the disagreements within the commission shone despite efforts to present a united front. Commission chair Charles Parlin introduced the plan and highlighted that it required no new constitutional change and would result in the abolition of the Central Jurisdiction. Brawley followed Parlin, but he noted that Amendment IX had been found wanting by the Central Jurisdiction. He reasserted that ending the Central Jurisdiction without removing all racial barriers within the church would be a failure in

25. 1964 General Conference *Journal*, 572–73, 1471–72.
26. Ibid., 459–69, 902, 1268–73, 1329.

furthering God's work in the world. Creation of a truly racially inclusive church could start a spiritual renewal, he concluded. Another sign of the tension over the plan was evident outside of the conference hall. In keeping with the example of civil rights demonstrations in the South, more than a thousand African American and white youth came to demonstrate on Saturday, May 2, 1964, against the continuation of the Central Jurisdiction. Bishops Golden, Mathews, and others met with them. Parlin dismissed the demonstration as being a publicity event by youth who did not really understand the issues. However, these young Methodists did show again that Methodist youth were impatient for the end of the Central Jurisdiction and were still interested in church affairs.[27]

The major challenge to the commission's plan occurred when Rev. Allen M. Mayes of the Texas Annual Conference of the Central Jurisdiction proposed amending the *Discipline* to require jurisdictional conferences to take no action that would condone continuation of racial discrimination within their bounds. The amendment originated from the memorials of the Committee of Five and sought to prevent transfer of an annual conference from the Central Jurisdiction into a regional jurisdiction and then indefinitely maintaining racial annual conferences. In effect, the Mayes amendment attempted to get the General Conference to adopt a one-step transfer and merger of annual conferences of the Central Jurisdiction into regional jurisdictions and their annual conferences instead of the two-step process outlined in the Plan of Action written by the Commission of Thirty-Six. Mayes and his supporters pointed out that the amendment was consistent with goals outlined in the Episcopal Address. The Central Jurisdiction would not be taking more of a risk than other jurisdictions, and racial discrimination should not continue after the end of the Central Jurisdiction. The General Conference would be establishing a clear policy of creating a racially inclusive church at the same time that it ended the Central Jurisdiction. Moreover, a one-step transfer and merger process might, in effect, establish a 1968 target for ending segregated annual conferences because few

27. Parlin wrote in a letter after the General Conference, "The pickets and demonstrators didn't know what they were talking about, ... they were working absolutely counter to what the Central Jurisdiction wanted" (Parlin to William N. Letson, May 11, 1964, Parlin Papers); *New York Times*, May 3, 1964, 78; 1964 *General Conference Journal*, 281–84.

observers expected the Central Jurisdiction to last beyond the coming quadrennium.[28]

Numerous critics of Mayes's amendment argued that the proposal would run counter to voluntarism and would delay desegregation. Laymen George Atkinson of the Western Jurisdiction and Leonard Slutz of the North Central Jurisdiction, who both served on the Commission of Thirty-Six, said that Mayes's amendment was dangerous because it held forth a lofty but unattainable goal. It would instead create new fears where cooperation was most needed, especially in the Southeastern Jurisdiction. Parlin joined the opposition by arguing that the Mayes's amendment violated the church constitution because it limited the powers of the jurisdictional conferences to determine the bounds of their annual conferences.[29]

The General Conference rejected the Mayes amendment. The conference then quickly approved an amendment from James S. Thomas, chair of the Committee of Five, to create advisory councils in each jurisdiction with representatives from each annual conference to meet and begin dialogue regarding transfers and mergers. These advisory councils would improve communication and facilitate desegregation.[30]

What is striking about the advisory councils is that they could have been created much earlier, albeit not without some opposition. Had they been created by the 1952 General Conference in advance of *Brown*, the councils might have cooled some southern white Methodists' reaction to the decision. If advisory councils had been started in 1956 they could have advanced the church leadership's understanding of how complex the mechanical problems of desegregation were. Advisory councils would have also been a forum for male church leaders to catch up with women in biracial contact and communication. They could have been a place for new ideas to filter up to the Commission of Seventy and Commission of Thirty-Six. Some contact between African American and white annual conferences in the South had occurred earlier, but it had been sporadic and did not achieve the continual dialogue needed to build trust and reconciliation. However, Methodists did not create advisory councils until

28. 1964 General Conference *Journal*, 317–20.
29. Ibid., 310–17.
30. Ibid., 309–20.

1964 when the Civil Rights movement was at its height, and walls of separation were already coming down, albeit slowly in the Deep South.

The 1964 General Conference also made a significant advance in removing financial impediments to desegregation. It created two special funds to minimize inequalities in ministerial pensions and annual salaries when annual conferences merged. The annual conferences of the Central Jurisdiction and the Rio Grande Annual Conference (a separate annual conference for Hispanic Methodists similar to the separate annual conferences of the Central Jurisdiction but part of the South Central Jurisdiction) had pension rates and minimum salaries that were considerably lower than the rest of the church. The Commission of Thirty-Six had recommended creation of a general church fund to increase pension funds, but it had not recommended a minimum salary fund. In creating both funds, the General Conference acknowledged that all ministers regardless of race should have economic security. Before desegregation loomed so closely, it was easy to ignore financial inequalities and to maintain that salaries and pensions were solely for annual conferences to determine. Once desegregation appeared certain, it was clear that the poverty of these annual conferences was no longer a local matter, but was also a national church concern.[31]

Another civil rights issue that came before the General Conference was establishment of a fund to aid ministers suffering because of their stand on racial matters. This issue came before the conference as a minority report of the committee on ministry, but the conference voted to substitute it for the majority report. Contributions to the fund were voluntary, so there were no national church funds budgeted, but contributions could be made to the fund by annual conferences, congregations, or individual Methodists. This contrasted poorly with the $500,000 provided for this purpose by the Presbyterian Church and $100,000 by the United Church of Christ. The Methodist fund would aid ministers or laymen who suffered economic deprivation due to their witness. Predictably, this fund drew vehement protests from Methodist segregationists, yet some southern Methodists were eloquent in their support. Bishop J. O. Smith

31. Ibid., 320–27.

of the Southeastern Jurisdiction defended the fund to one critic and added the postscript, "Incidentally, there is some reason to believe that this sort of thing was done for Paul, Peter, James and John."[32]

Besides working on racial church matters, the 1964 General Conference also considered a proposal to unite with the Evangelical United Brethren (EUB) Church, a 750,000-member midwestern denomination of German pietistic background that was similar to the Methodist Church in doctrine and polity. However, even here the issues of the Central Jurisdiction and race made their presence felt as W. Astor Kirk, secretary of the Committee of Five, moved that the ad hoc committee on the merger finalize the Plan of Union with the EUB without including any provision for the Central Jurisdiction. Kirk's motion passed. Since the merger was planned for 1968, this was yet another sign that Methodists intended to abolish the Central Jurisdiction in the next quadrennium.

Merger plans led the General Conference officially to suspend rather than end its meeting, so it could reconvene in 1966 in a special joint session with the EUB to approve their Plan of Union. At that time, the General Conference would also hear a report from the Commission on Interjurisdictional Relations (the successor to the Commission of Thirty-Six), known as the Commission of Twenty-Four, regarding progress toward abolition of the Central Jurisdiction and the desegregation of annual conferences. Action on the merger with the EUB and consideration of the Commission of Twenty-Four's report were the only two items on the agenda for the special session, which was slated for November 1966 in Chicago, Illinois.[33]

The 1964 General Conference concluded with the Central Jurisdiction intact, but with a plan for its abolition by voluntarism. This was hardly bold and innovative, but it was not an utter failure either.

32. Edwin Jones tried to tag the fund the "Civil Disobedience Relief Fund," but this disingenuous attempt to give the fund a provocative name failed; 1964 General Conference *Journal,* 749–47, 1539–40; Bishop J. O. Smith to Ralph C. Chester, June 22, 1964, Bishop John Owen Smith Papers, Special Collections and Archives, Robert W. Woodruff Library, Emory University, Atlanta, Georgia (hereinafter cited as Smith Papers).

33. 1964 General Conference *Journal,* 529–37. For an account of how similar these German piestists in America were to early Methodists, see Russell E. Richey, *The Methodist Conference in America: A History,* 69–71.

Methodists attempted to split the difference between contending forces in the Southeast by rejecting the one-step transfer and merger process while pressing ahead for the end of the Central Jurisdiction. The commitment to open local congregations did show that Methodists had lost all patience with those who maintained that Christianity and segregation could coexist. After the conference, James Thomas concluded that the Central Jurisdiction had made real progress in several areas. He specifically pointed to the *Discipline* being more emphatic about racial inclusiveness than ever before. No Methodist congregation could now assert that it could determine its own membership policy, and Methodist institutions must comply with church pronouncements. Methodists had also created a fund to increase pensions and salaries in merging annual conferences, and they excluded the Central Jurisdiction from plans of merger with the EUB. Finally, they established advisory councils in each jurisdiction to further the dialogue necessary to end racial separatism in all its forms in the Methodist Church.[34]

The 1964 General Conference in Pittsburgh was the last time that James P. Brawley and Charles C. Parlin worked together on church desegregation. Parlin, who had an influential role on both the Commission of Seventy and the Commission of Thirty-Six, served as secretary of the committee negotiating merger of the Methodist Church and the EUB. As chair of the Commission of Thirty-Six, he had attempted to speed the process of desegregation. However, the plan outlined in the first report had conceptual flaws and actually provoked a slowdown as the Central Jurisdiction felt compelled to redraw its conference boundaries. He had brought his considerable skills as a lawyer to persuade the contending parties together, but he had not exhibited much moral outrage over segregation. He prized Methodist unity so much that he refused to apply more pressure on his southern white counterparts to accept desegregation. Brawley, who had played such a significant role within the Central Jurisdiction, was scaling back his obligation as he approached his retirement. Parlin, the Wall Street lawyer, and Brawley, the college president, had each attained one of the leading positions in American society for a person of his race. Each had provided extraordinary

---

34. James S. Thomas to Dr. James P. Brawley, June 6, 1964, Brawley Papers.

lay leadership within the church and had devoted tremendous energy to church desegregation. Parlin left Pittsburgh quite pleased, and by July he was confident that all Central Jurisdiction annual conferences would transfer into regional jurisdictions by the end of 1965. Brawley did not record his thoughts about how close the church had come to fruition of a truly inclusive fellowship, one where race had no bearing. As an African American who for several decades had tirelessly fought for equality and had seen movement only recently, he was probably less confident than Parlin regarding how fast the church was moving toward racial inclusiveness. Nevertheless, Brawley had seen great change in Atlanta, where he was an influential community leader and probably felt that the church was moving in the right direction, albeit slowly.[35]

The victory for open Methodist churches came as Congress worked on the 1964 civil rights bill. This epochal legislation barred segregation in public accommodations and prohibited discrimination in employment as well as increased the federal government's role in the enforcement of desegregation of public schools and accommodations. As James F. Findlay Jr. has shown, mainline Protestant churches, especially through the National Council of Churches, played an important role in building public support for the civil rights bill and lobbied hard for its passage. The Methodist Board of Christian Social Concerns was integrally involved in applying pressure to Congress. At key junctures as the bill went through the House of Representatives, Grover Bagby, the associate general secretary of the board, sent letters to bishops and ministers urging them to mobilize support for the bill. As the bill moved to the Senate, he continued to write Methodist leaders about contacting their senators to support the toughest possible language and to apply pressure for cloture. As with the March on Washington, the board's Washington staff worked diligently with a coalition of civil rights organizations to make sure Methodists across the country used their influence to gain passage of the civil rights bill. Their actions, and those of others, were successful in overcoming the largely southern opposition. Congress

35. Parlin to Rev. D. Trigg James, July 14, 1995, Parlin Papers; see also Parlin to William N. Letson, May 11, 1964, Parlin Papers, and James S. Thomas to Brawley, June 6, 1964, Brawley Papers.

passed the bill, and President Lyndon Johnson signed it into law on July 2, 1964.[36]

Like Methodists in Pittsburgh, 1964 was also a time for the Democratic party to wrestle with how open it would be to all races. This confrontation also centered on Mississippi, although it was part of the larger voter registration drive in the South. In the summer of 1964, the Council on Federated Organizations (COFO), a coalition of civil rights groups, sponsored an effort called Freedom Summer. Freedom Summer focused upon voter education and registration and established "Freedom Schools" across the Delta region of Mississippi. College students from elite universities, particularly Yale and Stanford universities, came to Mississippi to aid in the voter registration process. Over three hundred ministers and rabbis of various faiths were also involved in Freedom Summer, although most spent only a week or two in Mississippi rather than the entire summer.[37]

One of the most ambitious projects of Freedom Summer centered on efforts to gain recognition of an integrated alternative group, the Mississippi Freedom Democratic party (MFDP), as a replacement for the segregationist state Democratic party. Both state delegations claimed to be the only legitimate Democratic organization in Mississippi at the August 1964 Atlantic Beach, New Jersey, Democratic party convention. Many northern Democrats sympathized with the MFDP and had no love for the conservative segregationists from Mississippi. President Johnson, however, wanted no floor fight or massive southern withdrawal at the convention. Using his powers as head of the party, he ordered liberal white Democrats to derail the MFDP challenge at all costs. He even personally prevented national television coverage of Fannie Lou Hamer's testimony before the credentials committee by hastily calling a White House press conference at the same time.[38]

The challenge to the all-white Mississippi Democratic organization ended in an unsatisfactory manner for both sides from Missis-

36. James F. Findlay Jr., *Church People in the Struggle: The National Council of Churches and the Black Freedom Movement, 1950–1970*, 48–75; Grover C. Bagby to Bishop Gerald Ensley, March 11, 1964; Bagby to Conference Christian Social Concerns Board Officers, March 1964; and Grover C. Bagby to large number of Methodists, May 27, 1964; Division of Human Relations and Economic Affairs, GCAH.
37. Dittmer, *Local People*, 242–71. See also Doug McAdam, *Freedom Summer*.
38. Dittmer, *Local People*, 272–302.

sippi. Democratic officials offered the MFDP two seats—for Aaron Henry and Ed King (the same Ed King who had organized the challenges to churches in Jackson), who were leaders of the MFDP party—but the MFDP delegation rejected this proposal. It felt like a slap in the face to people who had literally risked their lives for the principles of integration and equality. However, national party leaders did promise that all Democratic party organizations would be open to all voters regardless of race for the 1968 Democratic convention. Ironically, all but four of the regular Mississippi delegates, not inclined to vote for Lyndon Johnson anyway, walked out of the convention rather than accept the presence of even the two MFDP delegates.

Although the situations at the 1964 Methodist General Conference and the 1964 Democratic convention were different, both organizations wrestled with how to establish the principle that all persons, regardless of race, would be included. The Democratic party deferred achievement of this goal until 1968, while Methodists stated that the time to change was now. In both situations, national leaders wanted to bring African Americans and whites into the same organization with a minimum of disruption and without a mass exodus. Methodists had a tremendous advantage over the Democratic party because African American and white members shared a greater purpose through their faith in God. It was harder for Democrats to build a stable biracial coalition in the South, especially in areas like Mississippi, where many white Democrats simply abandoned the party for the more conservative Republican party. Barry Goldwater's opposition to the 1964 Civil Rights Act only accelerated this exodus.[39]

The Episcopal Church had its own struggle over opening its churches to all worshippers. Civil rights activists targeted Episcopal churches in several cities, including St. Augustine, Florida; Savannah, Georgia; and Selma, Alabama. At its 1964 General Convention, the church added two specific prohibitions against discrimination in the church to its canon law. One affirmed that all church members had equal status in every local church, and the other guaranteed that there could not be any "racial discrimination, segregation, and exclusion of any person in the human family, because of race, from

39. Ibid.

the rites and activities of the Church." However, lay delegates to the convention blocked passage of a resolution that endorsed the use of civil disobedience as a legitimate means of protest, which led lay delegate Thurgood Marshall to walk out in disgust. Continued civil rights pressure on several congregations forced the issue of openness in 1965. In Savannah, the local Episcopal congregation withdrew from the Episcopal Church entirely when the diocesan bishop tried to enforce the new canon law. In Selma, Alabama, during the height of voting rights demonstrations, St. Paul's Episcopal Church opened its doors to integrated worship, but ushers forced African American worshippers to sit in the back and to take communion last. The local bishop heard complaints about this treatment, but he only commented that it would give African American worshippers "humility."[40]

Although the focus of the Civil Rights movement in 1964 was upon the Congress and passage of the Civil Rights Act, this was also a time of new openness in churches and other voluntary organizations. For Methodists, the challenge to open church doors was a parallel to the national legislative struggle to open all public facilities. The church took concrete action that it hoped would keep it in step with the nation. Methodists also made another step toward working out a solution to the problem of the Central Jurisdiction and racial reconciliation. How far this step would take them was the challenge that lay before the new Commission of Twenty-Four, the Methodist bishops, and the entire church.

Passage of the 1964 Civil Rights Act and preceding events in the Civil Rights movement during the 1960–1964 quadrennium discredited the Southern Myth, although some white supremacists continued to live in denial. Methodists had begun looking beyond the Central Jurisdiction at their own racism. The larger question for American society was whether the Great Myth would also be shattered. Could American society move beyond the racial problems of the South to the larger and endemic forms of discrimination and prejudice? For Methodists, the big challenge was to finish the abolition of the Central Jurisdiction in a manner conducive to addressing the larger issues of openness and inclusion. Could the church move beyond merely keeping up with society in desegregation?

40. Shattuck, *Episcopalians and Race,* 146, 153–57.

7

The End of the Central Jurisdiction

FOR METHODISTS, the new quadrennium opened with a degree of optimism. While the 1964 General Conference remained committed to voluntarism as a plan of desegregation, it also did not include the Central Jurisdiction in its plans for the anticipated merger in 1968 with the Evangelical United Brethren (EUB) Church. The church clarified its *Discipline,* so beyond any doubt the church law declared all Methodist congregations and institutions open to all persons, regardless of race. Passage of the 1964 Civil Rights Act also meant that de jure segregation was dying even in the Deep South. Signed into law July 2, 1964, it was far-reaching in scope, opening all types of public facilities, including restaurants, motels, movies, laundromats, and parks to all individuals, regardless of race. For African Americans and other minorities, the legislation protected the rights first guaranteed in the Fourteenth Amendment. Employment opportunities for African Americans significantly expanded because the legislation created the Equal Employment Opportunity Commission and outlawed racial discrimination by those doing business with the federal government. Title VI of the act applied to education and denied federal money to any school district not in compliance with federal desegregation standards.

In most of the South, change was quickly evident. Andrew Young remembered being served courteously in a hotel in St. Augustine, Florida, where he had been rudely treated and denied service just weeks before. Whether willingly or under coercion, most southern white businesses complied with the law; if for no other reason, it now made good economic sense. Additionally, the economic impact of better job opportunities for African American workers was significant, especially in the first decade after passage. More importantly, the success of desegregation of public facilities and the widening of school desegregation undermined the forces of continued resistance. Predictions of dire consequences made by segregationists did not come true. Southern whites found desegregation easier than they had expected. For a few white southerners, the end of segregation may have actually been a relief.[1]

Despite the progress, enormous challenges remained. School desegregation had advanced in the border states in the ten years after the *Brown* decision, but in the Deep South the Supreme Court had been thwarted except for the most token integration. Texas and Tennessee led the states of the former Confederacy in terms of desegregation, but each had only 2 percent of schools desegregated; 99 percent of all African American students in the eleven ex-Confederate southern states still attended segregated schools. The slow pace of school desegregation indicated how successful southern segregationists had been in maintaining their power in the face of a slowly growing number of moderate southern whites who wanted interracial progress. The champions of Massive Resistance were no longer in control, but the system of thwarting desegregation was only just beginning to collapse.[2]

In terms of education, employment, and housing, most African Americans had experienced little change, regardless of where they lived. Expectations had increased, and there was a heightened sense of pride created by the Civil Rights movement, but so much more remained to be done. Very few African Americans in May 1964 felt that the struggle for equality was nearly over or that, in Gunnar Myrdal's phrase, "the American dilemma" was a thing of the past. The Great Myth of there being generally good race relations outside the South had not been even seriously examined because the Civil Rights movement had so consciously focused upon ending legal segregation in the Jim Crow South.

Within the Methodist Church, the Committee of Five's report to the 1964 Central Jurisdiction's conference highlighted the differences

1. Goldfield, *Black, White, and Southern*, 144–48; Bartley, *New South*, 370–75; for a more pessimistic assessment of the speed of compliance with the 1964 Civil Rights Act, see Dittmer, *Local People*, 273–77.
2. Gary Orfield, *The Reconstruction of Southern Education: The Schools and the 1964 Civil Rights Act*, 20, 45; Bartley, *New South*, 244–46, 249, 254–60, 372–75.

between African American Methodist leaders and the Commission of Thirty-Six's Plan of Action, which the 1964 General Conference had adopted with only minor changes. The Committee of Five's report pointed out that the Commission of Thirty-Six's plan "is based on the myth of 'voluntarism,' and hence it ignores the realities of The Methodist Church as a major social institution as well as the power of racialism as an operational principle of that institution." This was strong language meant to highlight that African American Methodists would not simply realign their annual conference boundaries as requested in the Commission of Thirty-Six's Plan of Action, lamely approve transfers into regional jurisdictions, and then simply hope for further desegregation. The attack on voluntarism was a reminder to the new Commission of Twenty-Four that despite the support for voluntarism among many white Methodists, especially in the South, it had little support among African American Methodists.[3]

The Committee of Five's report continued to call for a church where racial bodies did not exist even at the local level. The message given in the report and at the jurisdictional conference was that any method of abolishing the Central Jurisdiction that did not conform to this standard would encounter resistance from African American Methodists. While the Central Jurisdiction did look forward to the transfer of its annual conferences into regional jurisdictions, "the Central Jurisdictional Conference unequivocally affirm[s] its opposition to segregated annual conferences in regional Jurisdictions." In effect, the jurisdiction remained committed to the one-step transfer and merger process even though the 1964 General Conference rejected requiring it. However, the Committee of Five also expressed a willingness to accept a segregated annual conference in a regional jurisdiction if that jurisdiction agreed that merger would occur in the quadrennium of the transfer. This was an important qualification, but one that African American Methodist leaders failed to publicize.[4]

3. Central Jurisdiction Study Committee [Committee of Five], "Bridges to Racial Equality in the Methodist Church: Report to the Central Jurisdictional Conference," May 22, 1964, printed booklet, 16, Murray Collection.

4. Committee of Five, "Bridges to Racial Equality," 30, Murray Collection. Even in a November 1964 report to the Council of Bishops made by the Central Jurisdiction's College of Bishops, there was no mention of the transfer and merger process guidelines or whether flexibility was possible. Instead there was

The Central Jurisdiction did realign its annual conference boundaries so that none crossed the bounds of any regional jurisdiction. This paved the way for using Amendment IX to transfer annual conferences from the Central Jurisdiction to regional jurisdictions. Negotiations had already advanced sufficiently to permit the Lexington Annual Conference to transfer into the North Central Jurisdiction, and the Delaware and Washington annual conferences into the Northeastern Jurisdiction. In these discussions there was excitement and confidence that any problems encountered could be overcome. After several years of only limited use by African American Methodist congregations, Amendment IX was now beginning to bear some fruit, although it was only a start and the hardest negotiations were ahead. By the end of the summer, action was complete and three annual conferences of the Central Jurisdiction had transferred to two regional jurisdictions. The Central Jurisdiction decreased by 125,000 members, and two of its bishops, James S. Thomas (elected a bishop at the 1964 Central Jurisdiction conference) and Prince A. Taylor, transferred with these annual conferences and now presided over annual conferences in regional jurisdictions.[5]

The one-step transfer and merger provision of the Committee of Five's report quickly became a source of controversy. Charles C. Parlin, who attended the 1964 Central Jurisdiction conference, believed that most delegates did not realize that this particular feature of the report contradicted the Plan of Action approved by the General Conference. Several persons involved in the Commission of Twenty-Four thought that the one-step transfer and merger was a bargaining position by the Central Jurisdiction to apply pressure for a deadline ending segregated annual conferences. Indeed, the jurisdiction approved transfer of Delaware and Washington annual conferences

---

only a vague statement of willingness to negotiate on the issues and reference to the progress made in the North Central and Northeastern jurisdictions. This miscommunication contributed to tensions with hard-liners within the Southeastern Jurisdiction (Council of Bishops, Minutes, November 1964, Chicago, 59–62, CBP).

5. Thomas presided over the Des Moines Episcopal Area (Iowa) in the North Central Jurisdiction, and Taylor presided over the Princeton Episcopal Area (Northern and Southern New Jersey annual conferences). Meeting of the Special Committee Representing: The Commission of Thirty-Six and the Lexington Annual Conference, Chittenden Hotel, Columbus, Ohio, October 25, 1963, Parlin Papers.

into the Northeastern Jurisdiction even though they remained separate annual conferences for one year. Logistical details delayed merger with overlapping white annual conferences until 1965, but soon Methodists were hailing the experiences in the North Central and Northeastern jurisdictions as dramatic victories.[6]

The 1964 Southeastern Jurisdiction conference did not interpret the Central Jurisdiction's action favorably. Bishop Marvin Franklin of Mississippi informed the jurisdictional conference delegates that the Central Jurisdiction "went on record as being unequivocally opposed to the transfer of annual conferences to a geographical jurisdiction unless it can be assured that annual conference mergers can follow immediately. This seriously amends the action of the General Conference, and no such assurance can now be given." A special committee appointed by the conference to consider interjurisdictional matters recommended acceptance of the Plan of Action approved in Pittsburgh, specifically noting that it did not bind the jurisdiction regarding the timetable of the second step. Not satisfied, Judge John Satterfield, a Mississippian who served as legal counsel to the State Sovereignty Commission and led the state's organized opposition to the 1964 Civil Rights Act, got the conference to request an advisory opinion of the Judicial Council, the church's supreme court. The request concerned the constitutionality of the Southeastern Jurisdiction keeping transferred annual conferences intact until it desired to merge them with existing annual conferences.[7]

Satterfield represented those in the Southeastern Jurisdiction who feared that a future General Conference would force the merger of annual conferences once annual conference transfers were made. Their fear was reminiscent of the 1844 Methodist schism over Bishop

6. During 1964, both before and after the Central Jurisdiction's conference, its annual conferences approved transfer and merger of not only the Delaware, Lexington, and Washington annual conferences, but also their own transfer into either the South Central or Southeastern Jurisdiction. Although conference actions varied, most provided that the receiving jurisdiction merge annual conferences as a condition for transfer. Leonard D. Slutz to D. Trigg James, March 4, 1964, Parlin Papers; Parlin to D. Trigg James, July 14, 1964, Parlin Papers; D. Trigg James to Leonard D. Slutz, July 14, 1964, Parlin Papers.

7. Leonard D. Slutz characterized Satterfield's motion as "a slap in the face" toward the Central Jurisdiction, but Parlin disagreed. 1964 Southeastern Jurisdiction Conference *Journal*, 92, 134–35; Parlin to Slutz, November 27, 1964, Parlin Papers.

James O. Andrew's ownership of slaves. At that time, southern Methodists had left the church because, in their view, an overbearing General Conference was usurping power over matters beyond its legitimate interests. Satterfield and others saw national civil rights legislation as the national government overstepping its powers, and they worried that the national church was contemplating the same to achieve racial inclusiveness. Satterfield hoped that the church's Judicial Council would declare unconstitutional any such action by a future General Conference. This would give southern white Methodists the assurance that voluntarism was permanent and that they would not face coerced desegregation once they had transferred Central Jurisdiction annual conferences into the Southeastern Jurisdiction.

By 1964, Satterfield's position notwithstanding, the Southeastern Jurisdiction did harbor moderates who wanted to move forward with a minimum of quibbling over steps. Its Committee on Christian Social Concerns brought in a report that was more gentle and loving in tone. This report promised "we will extend the hand of fellowship to our brethren of the Central Jurisdiction when their conferences come to be member conferences in the Southeastern Jurisdiction and that we will strive earnestly to find the means as rapidly as circumstances permit in accordance with the procedure heretofore adopted by this conference so that eventually there will be no annual conference based solely on race." This was a cautious statement, but it was also the first endorsement by the Southeastern Jurisdiction of the principle of racially inclusive annual conferences.[8]

The clash between the Southeastern and the Central jurisdictions regarding the timing of annual conference mergers made the job of the Commission of Twenty-Four more difficult. The chair of the commission, Leonard D. Slutz, an Ohio attorney who had served on both the Commission of Seventy and the Commission of Thirty-Six, had high hopes for initiating transfers in both the South Central and Southeastern jurisdictions. He suggested to Central Jurisdiction leaders that transfers be made if at least one Central Jurisdiction annual conference merged immediately with an overlapping white annual conference. The suggestion attempted to continue use of Amendment IX and to inspire confidence that southern regional jurisdictions would merge white and African American annual con-

8. 1964 Southeastern Jurisdiction Conference *Journal*, 242–43.

ferences rather than keep them separate indefinitely. Slutz feared that if progress stopped, then the three jurisdictions might decide to wait until the special session of General Conference to be held in Chicago in 1966 to see what action it might take. If a wait-and-see attitude emerged, desegregation might halt after having just started.[9]

The Council of Bishops was also worried about the progress in desegregation, not just as it related to the Central Jurisdiction, but also as the church witnessed a new attitude towards race relations in the United States. Bishop Roy H. Short reviewed the actions of the 1964 General Conference and concluded, "If there was one concern that was obviously upon the heart and conscience of the General Conference it was the matter of race.... [T]he overall desire of the General Conference to move forward in this area was unmistakable." He cited the importance of episcopal leadership, but he noted the church was moving from one era in race relations to a new, fluid, and yet-to-be-realized era. "We must define more clearly our aims for the future and reconsider our former strategies.... Perhaps one of the finest contributions the bishops could make would be to give studied attention to some new definitions of aim in this whole field." Taking Short's recommendation to heart, the council decided to devote the major portion of its next meeting in April 1965 to reports on race.[10]

Progress on integration of conferences in the fall of 1964 and early 1965 was slow, partly due to the appeal to the Judicial Council by the Southeastern Jurisdiction that encouraged a wait-and-see attitude. Rather than decide the case in October 1964, the Judicial Council issued a delay to allow the Committee of Five to draft its own briefs relating to the case. In the meantime, the Commission of Twenty-Four tried valiantly to maintain the momentum, although Slutz wrote members in January 1965, "Frankly, I am much disturbed that things do not seem to be moving. I fear that the urgency that was felt last spring has diminished." This delay made the Commis-

9. Slutz to Dr. William H. Dickinson, August 6, 1964, D. Trigg James Papers, GCAH (hereinafter cited as James Papers); Slutz to Bishop Eugene M. Frank, September 14, 1964, James Papers; Slutz to Bishop Noah W. Moore, Jr., September 30, 1964, James Papers; Slutz to Bishop Charles F. Golden, October 1, 1964, James Papers.
10. Council of Bishops, Minutes, November 15, 1964, Chicago, 39, 40, CBP.

sion of Twenty-Four focus on inspiring dialogue among the regional advisory councils in the hope that regardless of the Judicial Council's decision the jurisdictional conferences would have already improved communication and developed a degree of trust.[11]

The bishops in the Southeastern Jurisdiction also polled one another regarding how far their conferences could go in creating a nonracial church. They believed that the Central Jurisdiction's annual conferences could be brought into the Southeastern Jurisdiction as annual conferences. Most agreed with Bishop Paul Garber, who presided over the North Carolina Annual Conference, that "this is about as far as we can go at this time," and with Bishop Earl Hunt, in western North Carolina, who thought, "I should not wish to risk a vote on this proposal until both clerical and lay leaders have had sufficient preparation and education on the issue." Only Bishop J. O. Smith of Atlanta felt his two Georgia annual conferences might go further in approving merger of annual conferences in that state. Yet he cautioned, "These same people [white Georgia Methodists], of course, will not be favorable toward a Negro District Superintendent or Bishop taking the place of what we now have. In other words, a general merger on the local level is some distance away."[12]

Bishop Smith brought up an issue that most of the bishops com-

11. Leonard D. Slutz to Dear Friends [Commisison on Interjurisdictional Relations], January 23, 1963, 5, James Papers.

12. These responses were intended to be used only by the Southeastern Jurisdiction College of Bishops. They were the equivalent of a private polling of southern governors regarding their assessment of race relations in their states. Eleven bishops responded: eight active bishops and three retired bishops. Only Bishop Short, who drafted and mailed the questionnaire, did not have a written response. Bishop Roy H. Short to Bishops Paul Hardin Jr. and H. Ellis Finger Jr., December 17, 1964, Roy H. Short to Bishop Paul Hardin Jr. and Bishop H. Ellis Finger Jr., December 17, 1964; Confidential, December 30, 1964 [labeled Harmon]; Confidential, December 30, 1964 [labeled Gum]; Bishop Paul N. Garber to Bishop Roy H. Short, January 6, 1965; Bishop Arthur J. Moore to Bishop Roy H. Short, January 6, 1965; Bishop James W. Henley to Bishop Roy H. Short, January 14, 1965; Bishop Earl O. Hunt to Bishop Roy H. Short, January 14, 1965; Bishop Paul Hardin Jr. to Bishop Roy H. Short and Bishop H. Ellis Finger, January 20, 1965; Bishop Marvin Franklin to Bishop Roy H. Short, January 21, 1965; Bishop Edward J. Pendergrass to Bishop Roy H. Short, January 27, 1965; Bishop J. O. Smith to Bishop Roy H. Short, February 3, 1965; Bishop H. Ellis Finger to Bishop Roy H. Short, February 4, 1965; all correspondence in Bishop Roy H. Short Papers, MSS 039, Archives and Manuscripts Department, Pitts Theology Library, Emory University, Atlanta, Georgia (hereinafter cited as Short Papers, EU).

mented upon, which was whether white southern Methodists were ready to have African Americans in leadership positions, either as district superintendents or bishops. While the bishops could foresee immediate cooperation between African American and white annual conferences regarding pastors' schools, Women's Society of Christian Service conferences, youth activities, and other functions, they all reported their conferences not ready for African American leadership. This was another indication that the gulf in the Southeast between African American and white Methodists had been so substantial during the two-and-a-half decades since unification that most white Methodists simply did not know any African American Methodist leaders. Prejudice prevailed under these conditions, especially since southern whites had always expected African Americans to show them deference.

Southeastern bishops were unanimous that should the Judicial Council or a future General Conference force immediate merger of annual conferences there would be mass defection in many areas and considerable trouble in the remaining portions of the jurisdiction. Yet, there was also considerable optimism about the changes going on in the Southeast. Bishop Walter Gum in Virginia spoke for many bishops when he wrote, "We are discussing this matter [merger of conferences] in most of our meetings. Our people feel that we must have a better understanding and relationship with the Central Jurisdiction. We need a little time. I am encouraged." Bishops also expressed optimism about African American worshippers. Bishop Hardin in South Carolina observed, "more and more of our South Carolina churches are opening their doors to any and all worshippers." However, this was still a cause of worry. A consistent refrain was that the national church should give the jurisdiction more time and show more understanding.[13]

13. Confidential, December 30, 1964 [labeled Harmon]; Confidential, December 30, 1964 [labeled Gum]; Bishop Paul N. Garber to Bishop Roy H. Short, January 6, 1965; Bishop Arthur J. Moore to Bishop Roy H. Short, January 6, 1965; Bishop James W. Henley to Bishop Roy H. Short, Jan, 14, 1965; Bishop Earl O. Hunt to Bishop Roy H. Short, January 14, 1965; Bishop Paul Hardin Jr. to Bishop Roy H. Short and Bishop H. Ellis Finger, January 20, 1965; Bishop Marvin Franklin to Bishop Roy H. Short, January 21, 1965; Bishop Edward J. Pendergrass to Bishop Roy H. Short, January 27, 1965; Bishop J. O. Smith to Bishop Roy H. Short, February 3, 1965; Bishop H. Ellis Finger to Bishop Roy H. Short, February 4, 1965; Short Papers, EU.

While the Southeastern Jurisdiction's bishops assessed their collective situation, the South Central and Central jurisdictions' advisory councils moved more swiftly and agreed upon a joint resolution to be submitted to their respective annual conferences in 1965. It would transfer the five southwestern Central Jurisdiction annual conferences into the South Central Jurisdiction and merge annual conferences "not later than 1968." In addition, they also wrote a separate resolution that approved the transfer and merger of the Central West Annual Conference into the Missouri East and Missouri West annual conferences of the South Central Jurisdiction. Here was a significant sign of progress in the South and one that might put new pressure on the Southeastern Jurisdiction to make similar progress. Although only the Central West Annual Conference was covered by a one-step transfer and merger process as recommended by the Committee of Five in 1964, the commitment to ending all separate annual conferences by 1968 was the type of guarantee that African American Methodists wanted. As in the case of the Northeastern Jurisdiction, which delayed by one year the elimination of the Delaware and Washington annual conferences, African American Methodist leaders were demonstrating flexibility in their efforts at furthering the goal of an inclusive church.[14]

In April 1965, the Judicial Council prepared to hear all the arguments relating to the Southeastern Jurisdiction's appeal for a declaratory decision, but before arguments could be made, the Council of Bishops requested and received yet another six-month delay. In explaining the gravity of the situation, the bishops expressed "our deep concern over the implications of the declaratory decision now under consideration, not only for the immediate future, but also for the future effectiveness of The Methodist Church." The Council of Bishops at the same time established its own seven-member committee "for the purpose of working out plans for making the transition from step one to step two." The bishops, as well as the Commission of Twenty-Four, realized that real progress depended upon agreement between the Central and Southeastern jurisdictions. The bishops hoped that by their intervention a formula could be devised

14. Resolution Approved by the Joint Interjurisdictional Relations Committees of the South Central Jurisdiction and Southwestern Area of the Central Jurisdiction for Presentation to All 1965 Annual Conferences of the Two Jurisdictions Concerned, undated, James Papers.

that would meet the needs of each side so that the church could move forward and so that racial practices would not be an issue that imperiled union with the EUB Church.[15]

The Council of Bishops devoted a large portion of its April 1965 meeting in Houston, Texas, to reports from each jurisdiction regarding race relations and church desegregation. These reports highlighted some points of difficulty and contained some new themes, suggesting a new understanding of the problem that racism posed for all Methodists and Christians in the United States. The structural problems were quite apparent, although Bishop M. L. Harris of the Central Jurisdiction curiously failed to discuss them in any depth. In the Northeastern and North Central jurisdictions, cross-racial appointment of ministers was still quite limited. Interracial congregations were also still rare and largely characterized as token integration. In the South Central Jurisdiction, opposition to transfer of the southwestern annual conferences of the Central Jurisdiction was largely limited to parts of Texas, Arkansas, and Louisiana, but there was general optimism that the transfers could be accomplished by the end of 1968. Yet there was still little acceptance of cross-racial appointments except in the Nebraska Annual Conference. In the Southeastern Jurisdiction, Bishop Paul Hardin Jr. pleaded with his colleagues for understanding and described how much change was going on in the Deep South, even though most went unreported by the media. Regarding abolition of the Central Jurisdiction, Hardin reiterated the actions of the 1964 Southeastern Jurisdictional Conference and criticized the action of the Central Jurisdiction in approving the report of the Committee of Five with its one-step transfer and merger recommendation. He concluded that "I believe that I can accurately declare that there is a strong feeling among the bishops of the Southeastern Jurisdiction in favor of taking, as quickly as possible, Step #1 as recommended by the General Conference, BUT WE NEED ADEQUATE TIME FOR PREPARING OUR PEOPLE FOR STEP #2, and this point must be emphasized."[16]

Beyond the discussion of the church structure, the bishops expressed several themes. One was awareness of the depth of the church's problems. This was especially true in the discussion of the

15. Council of Bishops, Minutes, April 20, 1965, Houston, Tex., 112, CBP.
16. Ibid. (emphasis in the original).

status of race relations in the Northeastern and North Central jurisdictions. Here the problem was not primarily between African American and white Methodists but the prejudice of white Methodists
against all African Americans. For example, with the large number
of African Americans entering northern cities, many churches found
their immediate neighborhoods in transition from all white to heav-
ily integrated or all African American. In these cases, Bishop Ralph
Alton of the North Central Jurisdiction confessed, "The pattern is
still either to relocate the church as to follow the migration of its
membership toward the suburbs or to draw its congregation from
an increasingly greater distance. For the most part, the ministry to
the rapidly increasing Negro population in our section of the country has fallen to other hands than Methodist." Bishop John Wesley
Lord, of the Northeastern Jurisdiction, noted that the problem centered on decent housing, good education, and equal employment
opportunity. These issues of equality and justice confronted all white
Methodists, not just the laity; as Bishop Vernon Middleton reported,
"unfortunately we have not been able to bring all our Methodist
preachers to believe that every neighborhood should be open to
anyone who can pay the price and wants to live there." The bishops
noted how deeply racist American society was and what a problem
the church faced in fighting de facto discrimination and prejudice.[17]

There was an open admission of both the church's previous failure and the importance of episcopal leadership if the church was
going to make significant progress. Bishop Prince Taylor, who had
transferred into the Northeastern Jurisdiction along with the Delaware and Washington annual conferences in 1964, openly described
the church's failure in race relations and called on his colleagues to
acknowledge that racism was not a sectional problem. Speaking in
theological terms of the church's mission, he asserted, "We are under
divine mandate to be out on the frontiers giving leadership in a
community of faith instead of being in the rear as custodians of the
status quo." If the mission of the church, he continued, was to bring
reconciliation even when church members practice un-Christian
ways, then the church must be creative in dealing with the situation
while never turning its back on its mission. Institutional size and

17. Ibid., 160–61, 174.

physical wealth should not be important. Bishop Short of the Southeastern Jurisdiction was only slightly less bold than Bishop Taylor. He, too, admitted that the church's problems were very deep: "particularly at community and local church levels, we are generally both South and North far from facing the full implications of the Christian position on race." Short told his colleagues that bishops needed to hold the church together as a family, regardless of its tensions.[18]

While the Council of Bishops was evaluating what it could do, Martin Luther King Jr. led a new civil rights campaign concentrated on voting rights in Selma, Alabama. These marches dramatized the struggle of African Americans to register to vote, but media attention skyrocketed after Alabama state troopers and forces under the direction of Sheriff Jim Clark brutally attacked marchers on the Edmund Pettus Bridge on March 7, 1965. Local and state police used tear gas and clubs against the nonviolent, peaceful marchers; the event was so intense and brutal it became known as Bloody Sunday. Television and newspaper cameras captured the savage attack, and there was an outcry of indignation at the excessive use of force. Martin Luther King Jr., who was not present on Bloody Sunday, issued a call for civil rights supporters in the South to come to Selma to join a march that he would lead, and thus join the struggle for voting rights. Many church leaders from various faiths and parts of the country responded heartily to his plea. The bishops of the Southeastern Jurisdiction noted the strife and issued a joint statement that affirmed voting rights for all Americans, condemned the use of violence, called for greater dialogue in race relations, and asserted that Christians were bound by their faith to work for improved racial justice. The march from Selma to Montgomery, Alabama, did take place after a delay, with a large clergy representation including Methodist bishop John Wesley Lord. Protected by federalized Alabama National Guard troops and U.S. marshals, the five-day march was one of the high points of the Civil Rights movement. It ended on the steps on the Alabama state capitol, where Jefferson Davis had taken the oath of office as president of the Confederate States of America in 1861. Just as important, the marches in Selma led President Johnson to call on Congress to pass comprehensive voting

18. Ibid., 145–46, 192, 197.

rights legislation. After the passage of the 1964 Civil Rights Act, denial of voting rights was the last bastion of segregationists.[19]

In the summer of 1965, as the Selma voting rights campaign was making headlines, Methodists were facing their own struggles. The need for creative leadership came crashing down upon bishops and other church leaders when the transfer of five Central Jurisdiction annual conferences of the southwestern episcopal area into the South Central Jurisdiction failed to win approval. The eight annual conferences of the Central Jurisdiction east of the Mississippi River voted against transfer, except for approving the transfer and merger of the Central West Annual Conference with the Missouri East and Missouri West annual conferences. The eight Central Jurisdiction annual conferences east of the Mississippi River did not want to be left to face the Southeastern Jurisdiction by themselves.[20]

The worst fear of church leaders was that the Plan of Action approved by the 1964 General Conference would fall apart and that the 1966 General Conference might approve a hastily devised plan that would abandon voluntarism. After almost a decade of dependence on voluntarism, any retreat would be humiliating and might result in serious divisions within the church. Moreover, there was a growing sense that the church simply had to move beyond the problem of the Central Jurisdiction. Race relations in the country were entering a new stage. In August, two events made this change apparent to all Americans. First, Congress passed the 1965 Civil Rights Act, usually called the Voting Rights Act. This legislation contained mechanisms for the federal government to supervise elections in parts of the country where patterns of discrimination were clear. It immediately applied to six southern states and parts of two others. Like the 1964 Civil Rights Act, its impact was quick and dramatic.

The other major change was less positive but no less significant. In Watts, a largely African American area of Los Angeles, California, where unemployment and poverty were endemic, rioting broke out. Triggered by excessive police force, the Watts riots were five days of rebellion against white control. The widespread burning of

19. Statement of Southeastern Jurisdiction Bishops, Louisville, Kentucky, March 23, 1965, Smith Papers; Fairclough, *To Redeem*, 241–51.
20. Commission of Twenty-Four, Minutes, July 1, 1965, Lake Junaluska, N.C., 2–5, Martin Papers.

buildings and looting of stores shocked government officials on all levels. It took nearly fourteen thousand National Guard troops to restore order, and, in the end, thirty-four deaths occurred and over a thousand people were injured. The Watts riots were an awakening to Americans who believed that military force would only be used against recalcitrant southern governors or that de jure discrimination was the sum of the racial problem in America.

The Civil Rights movement was moving beyond the problems of the South to the problems of the entire nation attacking de facto prejudice and discrimination. Church leaders had reached the stage that they recognized the complicity of white Methodists in society's broader race problems in education, employment, and housing. Although white Methodists were no more culpable than other white Americans, their professed beliefs provided no room for the deeply entrenched public policies that reflected popular prejudices and stereotypes. To move forward on these issues required completion of the dismantling of institutional barriers within the church. Discussion between the Southeastern and Central jurisdictions needed to produce a plan of reconciliation.

After long delay, the Central and Southeastern jurisdictions presented to the Judicial Council their most compelling cases regarding three separate appeals related to the transfer and merger process. The Council's nine judges entered into the fray with apparent enthusiasm, writing extensive opinions, both concurring and dissenting. In the first decision, Case 232, the judges decided that it was not possible to rule regarding a hypothetical case. This left unanswered whether a future General Conference action to achieve racial inclusiveness might conflict with the power of a jurisdictional conference to determine the borders of its annual conferences. The second case (233) originated from the Committee of Five, who wanted a ruling to determine whether the Central West Annual Conference could transfer and merge in one step with the Missouri East and Missouri West annual conferences. The Council decided that the one-step transfer and merger was possible under the church's constitution. In the third decision (234), the council upheld the right of the Southeastern Jurisdiction to approve a two-step transfer and merger procedure. Here the council noted that if merger of annual conferences after transfer was not a condition of the transfer agreement, then subsequent merger of annual conferences did change the bounds of those conferences and thus the church constitution required the approval of the jurisdictional conference.[21]

The Judicial Council's decisions shed no clarity on the merger process. Instead, the Council had dodged hypothetical questions and approved the constitutionality of both a one-step transfer and merger process and a two-step transfer and merger process. The judges decided that the church constitution did not favor one method above the other, and it really depended upon the terms of the transfer agreement whether there was any subsequent linkage with the issue of annual conference merger. Judge Leon Hickman summarized the three decisions for Parlin with the ironic observation, "We [the Judicial Council] really had a sharp battle about all this but have pretty well covered it up in the opinions."[22]

The Advisory Councils of the Central Jurisdiction and the Southeastern Jurisdiction at last met for the first time in December 1965. When they finally came together, the two councils examined the areas of cooperation that already existed in the southeastern region and where problems remained. Communications between African American and white annual conferences were either recently established or about to start, although instances of earlier cooperation existed among the Methodist Student Movement and Woman's Societies of Christian Service. Although these groups still existed along jurisdictional lines, they met interracially with their counterparts. Most, but not all, church-related institutions had moved to nonexclusionary policies in admission and employment. This was hardly surprising, however, since the 1964 Civil Rights Acts covered portions of their operation, and federal dollars spoke louder than church pronouncements. The reports also revealed great diversity within the Southeast with progress most evident in the border states of Kentucky, Tennessee, Virginia, North Carolina, and Florida. Progress was less evident in Alabama, Georgia, Mississippi, and South Carolina.

The discussion did not resolve the issue of conference merger, but councils did agree to have a ten-member subcommittee attempt to draft a common resolution. Here was a possibility that there might

21. *Decisions of the Judicial Council of the Methodist Church, 1940–1968,* 585–618.
22. Leon E. Hickman to Parlin, December 16, 1965, Parlin Papers; see also Bishop Roy Short to Bishop James W. Henley, January 27, 1966, Short Papers, GCAH.

yet be a plan for the transfer of annual conferences of the Central Jurisdiction into the Southeastern Jurisdiction. Such a plan would give confidence to African American Methodists in the Southeast, so they would probably approve the transfers and merger arrangement already agreed to in the South Central Jurisdiction. Methodist leaders had a new reason to hope that the Central Jurisdiction might end without further General Conference action. It was especially good news for the Commission of Twenty-Four, which did not want to draft a plan to force action by either side at the 1966 General Conference special session. A new plan would surely make the special session of the General Conference more difficult.[23]

The meeting of the drafting committee of the two advisory councils created powerful drama. One of the Southeastern representatives was Judge John Satterfield, a fervent defender of the old order in Mississippi. An ardent foe of the Civil Rights movement and an adviser to former governor Ross Barnett, Satterfield represented within the Southeastern Jurisdiction a recalcitrant opponent to annual conference merger by any specified date. One of the Central representatives was Rev. Joseph E. Lowery, a Southern Christian Leadership Conference vice president. A native of Mobile, Alabama, he had distinguished himself as a young minister within the Central Alabama Annual Conference for his leadership in civil rights. He had worked for Bishop Golden and written one of the influential position papers at the 1962 Cincinnati conference of the Central Jurisdiction. The Methodist Church brought Satterfield and Lowery together voluntarily to bridge their differences and produce a plan that would move African American and white Methodists to closer cooperation. They and their colleagues on the drafting committee had the task of discovering whether their common devotion to Jesus Christ could bind them together despite the gulf of years of mistrust and different values.

The drafting committee of the advisory councils failed to produce a resolution that both sides would agree to support. When the two advisory councils met again, they were no more successful. Voting regarding a target date was along jurisdictional lines and participants

23. R. Laurence Dill Jr., "Where Do We Go from Here?" December 8, 1965, 2, James Papers; Minutes of the Joint Meeting of the Advisory Councils of the Southeastern Jurisdiction and [the] Central Jurisdiction, December 7–8, 1965, Atlanta, 1965, 3, James Papers.

felt they had reached a complete impasse. No bridge could be constructed across the abyss between African American and white Methodists in the Southeast.[24]

The failure of the advisory councils to produce a satisfactory proposal regarding the merger of annual conferences created despair among some Methodist leaders. Bishop Edwin Garrison of the North Central Jurisdiction, who served on the Commission of Twenty-Four, confided to his colleague Bishop Charles Brashares that the situation regarding the Central Jurisdiction was at a dead end. He concluded, "I have a feeling that [this] could end in total catastrophe if we are not careful." Both among bishops and in the Commission of Twenty-Four there was a desperate search for new ideas and proposals to revive the process of transfers and mergers, but no constructive ideas seemed likely to bring the parties together, and another scheduled meeting of the advisory councils of the Southeastern and Central Jurisdictions was cancelled.[25]

By the summer of 1966, the national scene in civil rights was much more complex. Violence, once associated in the Civil Rights movement with southern whites attacking African Americans, changed as more riots broke out in northern cities. The Watts riot of 1965 was not an isolated event, but a reflection of a larger trend of frustration outside the South. In 1966, there were thirty-eight riots spread across the country in such cities as New York, Chicago, Cleveland, and San Francisco, as well as in smaller cities such as Omaha, Nebraska, and Lansing, Michigan. Seven people died, four hundred were injured, and property damage reached $5 million. All this unrest produced new calls for law and order, and California passed a strict riot act.[26]

24. Minutes of the Joint Meeting of the Advisory Councils of the Southeastern and Central Jurisdictions, February 25, 1966, Atlanta, 3–7, James Papers. See Bishop James W. Henley to College of Bishops of the Southeastern Jurisdiction, February 26, 1966, Short Papers, GCAH; and James to Slutz, February 25, 1966, James Papers. Regarding possible concessions, see Slutz to James, March 12, 1966, James Papers.

25. Bishop Edwin R. Garrison to Bishop and Mrs. Charles W. Brashares, June 2, 1966, Bishop Charles W. Brashares Papers, Bentley Historical Library, University of Michigan. James commented that a unilateral action by the Southeastern Jurisdiction annual conferences "would accomplish exactly nothing." James to Slutz, March 9, 1966; Slutz to James, March 12, 1966, 5, James Papers; and James to Slutz, March 16, 1966, James Papers.

26. Patterson, *Grand Expectations*, 662–68.

The riots in Chicago particularly illustrated the difficulties of bringing the Civil Rights movement's tactics and organizations from the South to the North. Martin Luther King Jr. and the Southern Christian Leadership Conference attempted to organize African Americans in Chicago for a campaign of marches like those that had earlier been so successful in the South. The targets were both the local Chicago Real Estate Board, which had for decades blocked open housing while the African American population of the city soared, and Congress, where open housing legislation was pending. King faced the determined opposition of the political machine of Richard J. Daley, mayor of the city since 1955 and a powerful voice in the national Democratic party. King quickly found that Daley had more resources than any southern sheriff or governor. Moreover, recruitment for a campaign in the northern urban environment was much more difficult than it had been in the South. There were more ethnic minority groups than just African Americans; the African American church, backbone to the movement in the South, was not as strong; and African American and white residents were more isolated from each other than in the South. Furthermore, northern African American youths were much more skeptical about nonviolence and more apathetic about civil rights agitation. Consequently, the results of the Chicago campaign were deeply disappointing. It was apparent that progress in the urban North was not achievable by simply transplanting tactics that had worked in the South.[27]

In the summer of 1966, a new slogan entered the American lexicon as young African Americans adopted the chant "Black Power!" First used in Mississippi in June, the term quickly became a wedge between young activists and older civil rights leaders, such as the NAACP's Roy Wilkins and the Urban League's Whitney Young, who dissociated themselves from it. They did not want to alienate white supporters of civil rights advances. Younger, more militant African American leaders, such as Stokely Carmichael, who was a new leader within the SNCC, saw the expression of African American nationalism and independence as more important than a biracial

27. Fairclough, *To Redeem*, 279–307; Garrow, *Bearing the Cross*, 489–525. The comprehensive study of the Chicago campaign is James R. Ralph Jr., *Northern Protest: Martin Luther King, Jr., Chicago, and the Civil Rights Movement*.

coalition. Only Martin Luther King Jr. maintained a dialogue between those committed to Black Power and those who rejected the slogan as counter to the ideals of the movement.[28]

Across the nation, this was a period of ferment, with much commentary about the country's racial problems. Within the Methodist Church, Bishops Golden and Thomas separately shared with their colleagues on the Council of Bishops their ideas regarding the Methodist response to the growing unrest and the lack of progress toward resolving the church's own racial problems. Golden's letter focused more on the situation within the church. He concluded that attempts of the Southeastern, South Central, and Central jurisdictions to agree on a plan were futile, and he noted the Council of Bishops had tried "to find a solution to the procedural problem in the achievement of our common goal of racial inclusiveness, but to date have failed." In addition, Golden warned that the church could improve its racial witness only by acting on theological and moral grounds, not what was good for one section of the country. For his part, Bishop Thomas noted that Methodists still had an opportunity to create a truly inclusive fellowship that would be unique in the United States. He reiterated that transfer and merger needed careful planning and a timetable rather than operating simply on goodwill or wishes. Inaction had too often replaced action because of the protests of the segregationists.[29]

For the Commission of Twenty-Four, the failure to negotiate any transfers from the Central Jurisdiction into either the South Central or Southeastern jurisdictions was troubling. The 1964 General Conference required the Commission of Twenty-Four to make a report on its progress at the 1966 General Conference special session. Although that special session was to consider merger with the EUB Church, the commission and other church leaders felt that it was clearly unacceptable to have made no progress in the two southern jurisdictions, especially since the 1964 Civil Rights Act and 1965 Voting Rights Act had ended de jure restrictions. If the Commission of Twenty-Four could not move the church further, then the

28. Fairclough, *To Redeem*, 309–31; Garrow, *Bearing the Cross*, 475–525.
29. Bishop Charles F. Golden to the Council of Bishops of the Methodist Church, August 31, 1966, Martin Papers; Bishop James S. Thomas to the Members of the Council of Bishops, August 1966, Garber Papers.

General Conference would likely try to impose its own settlement when it met in November 1966 in Chicago, Illinois.

The Commission of Twenty-Four decided to break the impasse by writing a single resolution for approval throughout the church. The resolution would include all the necessary transfers of annual conferences and bishops in order to abolish the Central Jurisdiction. Additionally, it would establish a target date of the 1972 jurisdictional conferences for the merger of all remaining racial annual conferences. Dubbed the "Omnibus Resolution" because it tried to include all portions of the church, the resolution attempted to split the differences between the Southeastern Jurisdiction and the Central Jurisdiction regarding the end of the racial annual conferences and voluntarism. The resolution was to be submitted to each annual conference, each jurisdictional conference, each college of bishops, and the Council of Bishops. It provided for the specific transfer and merger of two annual conferences of the Central Jurisdiction into the Southeastern Jurisdiction as a sign of the commitment to the merger of annual conferences as quickly as possible. The commission wanted a resolution that was ironclad in stating the intent of the church while leaving limited flexibility regarding timing of conference mergers. The resolution was designed to prevent any breakdown of the process as had happened during 1965 and 1966. The church, the commission believed, desperately needed closure on the issue of the Central Jurisdiction and racially separate annual conferences. Ironically, the Omnibus Resolution was as a statement of principles equivalent to the racial charter that Methodist women had written for themselves in 1952 and updated in 1962.[30]

Within the Commission of Twenty-Four, criticism of the Omnibus

30. The resolution included a provision for a special session of the Central Jurisdiction in 1967 so that the remaining annual conferences of the jurisdiction could elect a bishop to succeed Bishop M. L. Harris, who had died in October 1966. This was important to African American Methodists in the southeast because they looked forward to having two of their own bishops in the Southeastern Jurisdiction. Not to fill this position would deprive African American Methodists of an episcopal leader when they were particularly anxious about their status and influence in the church leadership. For a copy of the entire Omnibus Resolution, see 1966 General Conference *Journal,* 3076–79. (Although technically still a continuation of the 1964 General Conference, the meeting was held in Chicago in November 1966.)

Resolution chiefly came from Satterfield and Edwin Jones. They argued that the Omnibus Resolution abandoned voluntarism by establishing a target date, which in their minds was synonymous with a deadline. Yet Satterfield and Jones could not gain support from the commission's other Southeastern Jurisdiction representatives for the minority report they were contemplating writing. Rev. Francis Cunningham of the South Carolina Annual Conference wrote to Satterfield, "I believe it is important that our [jurisdiction's] approach be positive and that it be made in connection with discussion of the report . . . rather than as a minority report." However, Satterfield and Jones decided to make a minority report even if the other southern white commission members did not support them. Two members from the Central Jurisdiction, John T. King and Rev. Dennis R. Fletcher, abstained from supporting the Omnibus Resolution. They believed that the resolution should have established a firm deadline for merger of all annual conferences. Despite dissent by some representatives from both the Central and Southeastern jurisdictions, the Commission of Twenty-Four went forward with its proposed Omnibus Resolution. Leonard Slutz went to the General Conference with the hope that "if the strong majority of the entire church can establish a definite program[,] it will be accepted by Central even though less than they had wanted and by Southeastern even [though] more than some of them want to do now."[31]

The issues of desegregation and racial progress threatened to imperil the plan to unite the Methodist Church and the EUB Church, which had been the purpose of the 1966 special session of the Gen-

31. The Executive Committee of the Central Jurisdiction's Advisory Council issued its own critique of the Omnibus Resolution and also proposed amendments to it that together emphasized that the church should not be satisfied with a target date, but write into its laws a firm deadline of 1972 for the end of racially segregated annual conferences. The proposed amendments called for the end of the Central Jurisdiction in 1967 with a concurrent special session of the South Central and Southeastern jurisdictions. The Central Jurisdiction statement stressed that it had transferred four annual conferences and two bishops to regional jurisdiction since the 1964 General Conference. It was anxious to go further, but it needed a greater commitment from the general church toward the end of all racial structures. Francis T. Cunningham to John C. Satterfield, October 24, 1966, James Papers; Leonard D. Slutz to Francis T. Cunningham, October 27, 1966, James Papers; Executive Committee Central Jurisdiction Advisory Council, "Our Concerns, Our Convictions, Our Commitments," November 1966, 2–3, Garber Papers.

eral Conference. An ecumenical spirit had grown in the 1950s and 1960s; the National Council of Churches created the Consultation on Church Union from leading Protestant denominations. For Methodists, union with the EUB Church was both a quick way to boost membership and a way to broaden the church by uniting with a group that had an almost identical theology and a similar polity. For most Methodists, union would mean little besides the change in the name, because EUB membership was small and concentrated only in the Midwest. While Methodist leaders were enthusiastic about union, they feared that a combination of groups could thwart approval. The EUB Church might reject union if its leaders perceived that the Methodist Church was not making sufficient progress on racial practices. Because of its German American ethnic origins, the EUB Church was virtually without African American members; nevertheless, its membership had opposed racial discrimination over the years and was not going to compromise those principles now.

Another threat to the plan to unite with the EUB Church was that an "odd couple" might form between southern whites opposed to desegregation and African American Methodists and their allies opposed to the lack of an absolute deadline. Methodist leaders feared that their combined opposition might defeat the Plan of Union, even though their reasons for opposition were not in harmony. The issue of race was linked to consideration of EUB union and this made building support for the Omnibus Resolution crucial. On the eve of the 1966 General Conference, Methodist leaders had no certainty regarding the outcome of the Omnibus Resolution or the Plan of Union. Bishop Roy H. Short expressed his unease to his friend Dr. Harry Denman, "I dread the next two weeks as I never dreaded anything in my life."[32]

Part of Bishop Short's unease was that he had been selected to give the Episcopal Address to the special session. In picking Bishop Short, the Council of Bishops was affirming a new southern white leadership, one quite different from Bishop Arthur J. Moore, who had led southern bishops in the 1950s. For Bishop Moore, the major event of his career was the unification of the northern and southern churches. Although he had been active in the Southern Regional

32. Bishop Roy H. Short to Dr. Harry Denman, October 26, 1966, Short Papers, GCAH.

Council, he did not actively attack segregation in Georgia. Bishop Short was younger, his career was more tied to the post-*Brown* era, and he supervised not a Deep South state, like Bishop Moore, but Kentucky, where attitudes toward race relations were more varied. Bishop Short was anxious to desegregate his annual conferences and felt some frustration that the overlapping African American churches had not used Amendment IX to transfer. Although he apparently lacked close ties with leaders of the Central Jurisdiction, many Methodists respected him as a progressive southern leader who recognized the urgency for action.

In his Episcopal Address, Bishop Short noted that the single purpose of the special session was to consider the Plan of Union with the EUB Church. Yet he also noted that the Commission of Twenty-Four had a progress report to make and that it would additionally recommend new actions to end the Central Jurisdiction and all other racial structures with the Methodist Church, whether union was approved or not.[33]

While the address was largely devoted to explaining the issues to be considered surrounding union with the EUB, there was a striking parallel between the arguments for union and those for ending all racial structures in the church. First, the union would bring more Christians together in the same church to improve mission activity in the world. This would be a step for Christian unity and promote church efficiency and effectiveness. Second, union could combine the talents and traditions of each entity to bring about a new, richer church. Union would not be the same as merger or absorption of the smaller by the larger. Third, the world scene required that the church be more broad-minded and less provincial. All these arguments were also reasons for removing the remaining racially segregated structures within the Methodist Church.[34]

A challenge to the Omnibus Resolution came from Rev. Joseph Lowery, who moved to amend the final section so that all racially segregated annual conferences would end three months before the meeting of the 1972 General Conference. The difference in timing was not particularly large, but it was a definite timetable instead of a target date. Moreover, by specifying a date in advance of the Gen-

33. 1966 General Conference *Journal*, 2537–38.
34. Ibid., 2538–48.

eral Conference, Lowery's amendment provided a means of forcing action by the 1972 General Conference should any annual conferences fail to comply. The target date set by the commission did not dictate any action should any annual conferences fail to meet the target date, although Slutz argued that inaction would certainly be dealt with by the 1972 General Conference should it be obvious that merger was not going to take place.[35]

The debate over Lowery's motion hinged on the issue of voluntarism and continued faith in the good intentions of fellow Methodists. Lowery's motion had the virtue of being slightly stronger than the Commission of Twenty-Four's recommendation, but it was not a substantial change. For many delegates, the bottom line was that both proposals established 1972 as the date for action, although Lowery's deadline was earlier and more definitive. Slutz emphasized that the motion was not a major change and that the commission felt it had done a fair job of splitting the differences between the Central and the Southeastern jurisdictions. The General Conference rejected Lowery's motion and kept the end of jurisdictional conferences in 1972 as the target date.[36]

The minority report, presented by Satterfield, reasoned that the Commission of Twenty-Four's majority report had abandoned the church policy of voluntarism and replaced it with coercion. He predicted the loss of at least one million Methodists in the Southeastern Jurisdiction if the General Conference adopted the majority report. Jones, coauthor of the minority report, joined Satterfield in arguing that the 1964 General Conference had only approved a two-step process, that the Southeastern Jurisdiction had fully complied with the Plan of Action, and that adoption of the majority report would clearly go beyond what had been approved in Pittsburgh. Both asserted that the Omnibus Resolution was more than a progress report, which was all that the 1964 General Conference had authorized.[37]

Although the minority report did have defenders, support for it was weak. Even Southeastern Jurisdiction delegates criticized it. As one North Carolina delegate told the conference, "There are wrongs

35. Ibid., 2602–3.
36. Ibid., 2603–5, 2608–12.
37. Ibid., 2613–17.

to redress. There is a history from which it seems to me we must now turn decisively and without more delay." In concluding the debate, Slutz dismissed the criticisms of the minority report and urged delegates to affirm the majority report, which is exactly what the General Conference did. This action cleared the way for the EUB to approve union because it assured them that the Methodist Church was eliminating its racial structure.[38]

In perfecting the Plan of Union written by the Ad Hoc Committee on EUB Union, the 1966 General Conference did make one explicit deviation from the 1964 Plan of Action. The Plan of Union called for the transfer of one bishop of the Central Jurisdiction to each of the regional jurisdictions that as yet did not have an African American bishop. This meant that the Western Jurisdiction would receive a bishop from the Central Jurisdiction, and the Southeastern Jurisdiction would receive only one African American bishop instead of two as outlined in the 1964 Plan of Action and the First Report of the Commission of Thirty-Six in 1961. Under questioning from the General Conference floor, Parlin admitted that the change had been made without consultation with bishops of the Central Jurisdiction or its committee on episcopacy. Since each jurisdiction was also receiving one bishop from the EUB Church as a sign of unity and creation of a new church, the General Conference reasoned that each jurisdiction should also receive a bishop from the Central Jurisdiction as a sign of commitment to inclusiveness. However, another unspoken factor was concern about African American episcopal supervision in the Southeastern Jurisdiction. Transfer of one African American bishop to the Western Jurisdiction—who ultimately was Bishop Charles Golden—was also a way of decreasing the number of African American bishops to be received by the Southeastern Jurisdiction.[39]

The issue of union with the EUB did produce more reflection on racial structures in the new church. In consideration of the Plan of Union devised by the Ad Hoc Committee on Union, there were several attempts to prohibit racial annual conferences in the new church beyond the first quadrennium. This would be a deadline rather than a target date. Again, Lowery implored delegates to adopt this

38. Ibid., 2617–26.
39. 1966 General Conference *Journal,* 2673.

amendment as a means of not repeating the mistake of unification when the Central Jurisdiction was created under the assumption that flaws would be corrected in time. The history of the Central Jurisdiction showed that structures once created were difficult to abolish. However, the conference again rejected a firm constitutional deadline. Many African American delegates left their seats after the vote and went to the altar at the front of the assembly and knelt in prayer.[40]

Yet another attempt was made to link EUB union with elimination of all racial structures. Rev. Ray Ragsdale, a white minister, proposed as a substitute for the entire Plan of Union a commitment in principle to EUB union as soon as all annual conferences merged or a deadline for merger had been established. Ragsdale announced that he had a statement signed by over 160 delegates expressing dissatisfaction with the lack of a firm deadline. This was enough votes to block union with the EUB Church, but it turned out that many who signed the statement still preferred union with the EUB Church without a deadline over no union. Racism may have disturbed them, but they saw the two issues as separate. In the minds of most delegates, EUB union would not slow the creation of a racially inclusive church, and therefore there was no reason to slow union while working to end all racial structures. Major J. Jones, secretary of the Committee of Five, spoke of his strong support for both Ragsdale's attack on continuing segregation in the church and for EUB union. He concluded:

> Across Jurisdictional lines that yet separate us, across Conference lines which yet keep us from achieving oneness, my heart still yearns for true Union which is surely God's will for us all ultimately and finally.
> May God bless and increase this Union and may it ever bear fruits that would lead us ultimately into the company of God where we are indeed one family.[41]

Ragsdale's substitute for the Plan of Union was defeated, and the General Conference did approve the plan of EUB union by a vote of 749 to 40, with 5 abstentions. The EUB Church, in turn, approved

40. Ibid., 2655–58.
41. Ibid., 2764; 2655–58, 2740–42.

union with the Methodist Church. The 1966 General Conference closed with an outpouring of enthusiasm for the progress made in committing the church to greater racial brotherhood. In the waning moments of the conference, two southern white ministers, followed by a southern white layman, told the conference delegates of the growing southern support for creating an inclusive church and of the optimism in the region.[42]

Slutz and other leaders of the Commission of Twenty-Four must have been very pleased with the action of the 1966 General Conference. Although its progress report did have some defections from within the commission, it nevertheless had been accepted by the General Conference with no substantial changes. Particularly, the Omnibus Resolution received General Conference blessing as a means of binding the entire church into unified action. The church had again studiously avoided action that seemed too radical and instead remained true to a course that most Methodists would have called moderate. Many, but not all, African American Methodists would have preferred stronger action, such as that outlined in the Lowery amendment to the Omnibus Resolution, but they left Chicago knowing that the Central Jurisdiction would elect one more bishop before its dissolution and that the Omnibus Resolution would commit Methodists to further racial progress and brotherhood.

After the 1966 General Conference, the Commission of Twenty-Four optimistically resumed its work. It worked to insure that bishops would take a leadership role, that copies of the Omnibus Resolution would be distributed to the over twenty-five thousand annual conference delegates spread across the United States, and that a designated person (and an alternate) would manage both presentation and approval of the resolution in each annual conference. The bishops were especially singled out for leadership as a key to success. Rev. D. Trigg James, secretary of the Commission of Twenty-Four, noted to Slutz, "they [the bishops] cannot escape from this responsibility inasmuch as the resolution was passed with such a resounding majority by the General Conference." Nevertheless, opponents of the Omnibus Resolution did try to derail it, and many questions did arise regarding what would happen if various parts of the church failed to achieve the two-thirds votes required. Satterfield contin-

42. Ibid., 2773–74.

THE END OF THE CENTRAL JURISDICTION / 193

ued his campaign against any target date, even charging that the Omnibus Resolution included the Lowery amendment's timetable, which it did not. In a letter to all annual conference delegates in the Southeastern Jurisdiction in the spring of 1967, he contended, "We have long known that at some time and in some manner the dedicated integrationists in our Church would attempt compulsory action. This is now being attempted." Yet the criticisms of Satterfield and Jones were by now familiar to the Commission.[43]

Another serious attack on the Omnibus Resolution came from a group of Central Jurisdiction ministers. Eleven ministers from three annual conferences wrote a letter that criticized the Omnibus Resolution and charged that the 1966 General Conference had "totally ignored" the issues of racism. They also opposed the EUB merger plan because the Judicial Council had issued an opinion asserting that separate annual conferences or separate racial districts within a merged annual conference were possible during the twelve-year transitional period that the Plan of Union created. Bishop Edgar Love of the Central Jurisdiction, who temporarily replaced deceased Bishop M. L. Harris, characterized the letter of the eleven ministers as "an unethical move and tactic." He pointed out in his own letter to ministers and lay conference delegates that the Advisory Council of the Central Jurisdiction had voted by a two-thirds majority to support the Omnibus Resolution and urged favorable action by Central Jurisdiction annual conferences.[44]

There was indeed a struggle going on below the surface among African American Methodists over whether the Omnibus Resolution

43. James to Slutz, January 13, 1967, James Papers; see also Minutes of the Commission, January 1–2, 1967, Chicago, James Papers; Satterfield to Delegates to the Annual Conferences of the Southeastern Jurisdiction, April 25, 1967, James Papers. Satterfield urged SEJ delegates to vote against the Omnibus Resolution and EUB union, "both of which have the same racial effect" (Satterfield to Southeastern Jurisdiction delegates on the Commission, SEJ Council, and delegates to the SEJ conference, November 28, 1966, James Papers). See also Jones to Trigg [James], February 10, 1967, James Papers.
44. "Concerned Group on Racism in the Methodist Church" to All Ministers of the Twelve (12) Annual Conferences of the Central Jurisdiction, April 21, 1967, Garber Papers; Bishop Edgar A. Love to Pastors and Lay Delegates, May 10, 1967, Garber Papers. Slutz, in fact, believed that Golden was behind this effort at derailing the Omnibus Resolution; on his and James's suspicion of Bishop Golden's opposition, see James to Slutz, May 10, 1967, James Papers; and Slutz to Parlin, July 6, 1967, Parlin Papers. See also 1964 General Conference *Journal*, 2891–94.

provided enough certainty that the church was committed to inclusiveness. James P. Brawley wrote to John Graham, chair of the jurisdiction's advisory council, that critics of the resolution in his annual conference had argued that defeating it increased the power of African American Methodists to extract a more favorable plan, but he failed to see their reasoning and instead believed that now was the proper time to act. Delay seemed futile since the Central Jurisdiction was not part of the new church under the Plan of Union with the EUB Church, an action mandated by the 1964 General Conference. Graham, who hoped to be elected a bishop at the last meeting of the Central Jurisdiction, told Brawley that those who opposed the resolution were using his support for it as justification to oppose his episcopal candidacy.[45]

In 1967 annual conference sessions, the Central Jurisdiction gave the Omnibus Resolution an overall two-thirds approval, but the voting varied widely by annual conferences therein. While the twelve annual conferences constituting the Central Jurisdiction approved by 76 percent, the South Carolina and Tennessee-Kentucky conferences each disapproved by overwhelming majorities. The Georgia Annual Conference also failed to muster a two-thirds approval, but it did have 60 percent approval. Ironically, the three annual conferences in Alabama and Mississippi approved by close to 90 percent, even though this was where the organizers of opposition believed the plan failed to provide sufficient assurances of desegregation and inclusiveness. In addition, the North Carolina–Virginia conference approved by well over the two-thirds vote, probably because it had already worked out a transfer and merger agreement with overlapping white annual conferences.[46]

In the Southeastern Jurisdiction, supporters of the Omnibus Resolution were able to gain a narrow victory with slightly over 67 percent approval despite persistent opposition in much of the Deep

45. Brawley to Graham, June 6, 1967, Brawley Papers; Graham to Brawley, June 5, 1967, Brawley Papers.

46. In South Carolina, the vote was 35 for and 121 against, and in Tennessee-Kentucky the vote was 10 for and 131 against. Ten of the eleven ministers who wrote the letter opposing the Omnibus Resolution were in either the South Carolina or the Tennessee-Kentucky conferences. See "Concerned Group on Racism in the Methodist Church" to All Ministers of the Twelve (12) Annual Conferences of the Central Jurisdiction, April 21, 1967, Garber Papers.

South. Voting was highly favorable in the annual conferences of Florida, Kentucky, Holston [eastern Tennessee and southwestern Virginia], Louisville, Memphis, Tennessee, Virginia, and Western North Carolina. The North Carolina Annual Conference just barely failed to muster the two-thirds vote, and the Northern Georgia Annual Conference approved by over 63 percent. In six annual conferences (Alabama–West Florida, Mississippi, North Alabama, North Mississippi, South Carolina, and South Georgia) supporters of the Omnibus Resolution failed to gain a majority of votes.[47]

In voting on the Omnibus Resolution in the other regional jurisdictions, approval was achieved by lopsided votes. Even in the South Central Jurisdiction the approval rate was above 93 percent. Voting on the EUB union also received approval throughout both the Methodist Church and the EUB Church. Whether one pointed to the Omnibus Resolution or to the constitution of the new United Methodist Church created by the Plan of Union, the Central Jurisdiction would cease to exist after a special session in August 1967 to elect a successor to Bishop M. L. Harris. The voting in the spring and summer of 1967 had produced an end to a major symbol of Methodist racism.

The last meeting of the Central Jurisdiction took place in Nashville, Tennessee, August 17–19, 1967. It had a triumphant air as African American Methodists celebrated that one enormous obstacle to inclusive fellowship was coming to an end. There were many visitors present to join the proceedings, and there was much reflection over where African American Methodists had traveled, both before creation of the Central Jurisdiction and after, as a jurisdiction segregated from other Methodists. The conference also discussed where African American Methodists needed to go in the future. Bishop Golden, in giving the jurisdiction's last episcopal address, was unflinching. He stated that the Christian church began as a revolutionary organization and reminded his audience that its greatest leaders throughout its history have been revolutionaries. He continued that now the Methodist Church must become a revolutionary organization, or youth would abandon it. His remarks

47. Commission on Interjurisdictional Relations, "Dear Friends," from Slutz and James, June 27, 1967, Parlin Papers.

concluded with a strong reminder that for the new United Methodist Church to truly serve its African American members it must put enormous resources and energy into the urban areas of the country.[48]

Bishop Noah Moore, who presided over the annual conferences slated to transfer into the South Central Jurisdiction, preached the consecration sermon and was equally bold in attacking the sins of American society, especially economic injustice. How could the country pour money into the Vietnam War and yet not find money for revitalizing the economy of its urban centers? Moore said the government needed to act responsibly by creating a "Marshall Plan" to fight poverty, as recommended by Martin Luther King Jr. He observed that white Americans may not like militants such as Stokely Carmichael and H. Rap Brown, but providing jobs and decent housing would fight the conditions that produced such distrust and hatred for white America. Bishop Dwight Loder of the North Central Jurisdiction and representative of the Council of Bishops joined Moore by pointing out that the same Congress that appropriated $10 million for an aquarium in the District of Columbia had rejected $40 million for rat extermination in the nation's cities.[49]

The call for radical change heard from the bishops was in part a result of the massive cataclysm in American cities. Urban riots reached a new peak of violence in 1967, with the largest riots in Newark and Detroit. In Newark, a city with a large unemployment problem, twenty-five persons died as fires and looting raged. The next week witnessed an even larger outbreak, as Detroit erupted into an inferno and bloodbath with forty-three people killed and over $50 million worth of destruction. Some rioters shouted "Burn, Baby, Burn," but most riot victims were African Americans shot by nervous, trigger-happy National Guardsmen. President Lyndon Johnson had to send federal troops to restore order in Detroit. Congress rushed through a new riot act, but it refused to consider legislation to improve the conditions of urban cities. Public housing and education were inadequate, employment was difficult to obtain, and police brutality was ignored.[50]

48. 1967 Central Jurisdiction Conference *Journal*, 69–78.

49. Ibid., 111–14, 135–43; see also resolution on adjournment, 99–100.

50. John Morton Blum, *Years of Discord: American Politics and Society, 1961–1974*, 260–64, 267–70.

Riots and the new Black Power movement presented the racial problem in America in stark new images. White Americans outside the South faced the stark reality that racism in America might be more than a southern problem. For many white Americans, it was a new idea that the problem was national and could not be fixed by changing a few discriminatory laws. Instead, by 1967, it was becoming likely that improved race relations required fundamental action regarding employment, educational opportunity, and housing. These were areas where policies would not be cheap or cosmetic if they were to have efficacy. For most white Americans, the Great Myth was no longer so solid.

The Black Power movement, which had begun as a slogan during the 1966 Meredith march, revealed a new generation of African American leaders who rejected the model of the ideal American community that had prevailed among civil rights leaders for most of the twentieth century. Calling traditional civil rights leaders "Uncle Toms," the new African American leaders derided the idea of harmony with white Americans as a denial of the value of being African American. Burned by the compromises of white liberals and the violence that white society tolerated against African Americans, these new leaders revived African American nationalism. The Black Power movement also alienated many white Americans who felt that Black Power was largely a negation of anything to do with white Americans. Many liberal white Americans who had supported the Civil Rights movement in the South felt attacked by the Black Power movement. Civil rights organizations such as Martin Luther King's Southern Christian Leadership Conference began to suffer financial problems, especially as the Vietnam War replaced the Civil Rights movement as the most pressing national problem in the minds of many white liberals. Although it was never completely united, the Civil Rights movement became increasingly fragmented after de jure segregation ceased. De facto segregation and discrimination created new challenges, and there was no longer a consensus as to goals, tactics, or leaders. More troubling, the racial division in America was growing rather than diminishing. As noted by the Kerner Commission on Civil Disorders, led by Illinois governor Otto Kerner and appointed by President Johnson to report on the causes of the recent urban unrest, by the spring of 1968, America was rapidly moving towards "two societies, one black and one white—

separate and unequal." De facto divisions between the races might be as large and oppressive in nature as de jure differences had been at the height of Jim Crow.[51]

The successful abolishment of the Central Jurisdiction was another product of what one historian has termed a "rights revolution." During the 1960s, Americans expanded the notion of basic rights through a series of Supreme Court decisions, new federal government legislation, and grassroots citizens' movements. The Warren Court made a number of important decisions that protected the rights of individuals against government and societal infringements. Many of these decisions were controversial—none more so than those relating to prayer in public schools—but whether church members supported these decisions or not, the impact of them was to broaden individual rights. National legislation such as the Civil Rights Act of 1964 not only protected African Americans, but also specifically included women. Medicare and Medicaid expanded medical aid to the elderly and indigent populations. While not the same as national health insurance, the programs established a federal responsibility in an area that had been dependent upon local government and private charity. Finally, many citizens' groups did not wait for the government, but formed organizations to empower themselves. Women's organizations became a prime example of the new era, with the National Organization for Women (NOW) becoming the largest feminist organization. The concept of rights changed radically during the 1960s, and one victory in this revolution was the end of the Central Jurisdiction. In terms of American society, it was a small event, but for African American Methodists it was monumental. A dream long deferred had come to pass.[52]

The achievements during the quadrennium were impressive but still incomplete. Most important, the Central Jurisdiction was dismantled because it was not included in the new church constitution. All but three annual conferences of the jurisdiction approved their transfer into regional jurisdictions before 1968, and at least one con-

51. The official name of the Kerner Commission was the National Advisory Commission on Civil Disorders. Quote from *Report of the National Advisory Commission on Civil Disorders*, 1. On Black Power, see Steven F. Lawson, *Running for Freedom: Civil Rights and Black Politics in America since 1941*, 113–34; Robert Weisbrot, *Freedom Bound: A History of America's Civil Rights Movement*, 196–221.
52. Patterson, *Grand Expectations*, 565–77.

ference accomplished a transfer and merger into each of the regional jurisdictions that overlapped the Central Jurisdiction. Moreover, even in the Southeastern Jurisdiction, transfer of African American annual conferences had been approved by a two-thirds majority despite the target date of mid-1972 for merger of annual conferences. All this was done without a mass defection of southern white Methodists or African American Methodists. The minority report presented to the 1966 General Conference was not a serious threat, and while the Omnibus Resolution did not sail through the Southeastern Jurisdiction, it did not fail. Voluntarism prevailed for yet another four years, despite the efforts of some African American Methodists to extract a more concrete and detailed agreement. Nevertheless, despite the optimism of Slutz and many other Methodist leaders, a target date still left annual conference mergers indefinite and allowed for the possibility of yet another breakdown on the road to an inclusive church.[53]

For African American Methodists, the church was moving in the right direction, but they had to move in faith for the process to continue. This was the same dilemma African American Methodists had already experienced and that their ancestors had lived with continually. The new United Methodist Church offered all its members a new challenge and a new opportunity in terms of racial brotherhood. The challenge was enormous because the racial problems in society were compounding instead of diminishing. Advances in de jure equality increased the appetite of African Americans for de facto equality. Within the church, African American Methodists wanted inclusiveness to create a brotherhood that truly transcended all racial barriers. After the end of the Central Jurisdiction, this struggle continued with no less intensity. The new United Methodist Church would face the task of building a degree of racial brotherhood that neither the Methodist Church nor any large American church had achieved. This building of an inclusive church would not be easy, and it would require the church to be more aggressive in fighting racism in American society. Without true inclusiveness, the United Methodist Church would be a church without racial structures but with little genuine fellowship.

53. The Tennessee-Kentucky Annual Conference held a special session in February 1968 and voted to transfer and merge into the Southeastern Jurisdiction, reversing its earlier rejection of the Omnibus Resolution.

8

"Blest Be the Tie That Binds"

Blest be the tie that binds
Our hearts in Christian love;
The fellowship of kindred minds
Is like to that above.

—hymn by John Fawcett

THE UNITED METHODIST CHURCH, created by the merger of the Methodist Church and the Evangelical United Brethren Church in April 1968, confronted three layers of racial difficulty. The first problem was how to end the remaining racial structures in the new church, particularly the remaining racially segregated annual conferences in the Southeastern and South Central jurisdictions. In 1968, this was the most obvious racial challenge and the one for which there was the largest consensus for action. However, there was still considerable opposition in parts of the Deep South among white Methodists, who disliked even the plan of desegregation outlined in the 1967 Omnibus Resolution. Clearly, despite agreement that action had to be taken, there was no consensus on how to act. In addition, some African American Methodists rejected as inadequate the church's mid-1972 target date established for the end of racial structures.

The second racial problem concerned how to improve interracial harmony and fellowship among Methodists. The new church accepted the goal of being racially inclusive, but the practical meaning of *inclusive* was hotly debated. Among African American Methodists, there was anxiety over full acceptance in the life of the church. They did not want their white colleagues to ignore them. For African American ministers, the church would have to make substantial progress in inclusiveness before they would have equal professional opportunity. For African American laity, the church had to open itself so they were not marginalized. For both African American ministers and laity, tokenism now replaced rigid exclusion as the major challenge to inclusiveness.

The third racial problem confronting United Methodists was how to make the church an agent for racial justice and equality within American society. This was the most difficult, prophetic, and controversial of the challenges. Many United Methodists doubted that the church should clean up ghettos, educate African American people about their history, or concentrate its benevolent resources on inner city ministry. Nevertheless, to the most zealous advocates of racial inclusiveness, this was the truest call and greatest test of Methodism's convictions. If the church used its power and influence for programs and projects that reached mainly middle-class white people, then inclusiveness was shallow and without spiritual power—pious words followed by pitiful action. This was the most difficult challenge to the church because it confronted the Great Myth, which insisted that race relations remained a problem only in the South. For the church to tackle de facto discrimination and prejudice entailed great risk of alienating many white Methodists in all regions.

In February 1968, three hundred African American Methodists who were eager for the church to interpret inclusiveness in the broadest possible manner formed Black Methodists for Church Renewal (BMCR), the church's first ethnic caucus. Funded with the assistance of the Women's Division of Christian Social Relations, participants included James Farmer, who was a former national director of CORE and a Methodist minister's son, and SNCC leader Stokely Carmichael. BMCR saw itself as a prophetic movement calling the church to be a servant to society's neediest, instead of a comfort to the privileged. The new organization called for a church that supported African American liberation with local African American churches leading in the transformation of the inner cities. BMCR also charged that African American congregations were supporting Methodist benevolence funds that took money out of their community rather than assisting those in grinding poverty. BMCR wanted the church to adopt racial inclusiveness thoroughly and to undergo a radical change in its programs and practices. BMCR did not spare African American Methodists from its criticism. The BMCR conference findings confessed, "we have not always been relevant in service and ministry to our black brothers, and in so doing we have alienated ourselves from many of them," and "we have not always been honest with ourselves and with our white brothers. . . . Instead, we have told our white brothers what we thought they would like to hear."[1]

By the time United Methodists arrived in Dallas, Texas, for their first General Conference of the new church, significant changes had transformed the Civil Rights movement. On April 4, 1968, Martin Luther King Jr. was assassinated while visiting Memphis, Tennessee. King had gone to Memphis to support striking garbage workers at the request of Rev. James M. Lawson, an African American Methodist leader and a founder of BMCR, and against the wishes of his top aides, who wanted him to concentrate on the upcoming Poor People's Campaign. Because Lawson had been a close ally in the freedom struggle for a number of years, King responded to Lawson's plea for help.[2]

King's assassination set off a new wave of rioting across the country and left the Civil Rights movement without a single dominant voice.

1. Although there was already a Methodists for Church Renewal organization that had many common interests with the new organization, African American Methodists involved in BMCR did not want to depend upon any white-controlled organization to represent the needs and concerns of black people; see "Statement by Black Methodists for Church Renewal," 268, 268–73; James M. Lawson Jr., "Black Churchmen Seek Methodist Renewal," *Christian Advocate*, March 7, 1968, 24; Richey, *Methodist Conference*, 191–92.

2. The same age as King, Lawson had been a conscientious objector during the 1950s and had been dismissed from Vanderbilt Divinity School by the chancellor of the university in 1960 for leading civil rights demonstrations in Nashville. J. Robert Nelson, "Vanderbilt's Time of Testing," *Christian Century*, August 10, 1960, 921. At one point, twelve of sixteen divinity school professors threatened to resign because of Lawson's dismissal, but an eventual settlement of the crisis satisfied ten of those faculty members. For an account of the early career of Rev. James M. Lawson, see David Halberstam, *The Children*, 24–50, 60–62.

Already King had encountered numerous problems as he attempted to lead the movement outside the South. He died at a time when many younger militants found him passé and many white Americans found his attacks on economic injustice and the Vietnam War disturbing. Yet King's message of nonviolence, his eloquent appeals to both the Bible and American ideals, and his personal courage still commanded enormous respect. King's death was a severe blow to all who had faith in America's ability to redress its problems, and his death deprived American society of one of the most influential church leaders of the postwar period. The widespread rioting after King's assassination was larger than any previous unrest during the decade and seemed another sign that American society might disintegrate into continuous strife.

Another change in the ongoing struggle for civil rights was the continued growth of the Black Power movement. The early Civil Rights movement had built a loose alliance of African Americans assisted by the financial support and physical presence of white liberals. This biracial alliance was under great strain from several sources. One factor was the violence in the South, which largely attacked African Americans, although there were some white victims, also. There were at least thirteen killings in 1963, fourteen in 1964, and twenty in 1965. Violence against African American civil rights workers had taken quite a toll on many African American leaders, especially within the SNCC, and it fed perceptions among militant African Americans that ultimately the struggle for freedom depended solely on the efforts of African Americans. Black Power advocates in CORE and SNCC expelled white members in a move that many observers interpreted as racist.[3]

Additionally, the Vietnam War had escalated and divided the nation between hawks, who supported Lyndon Johnson's handling of the war, and doves, who opposed the war in Vietnam. Particularly after the 1968 Tet offensive, many Americans questioned their nation's role in the war. People who had accepted the "domino theory" expounded by President Eisenhower and others began to believe that the United States was in a quagmire with no way out. Many

3. Carson, *In Struggle*, 215–43; August Meier and Elliott Rudwick, *CORE: A Study in the Civil Rights Movement, 1942–1968*, 374–408.

Americans who compared the Vietnam War with World War II and the Korean War decided that Vietnam was not nearly as noble or moral. The antiwar movement grew considerably but at the expense of diverting attention away from civil rights and racial matters. The Tet offensive had also driven Lyndon Johnson from the presidential race after Johnson won the New Hampshire primary by an unimpressive margin over Minnesota senator Eugene McCarthy.

Mainline American churches found the war a difficult issue to confront. Most churches, including the Methodist Church, had supported the United States' anticommunist Cold War foreign policy. In lending their support to the cause of political freedom, American churches found it difficult to disengage from U.S. policies in Vietnam, even though U.S. actions in the Vietnam War did not resemble actions of the earlier wars. From a number of sides, American society was under severe stress, and many citizens, both white and African American, felt alienated and distressed.

The 1968 Episcopal Address in Dallas emphasized that the times demanded vigorous action by Methodists regarding both America's social and spiritual ills. The bishops recommended that Methodists make a special trip to the shattered areas of cities and visit the schools, stores, and apartments. For most Methodists, what they would see would be startling and deeply disturbing. The bishops judged that these conditions of poverty, crime, and hopelessness in a land as rich as America were "A failure of the imagination, of humane sympathies, of the will, of Christian convictions." They also asserted that the church had a mission of reconciliation and that the message could not wait.[4]

One response of the 1968 General Conference was the creation of a $20 million Bishops' Fund for Reconciliation. The fund, separate from traditional world service benevolence funds, established up to $20 million for programs that assisted those suffering from the poorest conditions and in most critical need. The national church would distribute half the funds, and half would remain in the annual conference from which the funds originated. This was Methodism's reaction to urban riots and social unrest, and it was an ambitious program launched to demonstrate the church's continuing relevance to the issues of the day. Because of the urgency of the task, annual

4. 1968 General Conference *Journal*, 231.

conferences were to raise the money immediately. Church leaders believed that tumultuous times required new benevolence for people whom the church had forgotten.[5]

Another sign of the zeal for action was the expansion of the Commission of Twenty-Four's recommendation for a successor commission. Instead of a commission that would largely oversee conference mergers, the General Conference authorized establishment of a Commission on Religion and Race, with a mandate to promote local church racial inclusiveness and to work "with various prophetic movements for racial and social justices." Instead of $25,000, as recommended by the Commission of Twenty-Four, the General Conference authorized $700,000 for the new commission. This was an enormous change and represented a new seriousness of purpose. This funding would permit the new commission to assist in the merger of the remaining racially segregated annual conferences, promote racial inclusiveness in local churches, monitor minority representation and employment in church agencies, and maintain relations with AME, AMEZ, and CME denominations.[6]

There was considerable controversy over the composition of the commission because the original motion, presented by Roy Nichols, an African American minister from New York, mandated that there be a majority of African American members on the new commission. This created friction with both those who wanted a broader minority representation (to include Hispanic, Native American, and Asian American Methodists), and those who questioned any guaranteed racial composition. The General Conference approved legislation that required each jurisdictional conference to elect two African American members and at least one other ethnic/minority member among their five representatives and that the commission elect three more African American members and one more ethnic/minority member for the seven at-large members. This guaranteed that the majority of the commission's members would be nonwhites. However, at the same time, the General Conference asked the Judicial Council to rule on the constitutionality of this quota system.[7]

The majority of the Interim Judicial Council concluded "that

5. Ibid., 1863–64.
6. Ibid., 1288.
7. Ibid., 405–7, 412–14.

mandated inclusion by race necessarily results in enforced exclusion because of race." This would thus violate the new constitution's provision that all United Methodists shared the full rights and privileges of membership "regardless of race or status." The dissenting judges argued that the General Conference did have the power to mandate a quota system. In their opinion, the dissenters noted that nothing in the church constitution prohibited "the General Conference from giving consideration to race in making certain that ethnic, national, and other groups are included in the work of achieving an inclusive color blind church." Moreover, they continued, "It is not realistic to conclude that, by the written declaration of the ideal of a racially inclusive church and a prohibition against exclusion, the result will be accomplished without positive, and in some instances, special action to correct the racial exclusion and separation historically created and currently existent in some aspects of the Church's life." After the Judicial Council's ruling, the General Conference changed the legislation so that the racial composition of the Commission on Religion and Race was recommended rather than mandated. This easily passed with the net result that the church accepted affirmative action in principle but rejected racial quotas. Essentially, the church arrived at the position that the U.S. Supreme Court would take in the 1978 *Bakke* decision, which affirmed consideration of race and gender but prohibited any quota system.[8]

The 1968 General Conference did encounter yet another attempt to discard voluntarism as a means of ending segregated annual conferences. Buoyed by the Omnibus Resolution's success and its provisions for ending segregated annual conferences by mid-1972, the Commission of Twenty-Four continued to advocate voluntarism. Some African American leaders and white liberals disagreed with both the commission's optimism and continued reliance on voluntarism. Therefore, William James, an African American minister from New York, offered a constitutional amendment that required an end to all segregated annual conferences "not later than the Jurisdictional Conferences of 1972." James pointed out that the church had provided a great deal of time, yet, despite some progress, there was still much yet to do. However, others, led by Commission of

8. Ibid., 967–68, 971, 972.

Twenty-Four's chair Leonard Slutz, argued that such a constitutional amendment was unnecessary and would be counterproductive by creating a new impediment to mergers. The conference decided to accept the continuation of voluntarism over an absolute deadline.[9]

Besides maintaining voluntarism, the General Conference also accepted the Commission of Twenty-Four's recommendation regarding pension and salary support for merging conferences. The national church had to accept more of the financial burden for mergers to take place in the Deep South because it had ignored very low pensions and inadequate minimum salary scales in the Central Jurisdiction for years. The resulting difference in pensions between white and African American annual conferences was substantial, especially concerning minimum salaries. The disparity in minimum salaries could derail annual conference mergers, because without substantial outside aid, white ministers voting for merger could also be voting to reduce minimum salary levels in their annual conferences.[10]

To deal with these financial problems, the General Conference authorized a new payment plan that would increase temporary funding assistance for both pensions and minimum salaries. The aid would start at 100 percent of the new burden on merging conferences and decline by five percent a year so that over a twenty-year period the national church would cease to provide financial aid to annual conferences. Annual conferences where there was no merger (because there was no overlapping annual conference) would send money to the fund, while annual conferences with a heavy burden would receive a credit entitling them to money from the fund. The plan encountered little opposition because the church wanted to minimize the financial strain on merging annual conferences.[11]

A final issue regarding greater racial justice was the economic power of the church and its employment practices. The General Conference endorsed Project Equality, an effort to gain adoption of fair employment practices by all major U.S. churches. Organized by the National Catholic Conference on Interracial Justice, Project Equality heightened awareness among churches regarding their

9. "Report of the Commission on Interjurisdictional Relations [Commission of Twenty-Four]," 1968 General Conference *Journal*, 1761–77, 1326, 811–17.
10. 1968 General Conference *Journal*, 1762–74.
11. Ibid., 424–30.

economic power and influence to open doors to minority employment, especially among businesses that dealt with national church bodies. In this area, the chief concern among Methodists was the Methodist Publishing House (MPH), the world's largest religious publishing concern, which critics charged discriminated against African American workers and had failed to join Project Equality before the General Conference. There had been criticism of the racial practices of the MPH for over a decade, but never an investigation by the national church. The conference appointed a special committee to investigate the racial and labor practices of the MPH and report back to the Council of Bishops. However, this decision came after enlarging the size of the investigative committee from five persons appointed by the bishops to sixteen members, with five of the sixteen recommended to be African American Methodists. The conference also ordered the MPH to include African American Methodists on its staff. Because of the abolition of the Central Jurisdiction and its newspaper, *The Central Christian Advocate*, there was no longer an African American editor on the MPH's managerial staff.[12]

The new United Methodist Church emerged from Dallas moving cautiously toward increased social action. Desegregation was the order of the day, but the church leadership expected annual conferences to work out the logistical details with the national church providing financial assistance. The church rejected a deadline that might upset many white southern members, but its patience was coming to an end. The mid-1972 target date had strong support. However, on the larger issue of establishing a more racially just society, the General Conference exhibited ambivalence. It authorized both a large program of reconciliation and renewal under the administration of the bishops and created an expanded commission to monitor the church's progress toward racial inclusiveness. Nevertheless, creation of the Bishops' Fund for Reconciliation did not ensure its success since the moneys would come from additional funds rather than from reallocated church funds. If those funds did not materialize, then the church's aid to the neediest would not dramatically change. The Commission on Religion and Race provided a new

12. Ibid., 577–81.

avenue for seeking racial justice within the church, but it was one agency within a large institution. It would need the active support of bishops, annual conferences, and local congregations to accomplish significant work.

There were similarities between the 1967 General Convention of the Episcopal Church and the 1968 Methodist General Conference. Presiding Bishop John Hines of the Episcopal Church believed that the inner-city crisis was acute and required a massive restructuring of church resources. Challenging the General Convention to respond in a dramatic way, Hines got the Episcopal Church to establish a special fund of $9 million over three years that would be used to fight poverty chiefly in the inner city. This money, which would come both from the general church funds and from the United Thank Offering of the General Division of Women's Work, would be distributed outside the normal Episcopal bureaucracy in the hope that it would be more efficacious in meeting the needs of the inner cities. At nearly one-quarter the national church's budget, the intent of the program was to make the largely white and affluent church relevant and caring. Yet this special program drew criticism from some African American Episcopal priests, who claimed it was led too much by white liberals and inadequately used the resources of African American priests and parishes, who were much more intimately knowledgeable about the needs of inner cities.[13]

Following the 1968 General Conference, the next step Methodists took toward reconciliation was the merger of African American and white annual conferences. By 1968, there was some prior experience and research to guide those involved in this task. Merger of the Delaware and Washington annual conferences of the Central Jurisdiction with the Baltimore and Peninsula annual conferences of the Northeastern Jurisdiction revealed that lay members were more opposed to merger than clergy, although clergy were more directly affected by issues of salaries and pensions. In addition, annual conference mergers seemed to have little impact upon inclusiveness on the local church level. Most important for building racial inclusiveness was the willingness of local congregations to reach out to all geographic residents of the immediate area. Most integrated congre-

13. Shattuck, *Episcopalians and Race*, 176–82.

gations were in urban areas undergoing the process of residential integration, and stable integrated neighborhoods were not common; white flight to suburbs was the general trend. The typical integrated congregation was, in fact, a church in transition from all-white to all–African American.[14]

At its root, the problem of few integrated, stable congregations was an attitude problem within local congregations. Was a congregation willing to address racial prejudice, and could it open its doors to all races? Was it willing to include African Americans in all church affairs and activities? A sermon or two would not make a congregation inclusive. It would require a conscious choice by the leadership, ratified by the general membership, to institute procedures to be truly open and inviting. Most local congregations lacked both the leadership and faith to take up this challenge.

A study of the merger of the West Texas Annual Conference of the Central Jurisdiction showed a different set of problems in rural areas. Here, most of the Central Jurisdiction congregations were small and remotely located, and merger agreements involved not one or two but six overlapping annual conferences. Moreover, the weaknesses of ministerial professionalism (there were many part-time ministers and ministers who had to depend upon other employment for income) in this annual conference made negotiations difficult. In West Texas, there was a high number of extremely small congregations (under thirty members) with little money to support even a part-time pastor. This situation was likely to produce restructuring, such as consolidating churches or even closing down congregations. If white administrators began these steps immediately after merger, there would be a belief among African American Methodists that merger had simply brought havoc to their congregations when, in fact, many of these churches were already in precarious positions. If an annual conference merger produced the realignment of parishes with more interracial congregations or ministers serving small churches regardless of race, then it could provide a new solution to a vexing administrative problem. However, many white Methodists in these

14. James H. Davis and Robert L. Wilson, "Towards a Racially Inclusive Methodist Church," National Division of the Board of Missions, Methodist Church, Philadelphia, Pa., January, 1966, 1–18, GCAH.

conferences understood merger as simply absorbing a small number of African American Methodists into their conference. This attitude did not produce genuine racial reconciliation.[15]

Nationally, the summer and fall of 1968 proved as tumultuous as the beginning of the year. Senator Robert Kennedy, a harsh critic of Johnson's Vietnam policies, became the front-runner for the Democratic nomination for president by winning the California primary in June. However, as he left the hotel ballroom after acknowledging victory in the California primary, he was shot and died the next morning. The Democratic convention in Chicago that summer became infamous for the police brutality against demonstrators assembled in Grant Park. Hubert Humphrey won his party's nomination but found his fellow Democrats dispirited and divided. Richard Nixon represented the Republican party, promising that he had a secret plan to end the Vietnam War. Although late in the campaign Humphrey closed the gap in public opinion polls, Nixon won the election. Third-party candidate George Wallace showed that a block of Americans considered both major parties too liberal. Although Wallace eventually received only 13.5 percent of the popular vote, he did significantly better than expected outside the Deep South with his tough rhetoric against hippies, antiwar demonstrators, and liberals. Nixon was less visceral than Wallace was, yet he tapped into the broad disgust among white Americans who were appalled and frightened by several years of urban riots and campus unrest. For liberal Americans, the shift in the political climate between 1964 and 1968 was profound and unsettling.[16]

Within this changing atmosphere, the Commission on Religion and Race organized late in 1968. It faced challenges because creating an entirely new staff was difficult and the persons involved were busy with annual and jurisdictional conferences, which met after the

15. James H. Davis, "Suggestions for the West Texas Conference in Preparation for Conference Mergers," Department of Research and Survey, National Division, Board of Missions, United Methodist Church, New York, N.Y., July 22, 1968, 1–22, GCAH; James H. Davis, "Next Steps for the West Texas Conference in Preparation for Conference Mergers," Department of Research and Survey, National Division, Board of Missions, United Methodist Church, New York, N.Y., January 8, 1969, 1–38, GCAH.

16. Patterson, *Grand Expectations*, 692–709; Matusow, *Unraveling of America*, 395–439.

General Conference. Rev. Woodie White, an African American minister from the Detroit Annual Conference, was selected the executive secretary of the commission. He had strong activist credentials. He had been among those Methodist ministers who had traveled to Jackson, Mississippi, and been arrested trying to integrate Methodist churches there, and he also had close links to the leaders of Black Methodists for Church Renewal. He was not afraid of saying that many white Methodists were racists and that much racism still existed within the church.[17]

White and the commission faced several daunting tasks. First, they wanted to promote merger of annual conferences, but they had little role other than as advisers. Second, they wanted to educate white Methodists regarding de facto discrimination at a time when African American militancy was putting more and more white Americans on the defensive. A part of this job included interpreting African American militancy to people who were quite skeptical that militancy had produced anything other than riots and lawlessness. Third, the commission had to gain the trust of other minority groups within the United Methodist Church, including Hispanic, Native American, and Asian American Methodists.

The commission's job of racial reconciliation was made more difficult by the proclamation of the Black Manifesto by James Forman in April 1969 at the National Black Economic Development Conference. Forman excoriated white America for its racial injustices, both past and present, and demanded $500 million in reparations from white churches and synagogues. Although Forman's demand was in character with Old Testament prophets and his militant tactics could be compared with Jesus driving the money changers from the Temple, most white churchgoers, including Methodists, greeted the manifesto with disdain or contempt. They particularly rejected its Marxist rhetoric, justification of violence, and demand for money to be controlled by a narrow group led by Forman. Their ire only increased as Forman and his followers began showing their serious intentions by disrupting church services and occupying the New York offices of the National Council of Churches. Many white

17. White's arrest in Mississippi was resolved in 1965. See Francis B. Stevens to Dr. Grover C. Bagby, November 29, 1965, GBCS.

Methodists were disturbed when some Methodist leaders wrote statements that praised parts of the manifesto. For example, *World Outlook*, the publication of the Board of Missions, editorialized in June 1969, "if we cut through the revolutionary rhetoric of the Black Manifesto (which isn't easy to do), it is clear that the churches have not begun to repent of their complicity in slavery, in the enslavement of the black man. . . . Perhaps this is God's way of reminding us that the Gospel makes radical claims upon us." The editorial concluded, "For our screams of rage may be only the pain resulting from the exposure of a moral nerve." BMCR leader James Lawson thoroughly repudiated Forman's justification of violence, comparing it to the violence of the U.S. government in Vietnam, but he praised the goals of the manifesto and called for a transformation of the church and its allocation of funds.[18]

The manifesto provoked a great deal of soul-searching within the church. Bishop Roy Short wrote several memos regarding the manifesto, pointing out that the United Methodist Church had established its Fund for Reconciliation the year before the manifesto. Additionally, Short noted, Methodist benevolence funds were not going to Forman or his organization, and he believed the church should pressure the government to do more for African Americans. Yet if there was any uncertainty among Methodist leaders as to the reaction of many church members to the Black Manifesto, they could get some indication from opposition to the Delta Ministry project of the National Council of Churches (NCC) in Mississippi. Begun in late 1964 in the poorest section of Mississippi, the project was an attempt by the NCC to aid African Americans in need of both economic development and political power. The NCC also hoped to initiate reconciliation between African American and white Mississippians, but the project leaders quickly found that white church leaders wanted nothing to do with it. Methodist bishop Edward Pendergrass became an outspoken critic of the Delta Ministry. Some local congregations began withholding funds designated for the NCC

18. World Outlook, "A Reparations Jubilee," 151, 152; James Lawson, "A Nonviolent Endorsement," 78–91; Findlay, *Church People*, 200–225. For liberal reaction to the manifesto, see *Christianity and Crisis*, May 26, 1969, 141–43; *Christian Century*, May 21, 1969, 701; *Christian Century*, June 18, 1969, 832–33; and *Christian Century*, June 25, 1969, 861, 866–67.

as a means of expressing disapproval of the Delta Ministry project. Other bishops also received a steady stream of letters criticizing the church's donations to the NCC, even though it was only pennies per member each year, and most of the NCC's activities were not as controversial as the Delta Ministry.[19]

Woodie White made interpreting the Black Manifesto to United Methodist Church leaders part of his mission. The Commission on Religion and Race reprinted the manifesto and gathered bishops and heads of church boards and agencies to study the document and consider possible responses. White distanced himself from Forman's Marxist rhetoric, but he supported the call for substantially increased economic aid for African Americans. His efforts were more than matched by BMCR, which endorsed the Black Manifesto and campaigned for, among other changes, a reallocation of Methodist higher education resources toward twelve church-related, African American colleges. Rejecting a Methodist Board of Education offer of $2 million in emergency funding, BMCR called for providing these institutions with $20 million annually over the next five years.[20]

While the manifesto threatened to divide Methodists further, merger of annual conferences still produced controversy, because of the instances of merger where African American Methodists received no leadership roles. For example, merger in Florida occurred in 1969, but no African American minister became a district superintendent in the new annual conference. This meant a white bishop had an entirely white cabinet in a supposedly racially inclusive annual conference. Writing in the church's *Christian Advocate*, White chided "[t]he audacity of white persons to claim they had the administrative skills and sensitivity to lead black people, but that black leadership does not possess the administrative skills and sensitivity to lead white people." By 1970, five other Southeastern Jurisdiction annual conferences had completed merger without appointing a single Afri-

19. Findlay, *Church People*, 142–43; for Bishop Roy H. Short memorandums regarding the manifesto, see "The Black Manifesto," "The Reactions in the Churches," "Observations," and "General Observations," Short Papers, EU.

20. Woodie W. White, "Executive Secretary's Report to the Commission on Religion and Race," not dated, 1–2; Bernard E. Garnett, "Black Protest: Will It Split the United Methodists?" Race Relations Information Center, Nashville, Tenn., November 1969, 2–3, Commission on Religion and Race, GCAH.

can American district superintendent. This did not bode well for reconciliation.[21]

The Commission on Religion and Race also found the task of encouraging merger of annual conferences difficult. Terminology was itself an issue, since it did not help to move beyond race if conferences were always designated as either white or black. In South Carolina, the two overlapping conferences referred to each other by the date of their founding, and in Louisiana the conferences became the Louisiana A and B conferences. Progress was slow and not without setbacks. In March 1969, a study document concerning merger in Alabama concluded, "There are still vast numbers of laymen and ministers who neither understand [n]or accept the proposal," and, it concluded, "Let our work, like prayer, be persistent." A merger plan in Georgia that had been accepted by the African American annual conference and the white northern Georgia conference was rejected by the white conference in southern Georgia, causing additional delay. In Mississippi, the two conferences formerly of the Central Jurisdiction and their two white overlapping conferences only began study of merger. Merger talks also dragged on in Arkansas and Louisiana. Progress came more slowly than the Commission of Twenty-Four had envisioned in its report to the 1968 General Conference. The Omnibus Resolution provided a general framework to encourage merger, but the Omnibus Resolution did not make compromise any easier on specific issues.[22]

The struggle for direction was quite evident at a special session of the General Conference held in April 1970 in St. Louis, Missouri, the fifth general conference in a decade. Even before the conference opened, there were signs of unrest. African American militants entered the preconference meeting of the Council of Bishops and engaged in a short shoving contest with the bishops. On Sunday,

21. White's disgust was surpassed by that of BMCR. It denounced merger agreements "in which white racism is accommodated and black people are negated and robbed of their humanity, integrity and dignity." Woodie W. White, "Black and White Merger at Any Cost," *Christian Advocate*, October 16, 1969, 9; BMCR, "Position Paper on Merger of Black and White Annual Conferences in the Southeastern and South Central Jurisdictions," February 20–23, 1969, 1, Commission on Religion and Race, GCAH; 1970 General Conference *Journal*, 843.

22. T. Leo Brannon, ed., "Study Paper for Tri-Conference Advisory Committee on Merger" March 18, 1969, 33, Commission of Religion and Race, GCAH.

the day before the conference, police arrested demonstrators at the Centenary United Methodist Church in St. Louis, the largest Methodist congregation in the city. The demonstrators had planned a "testimonial witness" in the midst of the Sunday morning service. The stage was set for a confrontation between those who wanted a more prophetic and revolutionary church and those who wanted no major changes.[23]

The Episcopal Address acknowledged the deeply distressing times, particularly the strong hold racism had on American society. Bishop J. Gordon Howard, speaking for the council, admitted, "Advances in eliminating racism do not come easily. Those in control do not readily relinquish privileges that they have enjoyed, and they exert pressures and restrictions which often are cruel." The bishops also entreated delegates to work for unity so that the church might be effective in the world. In this emotionally charged atmosphere, the bishops may have feared that demonstrators might disrupt the General Conference proceedings.[24]

On the second day, the General Conference voted to allow BMCR to make an appeal to the conference. About five hundred persons, mostly African Americans, entered the auditorium and encircled the delegates as James Lawson presented a series of demands for action. He called for the church to build reconciliation between African American and white Methodists by empowering African Americans both in the church and society through rechanneling Methodist wealth to aid those in greatest need. The church needed not only to increase funding dramatically, but also to allow African American people to control the use of those funds. Specifically, BMCR requested 25 percent of World Service annual funds be given to BMCR for its ministry to inner cities and that the entire balance of the Fund for Reconciliation ($5 million) go to BMCR for com-

---

23. The special session had been authorized at the conclusion of the 1968 General Conference in anticipation that problems might emerge regarding EUB-Methodist union. The Council of Bishops attempted to cancel the meeting, because union was going so smoothly that they believed the session was unnecessary and wasteful even if the special session had been authorized only for a short, five-day meeting. However, the Judicial Council ruled that the Council of Bishops lacked the authority to cancel the meeting. 1970 General Conference *Journal*, 362–65; Alan Geyer, "Mishmash and Renewal," *Christian Century*, May 6, 1970, 556–58.

24. 1970 General Conference *Journal*, 188.

munity self-determination. Additionally, it wanted $10 million for twelve Methodist-affiliated African American colleges and a special $1 million for a minority scholarship program. To insure greater representation of minorities in the governance of the church, BMCR wanted African Americans and other minorities to receive 30 percent of all board and agency positions as well the same percentage of jurisdictional and General Conference membership. Lawson implicitly acknowledged the audacity of these requests by comparing BMCR to the early Christian church in attempting to impact the lives of so many while starting with so few.[25]

To many Methodists, BMCR's proposal looked like a Methodist Black Manifesto. To turn so much money over to an organization that had no official church standing was not likely, and the amounts of money requested were not likely to be raised because the church offering goals were already not being met. Nevertheless, the conference seemed appreciative of the witness of BMCR and its dignified presentation. They were probably also relieved that the appeal was not like Forman's gun-toting invasions of some churches. BMCR's requests also probably strengthened the Commission on Religion and Race's calls for increased action. White and his commission made more modest requests, but BMCR emphasized the gravity of the need.

The report of the Commission on Religion and Race boldly stated, "White racism, subtle and overt, still pervades our Church." It also pointed out several flaws in efforts at merging the remaining racially separate annual conferences. The largest single problem was the continuing lack of communication between African American and white Methodists. Years of mistrust and the lack of formal communication had stymied efforts to be more inclusive, even where merger had taken place. Too often white Methodists believed that African American Methodists were joining "their" annual conferences, an attitude that fed the idea of tokenism. The commission stressed that mergers should create entirely new annual conferences, an open itinerancy, and the appointment of African American district superintendents. Apprehensions among African American Methodists included support for African American colleges and their community needs after merger. The commission also asked the General

25. Ibid., 188, 248–51.

Conference to prohibit any merging conferences from establishing different pension rates for African American and white ministers. No conference had done this, but apparently the idea had surfaced, so the commission felt the General Conference needed to prohibit this possibility.[26]

A study made by the Commission on Religion and Race examined the operation of Methodist homes and hospitals and showed the depth of institutional racism. The populations served by these institutions were overwhelmingly white and middle class. In part, this was due to economics, because many of the institutions bearing the Methodist name received only a small portion of their operating budget from the church, but it was also a consequence of the leadership of these institutions. The boards and directors of these church-affiliated institutions were 99 percent white Americans, which meant that minority concerns were not as likely to surface in decision making. The Commission on Religion and Race also highlighted the more overt racist action of some congregations in the South, which were opening their facilities to new private schools in the wake of public-school desegregation. Here the commission called for tough church legislation to enforce the new Methodist constitution's prohibition of racially restrictive programs.[27]

The General Conference also received the report of a special panel established in 1968 to investigate the racial and employment practices of the Methodist Publishing House. The study committee of the MPH was, in fact, an inquiry into the Christian ethics of one of the church's largest agencies. If the church were to be truly racially inclusive, its agencies would have to operate not by the standards of secular society, but by the standards of the church's teachings. The report revealed that the MPH had failed to live up to the church's social teaching.[28]

No area of this failure was more apparent than employment practices. The MPH study produced a grim picture of discrimination and racism. Of the 352 professional positions throughout the MPH, African American workers held only 1.1 percent of the jobs, but at the bottom of the employment scale, they held 78.6 percent of the

26. Ibid., 820, 838–45.
27. Ibid., 854–60, 866–68.
28. Ibid., 722–57.

jobs. In Nashville, Tennessee, where the MPH had its headquarters and the majority of its printing presses, African American workers comprised 97.7 percent of the lowest ranks of workers. One example of the discrimination cited by the committee dealt with the Stock Department, where African American workers made $2.30 an hour while white workers in the Mail Room, who did essentially the same job, received $3.13 an hour. When openings occurred in the Mail Room, rather than promoting stock handlers, managers hired new persons from the outside. The study committee recommended that workers who had been discriminated against receive financial compensation for past employment practices; that employed workers be given seniority when advancement possibilities occurred; and that the MPH intensify job training for lower-level employees. In addition, it suggested a full-time minority personnel manager to promote employment opportunities for minorities at the MPH.[29]

The study committee also investigated the MPH's dealing with Project Equality, which the 1968 General Conference had recommended that it join. The 1968 General Conference's action had not specified whether the MPH should join as a sponsoring organization or merely as a cooperating supplier. The distinction was important, because "sponsors" agreed to apply Project Equality's employment standards in choosing their suppliers, while "suppliers" would be required to show that they did not engage in any discriminatory hiring or promotion activities in their own internal employment practices. The controversy became more heated in October 1968 when the Board of Publications, on the advice of the MPH's president and publisher Lovick Pierce, voted not to affiliate with Project Equality even at the supplier status—an outright rejection of the 1968 General Conference's recommendation. This created a new wave of protests within the church, and the Board of Publications reversed its decision in March 1969 over the objections of Pierce and joined Project Equality, but only as a supplier. Obviously, joining as a sponsoring organization would have had greater impact, but the study committee, with some reluctance, concurred with the board's decision because of the difficulty in requiring compliance from suppliers. The study committee noted that the printing houses of five other denominations that had joined Project Equality in advance of

29. Ibid., 738–43.

the MPH had all joined at the supplier level, too. In sum, the special committee presented a gloomy picture of a major Methodist employer that operated with little consideration for social justice.[30]

The 1970 General Conference gave a mixed response to these reports and requests for reordering of priorities. Rather than give money to BMCR, the conference reallocated $2 million a year for 1971 and 1972 to the Commission on Religion and Race to use for assistance of minority groups. The funds would come entirely from other boards and agencies instead of a new appeal, which might not raise those funds. In response to the appeal for African American colleges, delegates voted to increase funding up to $2 million annually, but this was not a commitment of funds on hand. Instead, the conference authorized the money if the annual "Race Relations Sunday" offerings matched that total. Since giving to this designated offering had not exceeded $600,000 in any recent year, the commitment was far less than it appeared to be. Regarding minority representation within church boards and agencies, the conference narrowly defeated a constitutional amendment that would have given the General Conference the power to specify the number of minority representatives. The vote was 333 for and 169 against; 335 votes had been necessary to approve the amendment and submit it to annual conferences for ratification. This indicated that while a majority of delegates approved of affirmative action in principle, the church still would not allow any specified quota of minority representation. Finally, the General Conference disapproved of the use of Methodist facilities for private schools when the main purpose of those schools was to provide segregationist alternatives to newly integrated public schools.[31]

Many important items were still pending when the conference concluded because of a lack of a quorum; it was the first time that a General Conference had ever ended in this manner. Buried under an avalanche of memorials—typical for General Conferences—most committee reports never reached the floor of the conference for consideration. Also lost due to the abrupt end of the General Conference was official action on the report of the special committee investigat-

30. Ibid., 743–46.
31. Ibid., 231–38; 311–18, 322–26, 337; see also "Conference Acts...Tensions Relax," *Together,* July 1970, 11–17.

ing the MPH. This failure was the result of a novel stalling strategy led by Judge John Satterfield. On the fifth day, fearing that the church might be more responsive to a liberal agenda, Satterfield and others requested quorum calls as efforts were made to expedite consideration of items yet to be considered. On the third quorum call, Satterfield got his wish: the end of the General Conference.[32]

The conference had cost $600,000 and yielded only limited results. Inviting BMCR into the auditorium and listening to its demands was nearly as important as reallocating funds to the Commission on Religion and Race. The conference moved forward on building racial inclusiveness, but it did not take any major new initiatives. Regarding the merger of annual conferences, the General Conference only took the action of forbidding any merged conference(s) from establishing two different pension rates. Merger was still operating on the timetable established in 1968 that all racial structures in the church would cease by the 1972 jurisdictional conferences. The Commission on Religion and Race would continue to monitor progress and offer its advice, but it had no power to impose any solution to a conflict between overlapping conferences.

Georgia was an example of how tortuous the process of conference merger was at times. There, the white North Georgia and South Georgia annual conferences sought a merger agreement with the Georgia Annual Conference of the former Central Jurisdiction. Merger committees began work in 1968 and put a plan before all three annual conferences in 1969. The Georgia (African American) Annual Conference approved the plan by a vote of 116–7, as did the North Georgia conference, 624–217; but the South Georgia conference voted nonconcurrence with the plan by the lopsided margin of 400–289. A slightly modified plan was resubmitted in 1970, and the Georgia conference again approved, although with a decidedly less enthusiastic vote of 79–52. However, the South Georgia conference again voted against the plan, 351–313. The North Georgia conference, which met after South Georgia, had also rejected the modified plan but then chose to pursue a separate merger plan between it and the Georgia conference. This plan won approval by large majorities in both of these conferences, but it contained within it an all–African

32. 1970 General Conference *Journal*, 998–99; 337, 581; *Christian Century*, May 6, 1970, 557–58.

American district of congregations that overlapped the South Georgia conference. The plan also committed the newly merged conference to pursue an agreement with the South Georgia conference that would end this racial district as soon as possible. However, the Commission on Religion and Race found the arrangement sufficiently bizarre as to petition the Judicial Council for a ruling as to whether this plan of merger was valid. The Council ruled in July 1971 that it was constitutional because the plan was only a transitional arrangement toward a more inclusive church and that further action to erase this racial structure could be taken by the annual conferences, the Southeastern Jurisdictional Conference, or the General Conference.[33]

In Arkansas and Oklahoma, representatives of the African American Southwest Annual Conference failed to win acceptance of a merger plan with the overlapping white annual conferences because the Southwest conference maintained there should be an African American district superintendent in each new annual conference. Voting in the merger committee over this provision of the merger plan was almost strictly along racial lines, with only one of fourteen white members siding with the thirteen African Americans on the committee. In South Carolina, Bishop Paul Hardin Jr. took a vigorous role in working for a merger plan acceptable to both conferences, but negotiations begun in 1967 did not produce an acceptable plan until January 1972. Both White and Slutz were delighted with the news from South Carolina even though the merger plan retained separate racial districts until 1974. South Carolina was an important victory, because it was the largest single African American annual conference that merged with a single white conference. It also meant that the Commission on Religion and Race could report to the 1972 General Conference that racial structures still existed only in Mississippi, Alabama, and parts of Oklahoma and Arkansas.[34]

There was a great deal of impatience over the issue of conference merger. Bishop Kenneth Goodson, who presided over three Alabama

33. 1972 General Conference *Journal*, 636–43.
34. Leonard D. Slutz to Rev. Woodie W. White, January 20, 1971, and Woodie W. White to Leonard D. Slutz, February 1, 1971, Commission on Religion and Race, GCAH; Clayton E. Hammond, "Meeting of the Merger Committee of Southwest, Little Rock, North Arkansas, and Oklahoma Conferences," Fort Smith, Arkansas, March 22, 1971, Commission on Religion and Race, GCAH.

annual conferences that had yet to complete merger plans, admitted, "People are tired and weary of this issue and would like to have it settled and get on with the work of the Church." He continued in his letter to Slutz, "My own feeling... leads me to feel that the time has come for the General Conference to direct the Jurisdictional Conferences to constitute their areas as an inclusive Church in Jesus Christ." But instead of a plan imposed by the General Conference, the Commission on Religion and Race decided to propose to the 1972 General Conference that the jurisdictional conferences (Southeastern and South Central) merge annual conferences and that no conference be allowed to maintain any separate districts after 1973. This would put the burden of merger on jurisdictional conferences instead of the more remote General Conference, and it would allow separate structures in a conference to exist for only one transitional year. This plan had two distinct virtues. One, while foot draggers might complain yet again about the General Conference being a dictatorial, national government, this plan made jurisdictional conferences rather than the General Conference impose a final merger. Second, jurisdictional conferences might, in fact, come up with a better plan because they were closer to the situation, but they could not evade the deadline set by the entire church.[35]

The 1972 General Conference met in Atlanta, the first time the General Conference had met in the Deep South since the unification of the northern and southern forms of Methodism. Since 1944, the church had a nondiscrimination policy that had kept the General Conference out of the Southeastern Jurisdiction—the largest jurisdiction in the church—but recent changes in society ended this exclusion by 1972. The Council of Bishops wasted no time in considering the progress toward racial reconciliation. Early in the Episcopal Address, they noted that only four conferences of the former Central Jurisdiction had not reached merger agreements with overlapping white annual conferences. Yet the difficulty of merger was also apparent because all EUB annual conferences had voluntarily merged with overlapping Methodist conferences within four years instead of the twelve-year transitional period permitted under the plan of union. Ironically, it proved easier to unite annual conferences

35. Bishop Kenneth Goodson to Slutz, May 20, 1971, Commission on Religion and Race, GCAH; 1972 General Conference *Journal,* 1878–85, 708–14.

of two formerly distinct denominations than to unite racially separate annual conferences of the Methodist Church itself.[36]

The Commission on Religion and Race's plan to eliminate the last racial annual conferences came to an abrupt halt when the Judicial Council ruled the plan unconstitutional. The Council ruled that the General Conference could not require jurisdictional conferences to merge annual conferences, and that jurisdictional conferences could not impose merger on annual conferences. However, the Council did state that the General Conference could, on its own authority, impose a deadline for annual conferences to merge. This could be done by the 1973 annual conferences (it was already too late to expect the 1972 annual conferences to perfect a merger agreement). The church constitution gave the General Conference powers to determine annual conference boundaries in matters of supreme importance to the entire church, and eradication of racial structures indeed had such importance. The enabling legislation adopted in the union of the EUB and Methodist churches had provided a transitional period through 1972, but the General Conference could decide that this time had now expired. It could now impose a deadline and establish an arbitration process that would settle all outstanding differences should that deadline not be met.[37]

In line with the council's decision, the General Conference quickly drafted legislation that provided for a firm July 1973 deadline for all merger agreements. If the deadline was not met, a board of arbitration, consisting of the president of each of the involved jurisdictions' college of bishops, would resolve remaining differences. Part of the beauty of this arbitration board was that no one knew who its members would be, since the elections of jurisdictional colleges of bishops would be in the future. Slutz moved adoption of the new plan, concluding, "As we complete the elimination of racial structure, let us forever remember that we have not created a completely adequately fully inclusive church by this one act. We have taken a very important step, but think how much we have yet to do, and let us press on." At the 1956 General Conference, Slutz denied that the church was even segregated, but in the course of

36. 1972 General Conference *Journal,* 206.
37. Ibid., 710–13.

sixteen years, he and other white Methodists had grown aware of the depth of racism in their church and in American society.[38]

Still opposed to any plan that pressured conference mergers, Satterfield spoke in opposition, but when his five minutes ended, the General Conference refused his request for additional time. Another white Mississippi leader spoke against the deadline and board of arbitration, but a representative of one of the two African American Mississippi conferences argued that the plan would stop dilatory action. In the eight years since the first transfer and merger, the number of segregated annual conferences had slowly decreased, so that those who wanted more time had few supporters. Even within the Southeastern Jurisdiction, so much progress had occurred that delay had little support. Why would white Methodists in South Carolina, who had just agreed to merge, vote for additional delay in Mississippi, or why would northern Georgia white Methodists, who had merged with the overlapping African American annual conference, sympathize with recalcitrant white Methodists in southern Georgia? The church had slowly isolated all those who argued that more time was necessary. The majority spoke in an overwhelming manner for the report, and the delegates adjourned after singing "Blest Be the Tie That Binds."[39]

The General Conference also acted on several matters that had gone unresolved at the 1970 meeting. The entire Methodist Church affiliated with Project Equality as a sponsoring organization, which meant that all boards and agencies would not only review their employment practices for compliance with Project Equality's standards, but also choose their suppliers by those standards. This was a major step at widening the scope of affirmative action through the purchasing powers of the church. The church also accepted the report of the committee to investigate the MPH. The entire tenor of the report was much more positive than had been the 1970 report, in part because of changes in the top ranks of the publishing house. Loverick Pierce had stepped aside as president and publisher, and new affirmative action procedures had been implemented. Equally important, the Board of Publications had begun to supervise the

38. Ibid., 499.
39. Ibid., 499–503.

MPH in a meaningful manner, as recommended by the 1970 report, rather than act as a mere rubber stamp for approving the MPH's management.[40]

The General Conference also received reports from both the Fund for Reconciliation and the Fund for Black Colleges. Each had received increased funding at the 1970 General Conference. Bishop James K. Mathews, speaking about the Fund for Reconciliation, emphasized that its success was not measured strictly in the dollars spent, but also in the reshaping of church priorities and in the lives of people who had been earlier forgotten by the church. The work of the church was not finished, he said; instead, it had just begun. In reality, offerings for the Fund for Reconciliation reached only $13.5 million instead of the goal of $20 million for the quadrennium. Per capita, this was less than $1.50 for each Methodist during the quadrennium. However, the economic impact of the program was larger than the $13.5 million figure because many of the more than eight hundred projects created by the fund had attracted additional government and private foundation support. Funds for the Black Community Development program had been channeled to African American Methodist congregations to operate outreach programs in the areas of health care, education, welfare, housing, politics, economics, drug treatment, youth services, employment, prison reform, and communications. Reports to the General Conference also pointed out that the Black Community Development program had attracted thirteen project directors to seek ordination as ministers. This was an unintended blessing, given the critical shortage of African American ministers. It was also an indication that social-justice ministry and evangelism were not as distinct as some people believed.[41]

The report on Methodist African American colleges was a model of clarity and justification for these institutions. Historically, African American colleges have been the central institutions providing African American leadership in a variety of fields, including the ministry. Integration in higher education had created new competition, but it did not make these institutions obsolete. Most of the students at these institutions were African Americans who particularly wanted to attend a historically African American institution.

40. Ibid., 422, 1706–10.
41. Ibid., 391–93, 499–503, 1799–1833.

The largest problem facing these institutions was financial because, on top of the economic pressures on all private institutions of higher education, these schools had small endowments, low faculty salaries, and trustees who lacked adequate philanthropic resources to support institutional growth. The report agreed with the Carnegie Commission on Higher Education that recommended that private African American colleges aim to build their enrollment up to a thousand students to achieve an adequate enrollment base for their programs. The Commission on Black Colleges recommended to the General Conference a program of $5 million annually for the general education budgets of these institutions or approximately 25 percent of their combined budgets. Additionally, $1 million annually would be given for capital projects at these institutions. Together, the $6 million in annual contributions to these twelve institutions (one two-year college, ten four-year institutions, and Meharry Medical School) would be one means of obtaining greater racial justice. While acknowledging that the goal set by the 1970 General Conference had not been met (that of raising $5 million annually), the General Conference accepted this $6 million goal as "reasonable and attainable."[42]

Finally, the General Conference recognized that the ongoing work toward racial inclusiveness necessitated a permanent Commission on Religion and Race. Moreover, the legislation enlarged the organization of the commission by creating a Commission on Religion and Race for each annual conference throughout the church. This was both an affirmation of Woodie White's leadership of the commission and an admission that the church needed to keep itself honest. Racism in the church was far from defeated. The church needed continual vigilance to make progress in rooting out racism and working for racial justice in society. By waiting until 1972 to create a permanent annual conference body on religion and race, Methodists were acknowledging that ad hoc solutions were inadequate and could not produce the kind of dialogue and action that the church needed.[43]

Nowhere was the need for diligence more profound or apparent than in Mississippi. The political scientist V. O. Key noted in 1949

42. Ibid., 484, 1676–91.
43. Ibid., 498, 1180–84.

that "Northerners, provincials that they are, regard the South as one large Mississippi. Southerners, with their eye for distinctions, place Mississippi in a class by itself." For Methodists, Mississippi was the last battleground regarding racial structures. The four overlapping annual conferences, two in the northern and two in the southern portion of the state, had made only some guarded contact with one another. An active but small resistance group of white segregationists had established the Association of Independent Methodists (AIM) as a new Methodist denomination with the intention of removing entire congregations of the United Methodist Church. Although centered in Mississippi, AIM also formed congregations in Alabama and Tennessee. These dissidents not only were resistant to desegregation, but they also hated Methodist church money going to the National Council of Churches or to any other perceived liberal causes. Members of AIM were extremists who thrived on misinformation and ignorance, but they had a sufficient following to concern Methodist leaders.[44]

The two African American annual conferences in the state found their white counterparts unwilling partners. In 1971, the Upper Mississippi conference voted for merger, but the white Northern Mississippi conference overwhelmingly rejected merger. Opposition was particularly strong among the laity. The two southern conferences did not vote on a merger plan in 1971, but instead they chose to take matters more slowly and with less controversy. Supporters of merger formed a group called "United Methodists for Merger" to build lay support for merger. Chief among their arguments was that merger was inevitable, so it should be drafted voluntarily by Mississippi Methodists rather than imposed by the General Conference or its representatives.[45]

After the 1972 General Conference, the two African American Mississippi annual conferences both voted for merger without a single dissenting vote. Yet the two white annual conferences, facing a July 1, 1973, deadline imposed by the General Conference, only approved resolutions of intent to merge before the deadline. In August 1972, Mack B. Stokes became bishop of Mississippi with the over-

44. V. O. Key Jr., *Southern Politics in State and Nation*, 229; Branch, *Born of Conviction*, 260, 266.
45. Branch, *Born of Conviction*, 283–90.

riding challenge of merging annual conferences in less than one year or accepting binding arbitration. He wanted to establish close personal ties with all leaders in the four conferences while persuading the merger committees to work out a plan that was most likely to win approval. The merger plan drafted under Bishop Stokes's guidance provided for a one-year transitional period that had no structural change other than merging the four conferences into two while affirming that membership of boards and agencies would include members from all preceding conferences. Satterfield wrote an interpretive introduction that set out what the merger plan would and would not do; he now supported merger as the best possible course of action. In public statements, Stokes pointed out that the merger plan did not place a huge financial burden on the conference or change the means of operation of the local church. All four conferences accepted the plan in November 1972.[46]

Work then began on the reorganization of the new conferences according to the merger plans. The reorganization established a new level of conference administration by adding subdistricts under districts. District superintendents would be part of an interracial team of superintendents so that a white church might invite an African American superintendent, but no white church would be forced to have an African American superintendent. Some African American churches would have white superintendents. This plan was seen as transitional, but it encountered opposition from the Commission on Religion and Race, which believed the plan would preserve racial separation and segregated districts, although Bishop Stokes and some Mississippi leaders denied this was the plan's intent. The Commission on Religion and Race decided to challenge the plan before the Judicial Council. Meeting in April 1975 at Hilton Head, South Carolina, the Council ruled that the Mississippi merger plan was unconstitutional because the *Discipline* had no provision for a team of district superintendents. This forced the two merged Mississippi annual conferences back to the drawing board in May 1975. Both conferences established new districts, and Bishop Stokes then appointed one African American district superintendent in each conference. Mississippi Methodists at last ended the remaining racial structure in the Methodist Church and closed the door

46. Ibid., 283–90, 303–14.

on one era of Methodist history. The 1967 Omnibus Resolution had set as a target date mid-1972 for ending all racial structures in the church. This date was not met in Mississippi, but the church had finally achieved a goal that it had set for itself both in the Omnibus Resolution and in the Plan of Union with the Evangelical United Brethren Church. Prejudice still existed, and reconciliation was far from complete, but the process of merger had moved forward in every annual conference. As the Commission on Religion and Race reported to the 1976 General Conference: "We are not where we ought to be, but thank God, we are not where we used to be."[47]

The 1976 General Conference began with the Episcopal Address given by Bishop James S. Thomas. It was an affirmation for African American Methodists for him to be selected by the Council of Bishops to be their spokesperson. He entered the ministry in South Carolina in 1939 as the union of the Methodist Episcopal Church, the Methodist Protestant Church, and the Methodist Episcopal Church, South created the Central Jurisdiction. As chair of the Committee of Five during the 1960–1964 quadrennium, Thomas led the struggle to make the entire church go beyond abolition of the Central Jurisdiction to adopt a more comprehensive plan of ending racial distinctions. After being elected a bishop by the Central Jurisdiction in 1964, he transferred into the North Central Jurisdiction and served as a bishop in Iowa and later Ohio. In his career as a Methodist leader, he had been an outsider, a point man for the Central Jurisdiction, and now a voice of the church's bishops. It was both a personal triumph and sign of change among Methodists.

A particular emphasis in the address was on the status of ethnic minorities within Methodism. Expanding their concern beyond the needs of African American Methodists, the bishops called for increased aid to all ethnic minorities, whether African Americans, Asian Americans, Hispanics, or Native Americans. The bishops noted that decline in membership among these members was steeper than among Methodists generally. There was also concern about the need for ministers among minority groups, since more were retiring each year than entered the ministry. This had been a problem evident in the Central Jurisdiction, but the entire church

47. Commission on Religion and Race, "The United Methodist Church and Race: A Progress Report," [1976], 9, Commission on Religion and Race, GCAH.

"Blest Be the Tie That Binds" / 231

had not systematically addressed it, largely because it was perceived as a jurisdictional problem rather than a Methodist problem. The bishops were calling for the entire church to recognize that it needed to reverse its membership decline, but more specifically it had to shore up its efforts to grow among all segments of American society. Failure to do so would make the church a bastion of white Americans in a society that was increasingly open to nonwhites.[48]

The call for greater support for ethnic minority ministry was not a retreat from inclusiveness, although some white Methodists may have been confused. Instead, church leaders were coming to accept pluralism, the belief that each part offered something rich and beneficial to the whole church. This faith came in part from the church's experience in coming to terms with its own racism. Other ethnic minority groups, and a reevaluation of the contributions of women in the church, also contributed to the faith in inclusiveness. Additionally, the wider diversity in the church was a phenomenon that reflected American society as a whole, as politics and culture increasingly used the talents and contributions of a broader array of Americans.

48. 1976 General Conference *Journal,* 198–99.

9

"And Are We Yet Alive?"

And are we yet alive
And see each other's face?
Glory and thanks to Jesus give,
for his almighty grace.

—hymn by Charles Wesley

T HE RESPONSE OF THE Methodist Church to the changes in race relations focused on building consensus. For some, this arduous process of consensus building exemplified the irrelevance of American churches because Methodists followed social change rather than moving ahead of society empowered by their faith. The changes brought about by many courageous individuals in the Civil Rights movement and by the federal government made many of the church's actions seem like a ratification of others' work, instead of prophetic, anticipatory movement. Moreover, by the early 1970s, Methodists had only cleaned up the mess they had created during the Jim Crow period; the goal of racial inclusiveness remained elusive, especially on the local church level, where it mattered most. The United Methodist Church achieved a semblance of racial harmony by eliminating its organizational barriers, but there was not much to show beyond that. This new racial understanding was hardly an example of vibrant faith and witness to life lived according to the Gospel. The "good news" arrived late and in timid form. Where the first

Methodists were transformed by the Gospel, Methodists were now transfixed by it.

Such a caustic judgment, however, overlooks some of the Methodist experience in race relations between 1940 and 1975, and it exaggerates the brief interracial beginnings of American Methodism. During the Civil Rights movement, the church, like American society, made some significant shifts in its racial consciousness. Methodists moved from a church that marginalized African American members to a church that included African American members in all activities. Race still mattered, but it was now important to include all ethnic and minority groups rather than ignore them. Where previously racial equality had been a low priority or categorically rejected, it now became a high goal and was proclaimed throughout the church. Whites as well as African Americans, southerners as well as northerners, men as well as women, elders as well as youth, recognized the need for racial equality.

If there were a room where all the Methodists, dead or alive, who played a role in this struggle between 1930 and 1975 might gather to reminisce, it would be filled with talk about how the church had changed in race relations. The early bishops of the Central Jurisdiction, such as Robert E. Jones, would be delighted, if not thrilled, by the progress made. They began their careers in a church where white bishops ruled over African American annual conferences and in which there was no contact between African American and white southern Methodists. Bishop Charles Golden might grumble that racial inclusiveness was not complete, and he might still wonder whether he would be allowed to worship in all the Methodist congregations in Mississippi. However, John Satterfield might reply that, in fact, Golden could worship in Methodist churches across Mississippi, and he would point out that African American district superintendents had served in both Mississippi annual conferences. If Methodists still worshipped largely along racial lines, their activities beyond the local church were thoroughly integrated. They accomplished this without a mass exodus of members or a new schism. However, any joy or pride regarding the progress made by the Methodist Church necessarily would be tempered by changes in American society. The central question is not whether the Methodist Church changed its race relations, but whether its changes exceeded the changes made by American society. Here the evidence is much less clear, although not completely absent.

In contrast to the changes that occurred in Deep South politics, southern Methodists' unity across racial lines, despite its tentative nature, seems an important achievement. In 1940, the Deep South was so solidly Democratic that a racist tactic such as the all-white Democratic primary was tantamount to holding a general election. White support for the Republican party in the South was traditionally quite small (although some cracks occurred, such as during the presidential election of 1928 when Al Smith's nomination provoked revolt among some southern Democrats). However, after the 1964 Civil Rights Act and 1965 Voting Rights Act, large numbers of white voters, particularly male, began to defect to the Republican party. By 1972, the hemorrhage was significant at the national level and increasingly the state level as well. Methodists were able to keep a biracial membership in areas of the South where segregationist politicians earlier had dominated and where the Democratic party saw its strength sharply erode. Racial inclusiveness in the South became one of the success stories of the United Methodist Church, although it was least evident at the most challenging and significant level. Of course, some segregationist politicians also adapted to the new era of race relations. For example, George Wallace and Strom Thurmond, committed segregationists into the mid-1960s, showed remarkable resilience after the enactment of the 1965 Voting Rights Act.

A persistent problem throughout the postwar period was the decay of inner cities and the flight to suburbs. This was an area of weakness for the Methodist Church in every region of the country. Problems of the inner city also befuddled Catholics, whose membership was even more urbanized than the Methodist Church. White Methodists, other Protestants, Catholics, and Jews tended to abandon neighborhoods in residential transition. White flight was a persistent problem as metropolitan churches saw much of their membership join the exodus to suburbs, a new "promised land." Many urban Protestant churches, including Methodist churches, became citadels occupied by those who were unable to leave or who commuted to church as they did to work and other places. The Methodist Church was slow to develop strategies for inviting the "new neighbors"—mostly, although not exclusively, African Americans—

into the existing churches. For Methodists, this was a particular problem because African American and white ministers in most of the North were in separate annual conferences until the mid-1960s. Whether interracial ministerial teams in the 1960s would have slowed the flight to suburbs is unknowable, but Methodist structure impeded development of an alternative strategy to an immense social problem.[1]

Methodists began dealing with their racial structure during a period of unprecedented church growth. During the late 1940s through the early 1960s, Methodists and other mainline churches experienced immense expansion, whether measured in new members, church construction, or financial giving. This seemed a time of impressive religious revival and vitality as well. What was less evident and only slowly comprehended was that the religious revival was not very deep and was in part a celebration of American life—especially that of white, middle-class Americans. Americans experienced prosperity as never before, and many interpreted this material bounty as a sign of God's blessing. After all, the United States had just defeated Nazi Germany and Imperial Japan, and it was engaged in the fight against atheistic communism. Americans assumed they were also extending a beneficent influence across the globe. Americans did have anxieties in the early postwar years, but there was also great optimism. Science was producing progress and a better life. Many Americans assumed God's blessing was a critical factor in this prosperity and abundance. Methodists were not unique in seeing God's favor in their growth. This was an idea shared broadly, but not universally, across the American religious landscape.[2]

For Americans, one article of faith in their self-assurance was that the democratic process was inherently moral. Methodists translated this faith in democracy into voluntarism as a means of desegregation. Voluntarism as an idea celebrated freedom, a core American value that in the Cold War contrasted with totalitarian communism. Voluntarism wrapped the church's means of desegregation neatly in the flag and made advocates of faster action seem like radicals who not only threatened church unity, but also violated an American principle. The connection between freedom and voluntarism was a

1. John T. McGreevy, *Parish Boundaries: The Catholic Encounter with Race in the Twentieth-Century Urban North.*
2. Martin E. Marty, *Modern American Religion,* vol. 3, *Under God, Indivisible, 1941–1960.*

powerful weapon that allowed segregationists to keep critics at bay for at least a decade. Most white Methodists did not see through the absurdity of equating a segregated church structure with freedom. Even among those African American and white Methodists who supported desegregation, there was not solid support for a deadline that could be labeled coercive. Methodists deliberately built consensus through voluntarism so that schism would not occur, keeping the northern and southern Methodists united in a strong, national church.

However, unity did not translate into continued Methodist membership growth. Church membership began to decline in the mid-1960s, just as it reached a critical stage in race relations. The descent continued for over a generation. Some experts even forecast a completely different religious landscape for mainline churches in America because of changes in membership that began in the 1960s. Whether there is a connection between how Methodists handled race relations during the Civil Rights movement and the decline in membership is a thorny and complex question.[3]

In dealing with the issue of race, the Methodist Church did not became so liberal that it lost touch with its members. Obviously, there were members who were upset and felt, like Edwin Jones did, that the church was headed in the wrong direction. Others wanted a more progressive, social-action church, as envisioned by James Lawson. Yet the experience of Methodists shows that the church followed society with great care. The church fashioned compromises that provided hope to liberals while offering comfort to conservatives. The church's actions attempted to maintain a straight plumb line even while American society moved. Race was the first of many issues that pulled Methodists apart while the center became smaller as people drifted toward poles. Other social issues besides race besieged Methodists from several different fronts, making it more difficult to maintain unity.

Two examples of issues that further divided Methodists during the period of the Civil Rights movement are prayer in schools and feminism. In each, the liberal-conservative divide grew and the center

3. For an introduction to the changes in mainline churches in postwar America, see Robert Wuthnow, *The Restructuring of American Religion: Society and Faith since World War II,* and Wade Clark Roof and William McKinney, *American Mainline Religion: Its Changing Shape and Future.*

became more difficult to hold. When the U.S. Supreme Court ruled against prayer in public schools, many Methodist leaders who had generally supported the justices in school desegregation were confused and dismayed. Bishop John Wesley Lord, who enthusiastically marched for Methodists in the March on Washington, expressed his dismay over the 1962 *Engel v. Vitale* decision that struck down the New York State Board of Regents' prayer. He criticized the decision in a public statement that noted, "The Constitution bars indoctrination, but it does not require ignorance." The following year the Court barred required devotional periods in schools, a decision that further stressed many Methodist leaders. Conservatives, many of whom questioned the wisdom of the Supreme Court in school desegregation cases, used these decisions as further ammunition for their attacks upon liberalism.[4]

Feminism produced another wedge, as women demanded a larger role in the church and were no longer satisfied with a separate organization within the church. The 1964 Civil Rights Act, almost as an afterthought, explicitly covered women as a group protected from discrimination. Liberals saw this as another dimension of the rights revolution in American society. Methodists established an official Commission on the Role and Status of Women. The 1972 General Conference also approved three constitutional amendments that would take out explicit male language and replace it with gender-neutral language. While there was not major opposition to the creation of the commission or submitting the constitutional amendments, conservatives saw feminism as part of a greater social trend that included declining family values, increased divorce, and more sexual immorality.[5]

One of the largest segments of church loss for Methodists was among young people. While Americans were living longer, senior citizens increasingly dominated Methodist churches, an indication of deep trouble. This was especially disturbing because, during the

4. Bishop John Wesley Lord, "News of the Methodist Church in the Baltimore and Peninsula Conferences [press release]" June 26, 1962, 2, GBCS; see also "The Supreme Court Ruling against Prayer in Public Schools Marks Another Step in the Secularization of American Life," Bishop W. Ralph Ward, press release, June 29, 1962, GBCS; "A Pronouncement of the General Board of Christian Social Concerns on the Methodist Church on 'Worship in the Public Schools,'" not dated, GBCS; and Patterson, *Grand Expectations*, 444–45, 565, 567–68.
5. 1972 General Conference *Journal*, 471–73, 1732–59.

1950s and into the 1960s, Methodists had a strong and vibrant student movement on college campuses. By the late 1960s, the national Methodist student movement went into a deep decline. The generation of Baby Boomers failed to follow their parents' footsteps by bringing their own children to church. By losing young adults and children, it was as if the church lost most of an entire generation or more of believers.

This generation of Methodists began leaving the church during the struggle over the Central Jurisdiction. Many Methodist students during the 1950s and 1960s felt the church was moving too slowly on race relations. Methodist student organizations integrated faster than other parts of the church and lobbied hard for speedier church desegregation. Charles Parlin said that the student demonstrators at the 1964 Pittsburgh General Conference did not really understand the issues; but although he knew the *Discipline* more intimately, they saw the moral issues facing the church more clearly. Edwin Jones tried to slow down the integration of Lake Junaluska, a Methodist conference and vacation center in the western North Carolina mountains, because the idea of an integrated swimming pool raised fears of interracial marriage. Methodist youth saw this as using the church to prop up outdated social ideas. They wanted a church of transforming love rather than cultural conservatism.

There are many reasons to hesitate before proclaiming a reason to explain why Methodists lost young members. Maybe nothing that the Methodist Church did regarding race relations would have made a tremendous difference to the Baby Boomers and their children. Although some, like Bishop Golden, saw the church failing miserably to be relevant to this generation, it is difficult to see how a more radical church would retained a larger church membership. In 1972, George McGovern thought that he could defeat Richard Nixon by capturing the youth vote along with that of women and minorities. Instead, he carried only Massachusetts and the District of Columbia. He found that younger Americans were more divided than he had anticipated. Many were so opposed to what they described as the Establishment that they did not vote at all. Others were not so alienated, and they voted, like their parents, for Nixon. Methodists suffered from a similar divide. Alienated Baby Boomers found the Methodist Church too much a part of the religious Establishment. Its music was conventional and worship services seldom set people afire as they had in the early Methodist revivals. Many conservative Baby Boomers drifted to faster-growing, more theologically and socially conservative churches. For a variety of reasons, Baby Boomers declared their independence from their parents by finding their own church or opting for no church at all. For Methodists, this was an enormous loss.

The rights revolution that took place in American society also went on within the Methodist Church. However, the rights revolution also extended to individuals versus institutions. Many Americans, especially of the immediate post–World War II and later generations, did not want the institutional church to set limitations on their freedom of action. Conversely, those who sought limits opted for the more rigid and more conservative churches. Methodists were too conventional to benefit from the rights revolution that occurred in American society during 1960s and 1970s, or to benefit from the backlash against the rights revolution.

Methodists during the Civil Rights movement confronted two myths about race relations, a national and a southern myth. Both myths denied the reality of racial problems in the United States and the church. Slowly, church leaders came to understand that it was a mission of the church to bring truth to its members regarding the power of prejudice and racism in America. Methodists challenged themselves and American society to see the lies they lived by and to grow into new wholeness. Methodists struggled to discern the truth so that it might set them free. The church had within it prophets like Bishop Charles Golden and conservatives like John Satterfield. There were also dedicated individuals such as Charles C. Parlin, James P. Brawley, Dorothy Tilly, and Thelma Stevens. Most of the church leaders, ordained or lay, and members were relatively unknown Americans. They did what they could outside the glare of cameras or television to make the church and American society better, and they did significant work. In 1964, Bishop John Wesley Lord of the Washington, D.C., area, described for his fellow bishops the work of the Methodist Church in race relations: "The Church has been involved, not always successfully, but moving in the right direction. That we have not done more is our shame. That we have not been silent is our glory."[6]

6. Council of Bishops, Minutes, November 15, 1964, Chicago, 22, CBP.

Works Cited

MANUSCRIPT SOURCES

Barnett, Claude A. Papers. Archives and Manuscripts, Chicago Historical Society, Chicago, Illinois.

Brashares, Charles W. Papers. Bentley Historical Library, University of Michigan.

Brawley, James P. Papers. Atlanta University Center, Robert W. Woodruff Library, Atlanta, Georgia.

Candler, Warren Akin. Papers. Special Collections and Archives, Robert W. Woodruff Library, Emory University, Atlanta, Georgia.

Council of Bishops (The Methodist Church and United Methodist Church). Papers. General Commission on Archives and History (GCAH), United Methodist Church, Madison, New Jersey.

Edens, A. Hollis. Papers. University Archives, Duke University.

Garber, Paul Neff. Papers. Special Collections and Archives, McGraw-Page Library, Randolph-Macon College, Ashland, Virginia.

General Board of Church and Society (GBCS). General Commission on Archives and History (GCAH). United Methodist Church, Madison, New Jersey.

General Board of Global Ministries. Women's Division (GBGM-WD). General Commission on Archives and History (GCAH). United Methodist Church, Madison, New Jersey.

Harmon, Nolan B. Papers. MSS 134, Archives and Manuscripts Department, Pitts Theology Library, Emory University, Atlanta, Georgia.

Harrell, Costen J. Papers. Special Collections and Archives, Robert W. Woodruff Library, Emory University, Atlanta, Georgia.

James, D. Trigg. Papers. General Commission on Archives and History (GCAH), United Methodist Church, Madison, New Jersey.

Jones, Robert Elijah. Papers. Amistad Research Center, Inc., Tulane University, New Orleans, Louisiana.

Lake Junaluska Board of Trustees. Papers. Lake Junaluska Assembly, Heritage Center, Commission on Archives and History, Lake Junaluska, North Carolina.

Martin, William C. Papers. Bridwell Library, Perkins School of Theology, Southern Methodist University, Dallas, Texas.

Moore, Arthur J. Papers. Arthur J. Moore Methodist Museum, South Georgia Conference Archives, Epworth by the Sea, St. Simons Island, Georgia.

Murray, Peter C., Central Jurisdiction Collection. General Commission on Archives and History (GCAH), United Methodist Church, Madison, New Jersey.

Oxnam, G. Bromley. Papers. Manuscript Division, Library of Congress.

Parlin, Charles Coolidge. Papers. General Commission on Archives and History (GCAH), United Methodist Church, Madison, New Jersey.

Riggs, Lawrence. Papers. DePauw University Archives and Special Collections, Greencastle, Indiana.

Short, Roy H. Papers. General Commission on Archives and History (GCAH), United Methodist Church, Madison, New Jersey.

Short, Roy H. Papers. MSS 039, Archives and Manuscripts Department, Pitts Theology Library, Emory University, Atlanta, Georgia.

Smith, John Owen. Papers. Special Collections and Archives, Robert W. Woodruff Library, Emory University, Atlanta, Georgia.

METHODIST CHURCH JOURNALS AND PUBLICATIONS

Central Christian Advocate
Christian Advocate
Daily Christian Advocate (Methodist Episcopal Church)

General Conference *Journal*

Judicial Council of The Methodist Church. *Decisions of the Judicial Council of The Methodist Church, 1940–1968*. Nashville: Methodist Publishing House, 1968.

Quadrennial Reports of the Methodist Church

Southwestern Christian Advocate (SCA)

Together

Annual Conference Journals, 1940–1967

Central Alabama Annual Conference (CJ)

Central West Annual Conference (CJ)

Delaware Annual Conference (CJ)

Georgia Annual Conference (CJ)

Lexington Annual Conference (CJ)

Louisiana Annual Conference (CJ)

Mississippi Annual Conference (CJ)

North Carolina Annual Conference (CJ)

South Carolina Annual Conference (SEJ)

Tennessee Annual Conference (CJ)

Upper Mississippi Annual Conference (CJ)

Jurisdictional Conference Journals, Methodist Church (1940–1964) and United Methodist Church (after 1968)

Central Jurisdiction Conference *Journal*

North Central Jurisdiction Conference *Journal*

Northeastern Jurisdiction Conference *Journal*

South Central Jurisdiction Conference *Journal*

Southeastern Jurisdiction Conference *Journal*

Western Jurisdiction Conference *Journal*

NEWSPAPERS AND MAGAZINES CITED

Atlanta Journal and Constitution

Birmingham (Alabama) News

Chicago Sun-Times

Chicago Tribune

Christian Century

Christianity and Crisis
Life
Nashville Tennessean
New South
New York Times
Washington Post

References

Ahlstrom, Sydney E. *A Religious History of the American People.* New Haven: Yale University Press, 1972.

Alvis, Joel L., Jr. *Religion and Race: Southern Presbyterians, 1946–1983.* Tuscaloosa: University of Alabama Press, 1993.

Andrews, Dee E. *The Methodists and Revolutionary America, 1760–1800.* Princeton: Princeton University Press, 2000.

Bailey, Kenneth K. "The Post–Civil War Racial Separations in Southern Protestantism: Another Look." *Church History* 46 (December 1977): 453–73.

Barnes, Catherine A. *Journey from Jim Crow: The Desegregation of Southern Transit.* New York: Columbia University Press, 1983.

Bartley, Numan V. *The New South, 1945–1980.* Baton Rouge: Louisiana State University Press, 1995.

Bass, S. Jonathan. *Blessed Are the Peacemakers: Martin Luther King, Jr., Eight White Religious Leaders, and the "Letter from Birmingham Jail."* Baton Rouge: Louisiana State University Press, 2001.

Blum, John Morton. *Years of Discord: American Politics and Society, 1961–1974.* New York: Norton, 1991.

Branch, Ellis R. *Born of Conviction: Racial Conflict and Change in Mississippi Methodism, 1945–1983.* Ann Arbor, Mich.: University Microfilms, 1984.

Brauer, Carl M. *John F. Kennedy and the Second Reconstruction.* New York: Columbia University Press, 1977.

Brock, Edwin L. "Methodism's Growing Cleavage." *Christian Century,* August 24, 1955, 971–72.

Brundage, W. Fitzhugh. *Lynching in the New South: Georgia and Virginia, 1880–1930.* Urbana: University of Illinois Press, 1993.

Burk, Robert Fredrick. *The Eisenhower Administration and Black Civil Rights.* Knoxville: University of Tennessee Press, 1984.

Carson, Clayborne. *In Struggle: SNCC and the Black Awakening of the 1960s*. Cambridge: Harvard University Press, 1981.

Carter, Paul A. "The Negro and Methodist Union." *Church History* 21 (March 1952): 55–70.

Chappell, David L. *Inside Agitators: White Southerners in the Civil Rights Movement*. Baltimore: Johns Hopkins University Press, 1994.

———. "Religious Ideas of the Segregationists." *Journal of American Studies* 32 (1998): 237–62.

Collier, Karen Y. "An Examination of Varied Aspects of Race and Episcopacy in American Methodism, 1844–1939." Ph.D. diss., Duke University, 1984.

Commager, Henry Steele, ed. *Documents of American History*. 9th ed. 2 vols. Englewood Cliffs, N.J.: Prentice-Hall, 1973.

Culver, Dwight W. *Negro Segregation in the Methodist Church*. New Haven: Yale University Press, 1953.

Cuninggim, Merrimon. *Perkins Led the Way: The Story of Desegregation at Southern Methodist University*. Dallas: Perkins School of Theology, Southern Methodist University, 1994.

Cunningham, W. J. *Agony at Galloway: One Church's Struggle with Social Change*. Jackson: University Press of Mississippi, 1980.

Dalfiume, Richard M. *Desegregation of the U.S. Armed Forces: Fighting on Two Fronts, 1939–1953*. Columbia: University of Missouri Press, 1969.

———. "The 'Forgotten Years' of the Negro Revolution." *Journal of American History* 55 (June 1968): 90–106.

Daniels, Pete. *Lost Revolutions: The South in the 1950s*. Chapel Hill: University of North Carolina Press for Smithsonian National Museum of American History, 2000.

Dittmer, John. *Local People: The Struggle for Civil Rights*. Urbana: University of Illinois Press, 1994.

Du Bois, W. E. B. *The Negro Church*. Atlanta: Atlanta University Press, 1903. Reprint, New York: Arno Press, 1968.

Egerton, John. *Speak Now against the Day: The Generation before the Civil Rights Movement in the South*. New York: Knopf, 1994.

Fairclough, Adam. *To Redeem the Soul of America: The Southern Christian Leadership Conference and Martin Luther King, Jr.* Athens: University of Georgia Press, 1987.

Farish, Hunter Dickinson. *The Circuit Rider Dismounts: A Social History of Southern Methodism, 1865–1900.* Richmond, Va.: Dietz Press, 1938. Reprint, New York: Da Capo Press, 1969.

Ferry, Henry Justin. "Racism and Reunion: A Black Protest by Francis James Grimke." *Journal of Presbyterian History* 50 (summer 1972): 77–88.

Findlay, James F., Jr. *Church People in the Struggle: The National Council of Churches and the Black Freedom Movement, 1950–1970.* New York: Oxford University Press, 1993.

Garrow, David J. *Bearing the Cross: Martin Luther King, Jr., and the Southern Christian Leadership Conference.* New York: William Morrow, 1986.

George, Carol V. R. *Segregated Sabbaths: Richard Allen and the Emergence of Independent Black Churches, 1760–1840.* New York: Oxford University Press, 1973.

Goen, C. C. *Broken Churches, Broken Nation: Denominational Schisms and the Coming of Age of the American Civil War.* Macon, Ga.: Mercer University Press, 1985.

Goldfield, David R. *Black, White, and Southern: Race Relations and Southern Culture, 1940 to the Present.* Baton Rouge: Louisiana State University Press, 1990.

Gravely, William B. "African Methodisms and the Rise of Black Denominationalism." In *Perspectives on American Methodism: Interpretive Essays,* ed. Russell E. Richey, Kenneth E. Rowe, and Jean Miller Schmidt. Nashville: Kingswood Books, 1993.

———. *Gilbert Haven, Methodist Abolitionist: A Study in Race, Religion, and Reform, 1850–1880.* Ed. Commission on Archives and History of the United Methodist Church. Nashville: Abingdon Press, 1973.

———. "The Social, Political, and Religious Significance of the Formation of the Colored Methodist Episcopal Church." *Methodist History* 18 (October 1979): 3–25.

Halberstam, David. *The Children.* New York: Random House, 1998.

Hall, Jacquelyn Dowd. *Revolt against Chivalry: Jessie Daniel Ames and the Women's Campaign against Lynching.* Rev. ed. New York: Columbia University Press, 1993.

Hayden, J. Carleton. "After the War." *Historical Magazine of the Protestant Episcopal Church* 42 (December 1973): 403–28.

Heyrman, Christine Leigh. *Southern Cross: The Beginnings of the Bible Belt.* Chapel Hill: University of North Carolina Press, 1997.

Hildebrand, Reginald F. "Methodist Episcopal Policy on the Ordination of Black Ministers, 1784–1864." *Methodist History* 20 (April 1982): 124–42.

———. *The Times Were Strange and Stirring: Methodist Preachers and the Crisis of Emancipation.* Durham: Duke University Press, 1995.

Hill, Samuel S. *Southern Churches in Crisis Revisited.* Tuscaloosa: University of Alabama Press, 1999.

Hobson, Fred. *But Now I See: The White Southern Racial Conversion Narrative.* Baton Rouge: Louisiana State University Press, 1999.

Johnson, Donald Bruce, comp. *National Party Platforms.* 2 vols. Rev. ed. Urbana: University of Illinois Press, 1978.

Joyner, Charles. *Down by the Riverside: A South Carolina Slave Community.* Urbana: University of Illinois Press, 1984.

Kennedy, David M. *Freedom from Fear: The American People in Depression and War, 1929–1945.* New York: Oxford University Press, 1999.

Key, V. O., Jr. *Southern Politics in State and Nation.* New York: Knopf, 1949.

Klarman, Michael J. "How *Brown* Changed Race Relations: The Backlash Thesis." *Journal of American History* 81 (June 1994): 81–118.

Kline, Lawrence O. "The Negro in the Unification of American Methodism." *Drew Gateway* 34 (spring 1964): 128–49.

Kluger, Richard. *Simple Justice: The History of* Brown v. Board of Education *and Black America's Struggle for Equality.* New York: Vintage Books, 1977.

Knotts, Alice G. *Fellowship of Love: Methodist Women Changing American Racial Attitudes.* Nashville: Kingswood Books, 1996.

Korstad, Robert, and Nelson Lichtenstein. "Opportunities Found and Lost: Labor, Radicals, and the Early Civil Rights Movement." *Journal of American History* 75 (December 1988): 786–811.

Lawson, James. "A Nonviolent Endorsement." In *Black Manifesto: Religion, Racism, and Reparations,* ed. Robert S. Lecky and H. Elliott Wright. New York: Sheed and Ward, 1969.

Lawson, Steven F. *Running for Freedom: Civil Rights and Black Politics in America since 1941.* 2d ed. New York: McGraw-Hill, 1997.

Leonard, Bill J. "A Theology of Racism: Southern Fundamentalists and the Civil Rights Movement." In *Southern Landscapes,* ed. Tony Badger, Walter Edgar, and Jan Nordby Gretlund. Tübingen: Stauffenburg Verlag, 1996.

Link, William A., and Arthur S. Link. *American Epoch: A History of the United States since 1900.* 7th ed. New York: McGraw-Hill, 1993.

Loescher, Frank S. *The Protestant Church and the Negro.* New York: Association Press, 1948.

Luker, Ralph E. *The Social Gospel in Black and White: American Racial Reform, 1885–1912.* Chapel Hill: University of North Carolina Press, 1991.

Madison, James H. "Reformers and the Rural Church, 1900–1950." *Journal of American History* 73 (December 1986): 645–68.

Marsh, Charles. *God's Long Summer: Stories of Faith and Civil Rights.* Princeton: Princeton University Press, 1997.

Marty, Martin E. *Modern American Religion.* Vol. 3, *Under God, Indivisible, 1941–1960.* Chicago: University of Chicago Press, 1996.

Maser, Frederick E. "The Story of Unification, 1874–1939." In *The History of American Methodism,* vol. 3, ed. Emory Burke. Nashville: Abingdon Press, 1964.

Mathews, Donald G. "Evangelical America: The Methodist Ideology." In *Perspectives on American Methodism: Interpretive Essays,* ed. Russell E. Richey, Kenneth E. Rowe, and Jean Miller Schmidt. Nashville: Kingswood Books, 1993.

———. *Religion in the Old South.* Chicago: University of Chicago Press, 1977.

———. *Slavery and Methodism: A Chapter in American Morality, 1780–1845.* Princeton: University of Princeton Press, 1965.

———. "The Southern Rite of Human Sacrifice." *Journal of Southern Religion* 3 (Aug. 22, 2000), http://jsr.as.wvu.edu.

Matusow, Allen J. *The Unraveling of America: A History of Liberalism in the 1960s.* New York: Harper and Row, 1984.

McAdam, Doug. *Freedom Summer.* New York: Oxford University Press, 1988.

McClain, William B. *Black People in the Methodist Church: Whither Thou Goest?* Cambridge, Mass.: Schenkman, 1984.

McDowell, John Patrick. *The Social Gospel in the South: The Woman's Home Mission Movement in the Methodist Episcopal Church, South, 1886–1939.* Baton Rouge: Louisiana State University Press, 1982.

McGreevy, John T. *Parish Boundaries: The Catholic Encounter with Race in the Twentieth-Century Urban North.* Chicago: University of Chicago Press, 1996.

McNally, Michael J. "A Peculiar Institution: Catholic Parish Life and the Pastoral Mission to the Blacks in the Southeast, 1850–1980." *U.S. Catholic Historian* 5 (spring 1986): 67–80.

Meier, August, and Elliott Rudwick. *CORE: A Study in the Civil Rights Movement, 1942–1968.* Urbana: University of Illinois Press, 1975.

Miller, Randall M. "Slaves and Southern Catholicism." In *Masters and Slaves in the House of the Lord: Race and Religion in the American South, 1740–1870,* ed. John B. Boles. Lexington: University Press of Kentucky, 1988.

Miller, Robert M. *American Protestantism and Social Issues, 1919–1939.* Chapel Hill: University of North Carolina Press, 1958.

———. *Bishop G. Bromley Oxnam: Paladin of Liberal Protestantism.* Nashville: Abingdon Press, 1990.

———. *How Shall They Hear without a Preacher? The Life of Ernest Fremont Tittle.* Chapel Hill: University of North Carolina Press, 1971.

Montgomery, William E. *Under Their Own Vine and Fig Tree: The African-American Church in the South, 1865–1900.* Baton Rouge: Louisiana State University Press, 1993.

Morris, Aldon D. *The Origins of the Civil Rights Movement: Black Communities Organizing for Change.* New York: Free Press, 1984.

Morrow, Ralph E. *Northern Methodism and Reconstruction.* East Lansing: Michigan State University Press, 1956.

Myrdal, Gunnar. *An American Dilemma: The Negro Problem and Modern Democracy.* 20th anniversary edition. New York: Harper and Row, 1962. Reprint, New York: Pantheon Books, 1975.

National Council of Churches, Department of Racial and Cultural Relations. "Statements Adopted by Religious Groups Re[garding] Segregation in the Public Schools." Interracial Publication no. 84, October 1954, 1–32.

Oakes, Henry N. *The Struggle for Racial Equality in the Methodist Episcopal Church.* Ann Arbor, Mich.: University Microfilms, 1974.

Ochs, Stephen J. *Desegregating the Altar: The Josephites and the Struggle for Black Priests, 1871–1960.* Baton Rouge: Louisiana State University Press, 1990.

———. "The Ordeal of a Black Priest." *U.S. Catholic Historian* 5 (spring 1986): 45–66.

Orfield, Gary. *The Reconstruction of Southern Education: The Schools and the 1964 Civil Rights Act.* New York: Wiley-Interscience, 1969.

Orser, W. Edward. "Racial Attitudes in Wartime: Protestant Churches during the Second World War." *Church History* 41 (September 1972): 337–53.

Patterson, James T. *Grand Expectations: The United States, 1945–1974.* New York: Oxford University Press, 1996.

Pope, Liston. *The Kingdom beyond Caste.* New York: Friendship Press, 1957.

President's Committee on Civil Rights. *To Secure These Rights: The Report of the President's Committee on Civil Rights.* Washington, D.C.: Government Printing Office, 1947.

Ralph, James R., Jr. *Northern Protest: Martin Luther King, Jr., Chicago, and the Civil Rights Movement.* Cambridge: Harvard University Press, 1993.

Reimers, David M. "Negro Bishops and Diocesan Segregation in the Protestant Episcopal Church, 1870–1954." *Historical Magazine of the Protestant Episcopal Church* 31 (September 1962): 231–42.

———. *White Protestantism and the Negro.* New York: Oxford University Press, 1965.

Report of the National Advisory Commission on Civil Disorders. New York Times edition. New York: E. P. Dutton, 1968.

Richey, Russell E. *Early American Methodism.* Bloomington: Indiana University Press, 1991.

———. *The Methodist Conference in America: A History.* Nashville: Kingswood Books, 1996.

Roof, Wade Clark, and William McKinney. *American Mainline Religion: Its Changing Shape and Future.* New Brunswick: Rutgers University Press, 1987.

Shankman, Arnold. "Dorothy Tilly, Civil Rights, and the Methodist Church." *Methodist History* 18 (January 1980): 95–108.

Shattuck, Gardiner H., Jr. *Episcopalians and Race: Civil War to Civil Rights.* Lexington: University Press of Kentucky, 2000.

Shockley, Grant S., gen. ed., with Karen Y. Collier and William B. McClain, assoc. eds. *Heritage and Hope: The African-American Presence in United Methodism.* Nashville: Abingdon Press, 1991.

Sitkoff, Harvard. *A New Deal for Blacks: The Emergence of Civil Rights as a National Issue.* New York: Oxford University Press, 1978.

———. "Racial Militancy and Interracial Violence in the Second World War." *Journal of American History* 58 (December 1971): 661–81.

Smith, H. Shelton. *In His Image, But...: Racism in Southern Religion, 1780–1910.* Durham: Duke University Press, 1972.

Spalding, David. "The Negro Catholic Congresses, 1889–1894." *Catholic Historical Review* 55 (October 1969): 337–57.

"Statement by Black Methodists for Church Renewal." In *Black Theology: A Documentary History, 1966–1979,* ed. Gayraud S. Wilmore and James H. Cone. Maryknoll, N.Y.: Orbis Books, 1979.

Stevens, Thelma. *Legacy for the Future: The History of Christian Social Relations in the Woman's Division of Christian Service, 1940–1968.* Women's Division Board of Global Ministries, the United Methodist Church, 1978.

Thomas, James S. *Methodism's Racial Dilemma: The Story of the Central Jurisdiction.* Nashville: Abingdon Press, 1992.

Thompson, Ernest Trice. "Black Presbyterians, Education, and Evangelism after the Civil War." *Journal of Presbyterian History* 51 (summer 1973): 174–98.

Tilson, Everett. *Segregation and the Bible.* New York: Abingdon Press, 1958.

Tushnet, Mark V. *The NAACP's Legal Strategy against Segregated Education, 1925–1950.* Chapel Hill: University of North Carolina Press, 1987.

Tygiel, Jules. *Baseball's Great Experiment: Jackie Robinson and His Legacy.* New York: Oxford University Press, 1983.

Walker, Clarence E. *A Rock in a Weary Land: The African Methodist Episcopal Church during the Civil War and Reconstruction.* Baton Rouge: Louisiana State University Press, 1982.

Weisbrot, Robert. *Freedom Bound: A History of America's Civil Rights Movement.* New York: Plume, 1991.

Who's Who in Methodism. Chicago: A. N. Marquis, 1952.

Who's Who in the Methodist Church. Nashville: Abingdon Press, 1966.

Wigger, John H. *Taking Heaven by Storm: Methodism and the Rise of Popular Christianity in America.* New York: Oxford University Press, 1998.

Wiggins, William H., Jr. *O Freedom! Afro-American Emancipation Celebrations.* Knoxville: University of Tennessee Press, 1987.

Williams, William H. "The Attraction of Methodism: The Delmarva Peninsula as a Case Study, 1769–1820." In *Perspectives on American Methodism: Interpretive Essays,* ed. Russell E. Richey, Kenneth E. Rowe, and Jean Miller Schmidt. Nashville: Kingswood Books, 1993.

Willis, David W. "An Enduring Distance: Black Americans and the Establishment." In *Between the Times: The Travail of the Protestant Establishment in America, 1900–1960,* ed. William R. Hutchison. Cambridge: Cambridge University Press, 1989.

Wilmore, Gayraud S. *Black Religion and Black Radicalism: An Interpretation of the Religious History of Afro-American People.* 2d ed. Maryknoll, N.Y.: Orbis Books, 1983.

Wilson, Charles Reagan. *Baptized in Blood: The Religion of the Lost Cause, 1865–1920.* Athens: University of Georgia Press, 1980.

Wogaman, J. Philip. *Methodism's Challenge in Race Relations: A Study of Strategy.* Boston: Boston University Press, 1960.

World Outlook. "A Reparations Jubilee." Reprinted in *Black Manifesto: Religion, Racism, and Reparations,* ed. Robert S. Lecky and H. Elliott Wright. New York: Sheed and Ward, 1969.

Wuthnow, Robert. *The Restructuring of American Religion: Society and Faith since World War II.* Princeton: Princeton University Press, 1988.

Index

Abolition. *See* Slavery

Accommodation, 7, 28, 36, 46, 56

Advisory councils for race relations, 157–58, 160, 172, 180–82, 193–94

Affirmative action, 205–6, 220

African Americans: demographics of, 9, 36, 54–55; economic aid for, 52, 213–14, 216–17; goals of, 7, 37; lack of help by whites, 27–28; leaders of, 7, 197; living conditions of, 30–31, 36; nationalism of, 7, 183–84, 197; oppression of, 27–28, 29, 176; politics and, 28–29, 52, 69, 116; religious choice of, 11–12, 15, 20–21, 23–25; support for Civil Rights movement, 81, 108; in Union army, 18; white belief in fair treatment of, 52, 79; worship of, 21, 79–80. *See also* Central Jurisdiction; Methodists, African American

African Methodist Episcopal (AME) Church, 15, 18, 20–21, 102, 205

African Methodist Episcopal Zion (AMEZ) Church, 15, 18, 20–21, 102, 205

Afro-American Presbyterian Church, 51

Alabama, 105–6, 125, 177, 222–23, 228

Allen, Richard, 14–15

Alton, Bishop Ralph, 176

Amendment IX: Methodist desegregation through, 84–87, 90, 102–4, 121–22; limitations of, 99, 155; support for, 89, 97, 113–15; use of, 88, 97–98, 103, 110–11, 168, 170.

See also Annual conference transfers and mergers

American Dilemma, An (Myrdal), 46, 55–56

American Revolution, 12, 16

Ames, Jessie Daniel, 30, 58

Andrew, Bishop James O., 17, 170

Annual conferences: biracial, 21–22; call for integration of, 62–63, 167; of Central Jurisdiction, 44, 45, 73–74, 98, 132–33, 140; Central Jurisdiction adjusting boundaries of, 132, 136, 168; condemning discrimination, 81–82, 156–57; differences in finances among, 104, 123, 207; integration of, 122, 151, 172, 200; on Omnibus Resolution, 192–95; overlapping African American and white, 118–19; on Plan of Union, 35–36, 42–43; ratifying changes in constitution, 73–74, 84–86, 90, 113

Annual conferences, Methodist Episcopal Church, South, 19

Annual conference transfers and mergers, 67, 84–86, 117, 126; assistance with, 157–58, 180–82, 212; completion of, 198–99, 229–30; deadline for, 208, 223–25; of EUB with Methodist, 223–24; financial implications of, 158, 160; importance of, 174–75; need to integrate after, 98, 140–41, 214–15; one-step process for, 151, 156–57, 160, 167–70, 175, 179; plans for, 85, 121–23, 129, 132–33, 150, 174, 185;

253